When Hollywood Says Yes How Can America Say No?

When Hollywood Says Yes How Can America Say No?

Gene Wolfenbarger

New Leaf Press

First printing: February 1998

ISBN: 0-89221-376-0

Printed in the United States of America.

**To Karen
The leading lady in my life**

Table of Contents

Foreword

The family is the foundational building block of society and its health is a prerequisite for a healthy and prosperous nation. No nation has ever been stronger than its families.

Today our widespread rejection of the historic faith of our fathers, however, and because of a loss of commitment to the family, we are seeing an erosion which can result in our decline as a great country. Never before has the American family been in so much trouble. There are many contributing causes, such as the deterioration of our public education system, the prevalence of secular values to the downplaying of our religious heritage, and problems with our public health system and the rise of homelessness in our society. Drugs are an increasing blight on America.

Terrible attacks are being leveled against the family by extreme feminists, homosexual activities of both sexes, and by those who have downgraded ethical absolutes and "family values" in our society.

No single institution in our society has done more to undermine time-honored traditional American moral and spiritual values than the Hollywood motion picture industry. I am not firing a broadside at everyone in the entertainment business. There is a strong contingency of dedicated Christians, serious moral Jews and sincere believers in traditional values working in Hollywood, but they are a relatively small minority. By far the overwhelming majority of those who finance, produce, direct and develop motion pictures and television shows are ready to pander to the lowest common denominator, when it comes to morality, ethics, religion and character.

For the first six or seven decades of movie-making, religious themes were generally treated with respect and dignity. Cecil B. DeMille, an Episcopalian, kept a Bible on his desk and read it frequently. Movies like *The Ten Commandments, Ben hur, King of Kings, The Bible* and scores of others, very popular in their times and now shown on television occasionally, may not have been theologically perfect, but were produced with a high degree of appreciation for religion. In the last 20 or 25 years, the Hollywood movie industry has gone on the attack against religion, especially Christianity, debasing, ridiculing and twisting biblical themes. *The Last Temptation Of Jesus Christ*, a financial disaster, is a case in point.

In the area of morals, nudity, sexual promiscuity, adultery, homosexuality and lesbianism have permeated the industry. Such things, formerly frowned on, are now presented in a favorable light.

Graphic, ugly violence is more common than ever. Blasphemy, cursing and obscenity have polluted conversations in many dramas on film brought by television into your living room.

Some courageous reviewers like Michael Medvid have spoken up and written about the immoral cesspool displayed in Hollywood's portrayal of life.

What can Christians do?

We must rise up in the cause of biblical and traditional righteousness. There is still "a moral majority" out there, but unless there is a revival in America and a return to moral and ethical values, there will soon be an "immoral majority".

Evangelist Gene Wolfenbarger has prepared this excellent book to help parents and young people cope with the flood of evil flowing from the Hollywood entertainment industry. Read it carefully.

There are many of us involved in this "prophetic type ministry," crying out against moral and social evils, as did Isaiah, Jeremiah and all the Old Testament prophets.

You can join the ranks of millions who are not only appalled at what the movies and television are doing to our youth, but who are ready to oppose it with vigor and dedication.

Digest the contents of this book. Share these things with your own family.

The children and teenagers rescued from falling into immorality, perversion, drug addiction, violent crime, wild rebellion and destruction may be your own.

—Dr. Jerry Falwell
Pastor, Thomas Road Baptist Church
Chancellor Liberty University

Introduction

Never in the history of America has the entertainment media, particularly the motion picture and television industries, been more blatant and open about remolding the moral, cultural and even the religious life of our society than today.

Gone is respect for religion, such as the DeMille biblical epics used to project or films that appealed to millions of Catholics and others, like *Going My Way* or *The Song of Bernadette*. Pictures like *The Bible, The King of Kings* and *The Greatest Story Ever Told* are not being filmed at all.

Instead Hollywood dishes up *The Last Temptation of Christ*, a sordid story that besmirches Jesus and offends millions of Christians. That one lost a lot of money, but Hollywood continues to attack religion.

Whereas there was some discretion a few decades ago in depicting illicit relationships in a story, Hollywood now serves up nudity, obscenity, blasphemy and adultery with little regard for moral values or the traditional ideas of right and wrong.

Forty years ago the movie *The Ten Commandments* seemed to encourage keeping them. Now much of Hollywood is searching for new and dramatic ways to encourage to break them.

The lowest common immoral denominator seems to be the standard for much of today's entertainment.

Until recent years most people believed they could count on the Walt Disney people to present wholesome family fare. Now Michael Eisner and his ilk have corrupted the Disney tradition and with their subsidiary film companies have taken a leading role in corrupting good morals, promoting homosexuality as an acceptable lifestyle (because of AIDS it is more of a deathstyle than a lifestyle), and generally degrading even further the moral life of America.

For decades Disney was a name America's families could trust. Disney meant wholesomeness. Disney meant laughter. Disney meant quality entertainment without sex, violence and profanity. But more than anything else, Disney meant children. Sadly, "the times, they are a changing."

What is insidious about today's Disney is that they are

living off the reputation of the past. Disney is making millions off of family fare and then sinking it into movies, television programs and printed material that assails the very values of these same families. Disney has hoped that decent minded Americans would not make the connection. They have.

The Assemblies of God, the Church of the Nazarene and the Southern Baptist Convention (15,000,000) strong have expressed public moral concern for what Disney is now doing, some calling for a full boycott of Disney enterprises.

Disney is now taking the heat for its open support for the gay lifestyle. Alveda Celest King, niece of Dr. Martin Luther King, Jr. and now chairman and founder of King for America, Inc. has also taken Disney to task for changing its once wholesome image.

Homosexuality, violence, anti-Christian themes, incest, graphic sex, drug use, profanity and obscenity. All these now share a strange legacy with *Pinocchio, Snow White, Peter Pan* and *The Little Mermaid* as hallmarks of the Walt Disney Company.

Never before in the history of America is a book like the one you hold in your hand more needed. Study it carefully. Resolve not to surrender to the Hollywood Moguls of Immorality who would carelessly disrupt and destroy America's moral heritage and character for "the almighty dollar."

Being informed is absolutely essential, if we are to take our stand for God, for America as we have known it, and for all things good and wholesome. Internal moral decay, now being touted by much of Hollywood as normal and universal can lead, indeed to the decline and fall of America.

—Don Wildmon
President, American Family Association

What Evangelist Tim Lee Says...

As a personal friend and fellow evangelist, I have been involved in the life of Gene Wolfenbarger, Jr. for eleven years. He is deeply responsive to our Christian world and he is courageously immersed in the challenge of our times. Like the ancient prophets, he loves the people enough to warn them of their errors and to hold our country to its highest standards. With a national fervor and a love for America, Gene has set the trumpet to his mouth regarding the moral contamination being produced by Hollywood, television and the movie industry. We will all agree that the national strength of our country is important, but so is the spirit which informs and shapes our minds and the characters of our citizens. It is often the spirit behind a country or an establishment that defines its true purpose. The wickedness of Hollywood's spirit has plunged America into a moral and cultural crisis and destroyed her legacy of decency, honesty, and integrity. That we have allowed this crisis to develop to this extent is a tragic indictment of the blindness and complacency of Christianity.

As you read this book, you will be introduced to an innocent young girl named Callie. She will quickly win your affection and keep you turning the pages as her life unfolds before you. Between chapters, Callie grows from a winsome nine-year-old to a chaste, eager teenager in a world that is daily and moment-by-moment influenced by Hollywood. Callie's story will continue in your thoughts for days after you have finished reading the last chapter. She is startling proof of our need to accept the challenge presented in this book.

You will want to join in the ranks of those already gathering across this nation to pull down the strongholds of Hollywood through unity, prayer, and fasting. Let us say with one voice to Hollywood: "We serve notice on your method of concealment by openly producing films with explicit sex, graphic violence, and filthy language. Your method has come to an end. Such movies weaken our characters, destroy our minds, paralyze our society, and enslave our children."

—*Dr. Tim Lee*
Evangelist

What Tom Elliff Says...

Free speech is a treasured and protected privilege for every American citizen. But with that privilege comes the responsibility of using it in a manner that encourages and lifts moral standards rather than diminishing them. When the privilege of free speech is used to debase and demean traditional, Bible-based family values, it is imperative that the Christian community speak out loudly.

It is no secret that Hollywood, more than any other city in our nation, is Satan's epicenter of moral debasement, constantly shaking and attempting to destroy the spiritual foundations upon which this nation was built. I am grateful for every attempt to expose the truth about Hollywood in an uncompromising fashion.

It is time for believers to take seriously our Lord's exhortation to be "salt and light" in the midst of a wicked and perverse generation. Christ, and only Christ, is the answer for our sin-cursed society. Our pattern should be John the Baptist, a man for whom Christ reserved His highest praise. John pointed his generation to Christ while, at the same time, crying out against the immorality of his day. He was more concerned with eternal values that earthly praise. May we all be so convicted...and so convincing.

—Dr. Tom Elliff
Pastor, First Southern Baptist Church
Del City, Oklahoma

Part I
The Creation

"Film and visual entertainment are a pervasively important part of our culture, an extremely significant influence on the way our society operates. People in the film industry don't want to accept the responsibility that they had a hand in the way the world is loused up. But, for better or worse...films and television tell us the way we conduct our lives, what is right and wrong. It's important that the people who make films have ethics classes, philosophy classes, and history classes. Otherwise, we're witch doctors."

— Filmmaker George Lucas
(Star Wars, Raiders of the Lost Ark),
speaking at USC Film and
Television School in 1981

Chapter 1

Casting Its Shadow

Fall 1989

The Amberson Theater stood like a regal old queen on Main Street. It looked splendid and stately with its restoration now completed. Repairs on the theater had been both costly and luxurious, but everyone agreed that the finished structure was well worth it. Saved from destruction by some zealous lovers of the arts, the imposing theater guarded within its walls the extravagance of Hollywood's Golden Age. Tonight, excitement flowed out of the massive double doors, onto the sidewalks and into the eager crowd. An air of expectancy surrounded the opening night visitors as they moved as rapidly as they dared through the lines.

Nine-year-old Callie held Aunt Heather's hand as they walked through the doors. She smothered a giggle of anticipation as she bumped and elbowed along with the spirited crowd, anxious to get inside. Aunt Heather squeezed Callie's hand signaling her own pleasure.

People had always said that Callie favored the candid, lovely Heather Prescott more than her own mother—except for the color of their hair, that is. Aunt Heather was the pastel color of spring with blond hair and blue eyes, while Callie was the fiery, tempestuous fall with dark brown hair and sparkling hazel eyes. Everything about Callie's young person was honey-gold and warm in tone. She had a ready laugh and a welcome acceptance of everyone she met. Few people failed to succumb *to the magnetism of her innocent spirit and earthly charm.*

The smell of fresh buttered popcorn and the sound of cola gushing into paper cups assaulted Callie's nose as she entered the lobby of the theater. Yet more alluring than the aroma of popcorn was the sight of the ceiling-to-floor, maroon velvet curtains with gold bullion fringe, and the plush, flowered carpeting beneath her feet. On the walls were bigger-than-life, gilt-framed pictures of movie stars whom Callie did not recognize. All of Hollywood's Golden Age stars were there: Humphrey Bogart, Clark Gable, Greta Garbo, Cary Grant, Bette Davis, Gary Cooper, Spencer Tracy, Ingrid Bergman and a host of others stared down at Callie. Dropping Aunt Heather's hand, Callie wandered slowly from picture to picture. She stood mesmerized in the presence of Tinsel Town royalty—especially the child star, Shirley Temple, with her dimpled smile and bouncing curls. Callie admired them all and proved such by measuring out equal amounts of time gazing up at each cinema celebrity. While standing patiently in line for their refreshments, Aunt Heather smiled benevolently as she kept a watchful eye on her young niece gazing at the celebrities. The magical world of Hollywood's fantasy factory consumed Callie.

"Be careful and don't spill your soft drink," whispered Aunt Heather, as they walked up the balcony stairs. A few minutes later they entered the spectacular gilded theater that seated almost a thousand people. A well-drilled usher in a new uniform greeted them and directed them to their seats.

Callie eased down onto the lap of a velvet cushioned seat. This was such a special night. Aunt Heather had flown in especially from her publishing job in New York just to keep her promise to Callie—to accompany her to the grand opening of the restored Amberson Theater. Callie's innocent eyes quickly took in the surroundings of elegance; the cavernous theater was a thing of grace and beauty, exquisite and faultless, as elegant as any palace she had ever seen in a picture book. Callie's youth hindered her knowledge of high-renaissance architecture with its columns, its statutes and its high-vaulted ceilings; she only knew that she loved this classical temple of drama with its crowd of buzzing people surrounding her. Everything about this moment held for her a promise of anticipation. Everything about the theater promised her that she could trust what she was about to experience. The Austrian draped stage curtain ascended upwards revealing the mammoth silver screen. The lights dimmed and Callie's young heart beat a little faster as the mysterious darkness of the theater wrapped her in its arms. A holy hush now fell over the crowd. Squeezing her arms to her sides with enchantment, she leaned over and whispered to Aunt Heather:

"It's starting now."

"Shhh."

Callie savored this special moment of theatrical darkness. The music encompassed her ears and then moved inside her skin until her heart soon beat in rhythmic harmony to its melody. The elegant maroon curtains stopped their reverential rise, unveiling the hidden object of worship. The immense screen stood ready to receive the projected images. Callie's senses danced with excitement. Twin tastes of buttered popcorn and chocolate-covered raisins fought for supremacy inside her mouth. Then taking one long sip of acid soda, Callie drowned both the popcorn and raisins into oblivion.

Like most children, and adults, Callie loved the movies. When she was watching a movie, she did not have to think—although she was a straight A student in school. She did not have to use her brain. Not here. Later she would have to remember what nine times nine was and whether a noun was proper or common. Later she would have to stretch herself physically to beat Susy in the fifty-yard dash. All of that would come later. For now—she could simply watch and listen. Her senses were about to consume a sumptuous meal of technical make-believe.

God Knew The Ending

In the beginning, God knew the ending. He never slumbers or takes an afternoon nap. There is no incident, milestone, phenomenon, circumstance, happening or event, whether good or bad, that has ever occurred in the history of man that took God by surprise. From the beginning of His creation of man, God knew the ending.

Because of its content, some material in this book may weigh heavily upon your mind. It is for this purpose that I start with the reminder that from the beginning, God knew the ending. After reviewing the first manuscript draft of this book, my pastor, Gary Coleman, stated, "I felt as if I needed to go take a bath after reading it." So if the material of this book becomes "heavy" for some of you, then remember the ending of the Bible—we win!

In the Beginning—Hollywood

Mrs. Horace H. Wilcox, the wife of a developer, gave Hollywood its name in 1887. It was incorporated in 1903 and became part of Los Angeles in 1910. When we make reference to Hollywood today, however, we refer to the industry of film-making at large and not to the town located in southern California.

Mostly first-generation Jewish immigrants from Eastern Europe developed the movie colony in Hollywood during the first decade of the twentieth century. Some of these were a former junk dealer (Louis B. Mayer who headed the greatest studio of them all, Metro-Goldwyn-Mayer or MGM); a furrier (Adolph Zukor of Paramount Pictures); a clothing salesman (Carl Laemmle of Universal Pictures); a glove salesman (Samuel Goldfish, later changed to Samuel Goldwyn of Metro-Goldwyn-Mayer); a street hustler (Harry Cohn of Columbia Pictures); a garment manufacturer (William Fox of Fox Film Corporation that later merged with Twentieth Century Pictures to become 20th Century Fox); and bicycle repairmen (the Warner brothers of Warner Brothers). These Jewish entrepreneurs believed that the nickelodeon, a theater that presented entertainment for the price of a nickel, would be a source of profit to them. By 1910, there were some 10,000 of these nickelodeons in America that boasted of having as many as 80 million customers a week.

With the promise of cheap land and year-round sunshine, these East Coast Jewish tradesmen founded their fledgling film empires in Southern California. This state not only had the sunshine, but it offered distinct and diverse locations for filming—deserts, forests, beaches, mountains, valleys and lakes. These spots were plausible stand-ins for locations any-where in the world. Some of the early studios were often open-air stages among the orange groves in Southern California, while others were former warehouses or empty sheds. Yet some of these film companies would produce several films a week at times. These Jewish tradesmen succeeded in turning their risky operations into celluloid empires.

In those early years, Thomas Edison had the patent for the Latham Loop that was used in the cameras or projectors. Edison himself owned one movie company. He vigorously fought those who illegally used his loop in their cameras. Showing no mercy, he sued everyone that his troop of spies caught. Edison would have his own problems, however, when demands for censorship started flowing in after he produced *The Kiss* in 1896. It was a closeup shot of a man and woman kissing.

In 1908, some of the first movie companies formed the Motion Picture Patents Company. This company ultimately claimed exclusive rights to photograph, print and develop motion pictures. They followed the inclination of American business at that time which was to group companies together in huge corporations—or "trusts." During those years, railroad companies, food packagers and steel magnates monopolized specific areas of business. The movie industry tried to do the same thing; however, there were no precedent rules for the filmmaking industry to follow. They had to learn as they developed. In the beginning, those eager entrepreneurs had no conceivable idea that America would lead the world in moviemaking.

The Shadow of Babylon

Probably the oldest of the movie companies in Hollywood was one called Biograph. The main director for Biograph was D.W. Griffith. He revolutionized the production of motion pictures and founded the modern technique of movie art. Some of his innovations are still followed to this day. He introduced the close-up figure, the fade-out, sustained suspense, distant views, restraint in expression and the switchback. He shaped the foundation of the basic elements of film-making. Singlehandedly, he raised motion picture acting to a higher plane of genuine art. It was Griffith who instituted rehearsals.[1]

As the *Leonardo da Vinci* of Hollywood, Griffith gave cinema its social respectability among the intelligentsia. He was looked upon as the god of Hollywood. One of Griffith's extravaganza films was entitled *Intolerance*. It portrayed the colossal court of the Old Testament Belshazzar. Griffith recruited four thousand extras to play roles as Babylonian dancers, eunuchs, soldiers, slaves, and handmaidens. He paid them the excessive price of two dollars a day, including a box lunch and carfare to the movie site. Next to a dusty trail called Sunset Boulevard, Griffith erected his cardboard Babylon. He insisted on having eight white elephants perched upon mammoth pedestals. The crew and set of *Intolerance* were quite the spectacular sight. Mountains of scaffolding and hanging gardens enclosed the massive set. Rising high above the make–believe illusion of Babylon, Griffith's eight white elephants guarded the elaborate set below them like elephantine sentinels.[2]

Griffith's *Intolerance* spanned 2,500 years and his chief

aim was to show how truth had always been threatened by hypocrisy and injustice. Yet the only target he succeeded in hitting was a confused audience. *Intolerance* failed miserably. Belshazzar's court finally sprouted weeds. The towering Babylonian columns crumbled and its painted walls peeled beneath California's scorching sun. Yet even when the set was abandoned, the illusion of ancient Babylon still towered above the city. The Los Angeles Fire Department condemned the crumbling set as a fire hazard. Still, the pompous Babylon remained. On one hand, Griffith's Babylon became a reproach to the rapidly-expanding Tinsel Town. On the other hand, it became a challenge for others to try and surpass its magnitude.[3] Wisdom cried out in the streets of Hollywood during those beginning years. From its very beginning, the fantasy factory had Babylon casting a long and haunting shadow over it. The Babylonian shadow of decadence and immorality remains to this day.

More than the art form of moviemaking developed during Hollywood's beginning—there was a pattern being forged for its rising personalities. Initially, the first film players worked on both sides of the camera and they received no credit for their roles in the movies. However, some of the film players eventually became familiar to their audiences and the producers quickly recognized that a familiar face could be a definite asset. When word poured in from all over the country that crowds were flocking to see their favorite film players, these familiar faces became more than hired help. Almost overnight, Hollywood birthed the *Star System*. Just as rapidly, the stars' salaries started to rise. The stars quickly developed the art of both having fun and making money. The pace of their lives may have been hectic in making movies, but they comforted themselves with *joy powder* as they called cocaine in those days. English drug expert Aleister Crowley passed through Hollywood in those early days and made note of its inhabitants as "the cinema crowd of cocaine-crazed sexual lunatics."[4]

From its earliest days, a dichotomy hovered around Hollywood. Most preachers maligned the new movie industry. Yet others outside the religious crowd gave it their blind allegiance. Hollywood became synonymous with two words: *sin* and *glamour*. Some branded it as a new Babylon whose evil influence rivaled the legendary depravity of the old Babylon. It was located in the county of Sodom and the state of Gomorrah. Newspapers screamed through their editorials about the outrageous new movie stars and how involved they were in sex and dope. Yet the deaf public flocked by the thousands into the movie theaters. The public's romance with Hollywood ripened into a decadent love affair that has lasted for almost seven decades.

The gossip columnists of Hollywood had not yet stepped forward, but gossip circulated widely through Illusion City.

As lightly as the wind carries feathers, rumors floated around everything and everybody. Griffith was supposed to be obsessed with young female children. Directors were not the only ones targeted. Another rumor appeared with the photographic proof of a popular male star who had posed naked.[5]

Then in September 1920, they awakened the head of Selznick Pictures early one morning with a cablegram from Paris. One of Selznick's top stars, Olive Thomas, a sprightly Ziegfeld Follies' queen, had been found poisoned to death in a Paris hotel. The valet had used his key to enter the suite and was greeted by the sight of a sable opera cape spread out on the floor. Sprawled out on top of the sable was a nude, dead woman. In Olive Thomas' hand was a bottle of mercury granules. Newspapers around the world became embroiled in the controversial death of the beautiful, wealthy, and young 20-year-old star. The next year, another scandal dropped Hollywood to its knees.[6]

This time it involved Roscoe "Fatty" Arbuckle who had been a hefty plumber's assistant. The comedy producer of the Keystone Kops, Mack Sennett, offered the plumber a job on the spot when he unclogged Sennett's drain. Arbuckle rose to his fame as the 266–pound Keystone Kop, making the grand sum of three dollars a day. Arbuckle played with Charlie Chaplin in several films, but when Chaplin left the company they promoted Arbuckle to even greater stardom. He later signed on with Paramount.[7]

In September 1921, Arbuckle and some friends drove two carloads up to San Francisco for a Labor Day party. After renting three rooms in a swank hotel, and using the attendant as his bootleg connection for alcohol, Arbuckle's party quickly swelled to more than fifty people. Almost immediately, guests began shedding blouses and trading pajama bottoms. Empty bottles piled up like pyramids. At one point in the night, the drunken Arbuckle grabbed an aspiring starlet named Virginia Rappe and steered the tipsy woman toward a bedroom in Suite 1221. What happened within the suite's walls would bring the luxurious room a fame of its own.[8]

Guests later testified about piercing screams coming from the bedroom. Once they heard Arbuckle yell, "Shut up or I'll throw you out the window!"[9] Then they heard weird moans escaping from behind the closed door of the bedroom. The guests finally pounded on the door until the plastered Arbuckle burst forth in torn pajamas. Giggling, he told the other women to: "Get her dressed . . . she makes too much noise."[10]

The women testified later that Arbuckle so ripped Virginia's clothes to shreds that they could not distinguish between her underclothes and her stockings. Shortly after being taken to a hospital, Virginia whispered to a nurse, "Fatty Arbuckle did this to me. Please see that he doesn't get away with it."[11] She then slipped into a coma and died shortly after that. Investigation results of the murder and rape shocked the country. Fatty Arbuckle, favorite of the small children, a champion of slapstick comedy, had ravaged Virginia with some sort of bottle after becoming enraged at his own drunken impotence.

Then within six months, another Hollywood murder sent shock waves through the film colony. William Desmond Taylor was found murdered in his bungalow court apartment. He was Chief Director at a subsidiary of Paramount. Since the murders both occurred within six months of each other, Hollywood, but especially Paramount, found themselves again the target of public outrage.[12]

The Hays Office

After these three incidents, public fury reached a frenzied pitch of incense against Hollywood. America cried out for the movies to reform. In answer to the public outcry, Hollywood itself hurriedly and magnanimously appointed Will H. Hays as the leader of its new formal censorship code. Hays was a staunch Presbyterian elder, a Republican who had served as President Harding's Postmaster General. In March 1922, a press conference informed the country of Hollywood's new moral intentions. Hays told the people:

> "The potentialities of motion pictures for moral influence and education are limitless. Therefore its integrity should be protected as we protect the integrity of our children and our schools, and its quality developed as we develop the quality of our schools . . . Above all is our duty to youth. We must have toward that sacred thing, the mind of a child, toward

that clean and virgin thing, that unmarked slate—we must have toward that the same responsibility, the same care about the impression made upon it, that the best teacher or the best clergyman, the most inspired teacher of youth, would have."[13]

The Hays Office issued its first dictate. Purification was coming to the films. They would scissor screen immorality. There would be no more improprieties, no more lingering, lusty kisses, no more carnality. They would insert clauses regarding the stars' morals into all future contracts.

Smiling as they stood behind Hays and listening patiently to his speech, the Hollywood moguls nodded their heads in political agreement to everything that the staunch Presbyterian said. Then they returned to their studios and continued in their pursuit of private profit, turning a deaf ear to what the American public wanted. The fantasy factories took a gamble. They believed the public would choose their love for the movies and the stars in spite of their disapproval of sexuality on the screen and the scandals off it.

Fifteen years passed before more decisive actions occurred. When *bad girl* Mae West arrived in Hollywood, she paraded sex on film through her suggestive lines and erotic implications. West's practice of handling a gangster on the screen was: "Is that a gun in your pocket, or are you just glad to see me?"[14]   This new sex star's promiscuous assertions stirred up Chicago's Cardinal Mundelein. They viewed Mae West as a menace to their young people.

In October 1933, six months after the release of Mae West's *She Done Him Wrong*, the Catholics formed a National Legion of Decency.   They followed the advice of George Washington in his farewell address to the country: *"forbid...to expect that national morality can prevail in exclusion of religious principle."*[15] Once the Catholics stepped up to the front line of the battle against Hollywood, the Protestants and Jews guarded their flanks. The Federal Council of Churches issued the ultimatum for movie makers to clean up their movies or else face federal legislation. After fifteen years of receiving threats and warnings, the magnates of Hollywood realized it was time to do something more than put Hays up as a front for their good intentions. They feared that the government would step in with its regulations.

Revision of Production Code

A Jesuit priest, Father Daniel A. Lord, went to Hollywood to confer with Hays about the current censorship code under which he was operating. Father Daniel Lord employed Martin Quigley, to write a new set of restrictions. The Hays Office adopted this new censorship code in June 1934 and Joseph I. Breen was installed to enforce the new Production Code Administration (PCA). The Hays Office now had the power over the actual creation of films. Joe Breen would have a new weapon with which to execute the power of the PCA. Producers agreed never to distribute a film that lacked the Hays Office's *Seal of Approval*. A formidable power now rested in the hands of the Hays Office. The Production Code became the immutable commandments of the movie industry. From that time forward, all sex ended up on the cutting floors at the studios.

Critics of this time when Hollywood was under the control of the Production Code declare that Hays office stifled artists because of "a pious little group who feared for the souls of men."[16] They moaned about the injustice of a committee that checked every film for all offensive material.

> "Behind closed doors, a group of men had the power to lay their hands on the creations of artists, to twist them this way and that, to satisfy the mandates and morals of a pious little group who feared for the souls of their fellow men. It was all done in the name of public morality and the greater good; but the film censors were always a step behind the public and were doomed to fight a rear-guard against maturing tastes, until they were forced, kicking and screaming, into a long retreat."[17]

Yet Hollywood produced most of its "classic films" within the limitations of the Production Code. Time-honored films such as *Gone With The Wind; Casablanca; Mutiny on the Bounty; It Happened One Night; The African Queen; For Whom the Bell Tolls; Mrs. Miniver; The Grapes of Wrath; Key Largo; From Here to Eternity; High Noon; East of Eden; The*

Philadelphia Story; All Quiet on the Western Front; You Can't Take It With You; How Green Was My Valley; Mildred Pierce; Miracle on 34th Street; Johnny Belinda; Treasure of Sierra Madre; All the King's Men; Giant; The Good Earth; On the Waterfront; Boys Town; Come Back, Little Sheba; Sergeant York; Rebecca; The Song of Bernadette; A Place in the Sun; and The Best Years of Our Lives—many of these films won more than a few awards for film excellence. The Hays Office put its seal on all these movies.

Shortly after World War II, Hollywood gave the Presbyterian "pope," Will H. Hays, half a million dollars in severance pay, along with his walking papers. Will Hays left, but Joe Breen carried on business as usual in the Hays Office, faithfully administering the Production Code. With renewed vigor, Hollywood then engaged in a concerted effort to dupe Joe Breen and the restrictions of the Code.

"When the finishing touches are put on the romance of American business, one of its finest chapters will tell the story of the general Will Hays. He taught Hollywood's fiercely individual captains to meet at the conference table and cooperate sanely for their common purposes. Above all, from the point of view of the average citizen, he waged a constantly gaining battle for good, clean movies."

— *The Indianapolis Star*[18]

In 1946, Alfred Hitchcock filmed *Notorious*, starring Ingrid Bergman and Cary Grant. This film tackled the PCA's restrictions regarding the kiss on the silver-screen. The Production Code never allowed a kiss to last longer than a few seconds, but Hitchcock and his stars found a way around the regulation. *Notorious* shattered all former kissing scenes with the longest embrace in movies. The scene shows Ingrid Bergman and Cary Grant embracing each other with their faces only inches apart. They kiss softly, but careful to observe the Code's three second limit. All the time, Bergman is lightly touching Grant's ear and gazing adoringly into his eyes. She continues to plant light, feathery kisses upon his lips as they walk toward a door in each other's embrace. A close-up of the couple continues as Grant picks up the telephone and speaks to someone on the other end of the line. Their embrace never breaks. When the telephone comes between them, Bergman maneuvers around it and persists in her intermittent, faint kisses upon Grant's lips. The kissing scene, with not one kiss lasting more than three seconds, succeeded in extracting approval from the PCA. It gave the audience a lengthy, passionate moment of on-screen intimacy. For the standards in those days, the scene was sensational. By today's standards of movies, however, the scene would appear almost innocent to us.

Over the next several years, Joe Breen suspected an organized effort to undermine his efforts to uphold the Code. Rumors circulated about how directors bragged about what a real chore it had been, yet they managed to get all the sin into their scenes. European films infiltrated America's *art houses*. These foreign films featured explicit nudity and their kissing scenes were assuredly not limited to three seconds.

"Hollywood has hastened its own decline by alienating millions of Americans beyond the age of thirty through its insipid handling of love, sex, marriage and divorce."

— Critic, Gilbert Selders[19]

"Our fear of what the censors will do keeps us from portraying life as it really is. We wind up with a lot of empty little fairytales that do not have much relation to anything. Why should people go out and pay money to see bad movies when they can stay home and see television for free?"

— Studio Head, Samuel Goldwyn[20]

The Fifties may have arrived soaked in innocence, yet that decade tottered America on the brink of massive change. McDonald's unveiled its famous double arches for the first time in Arizona. America's landscape painted itself with television antennas. A national survey showed that

Americans watched 27 hours of television a week. Those statistics alarmed more than a few people. Daniel Marsh, president of Boston University, said: "If the television craze continues, we are destined to become a nation of morons."[21] Television networks continued to gain ground, however, and movie attendance plunged to an all-time low. The Golden Age of Hollywood was over. The studios began to panic. Critics and the studios blamed Joe Breen and the Production Code for the falling ticket sales.

Hollywood tried desperately to lure the public out of their living rooms and back into the theaters. The fantasy factory tried everything—Cinerama, Cinemascope, 3-D and even attempted Smell-O-Vision. Yet the studios knew that nothing sold as well as *good old-fashioned sex*.

In 1951, Warner Brothers Studio hired the unknown Marlon Brando to star in its film, *A Streetcar Named Desire*, along with *Scarlett O'Hara*, Vivien Leigh. Joe Breen fought vigorously to cut some of the film's scenes that radiated a level of sexuality never before seen on the screen. The three elements that the PCA resisted were homosexuality, nymphomania and rape. Director Elia Kazan fought for the integrity of his *art* and refused to cut any part of the film. Then the Catholic Legion of Decency moved to the forefront and threatened a national boycott of the movie. When that happened, Warner Brothers bowed to some of the PCA's requirements and cut some of the scenes. Some of the more sexually-implicit scenes fell onto the cutting floor of the studio. Kazan denounced the *self-appointed moralists* of the Catholic church. To avoid a condemned rating from the Legion of Decency, Warner Brothers made the cuts without consulting Kazan. He was outraged. Again, when those scenes that were cut are viewed by us today, they appear so naive in comparison to what Hollywood now produces.

In spite of the cuts, however, the film electrified the nation. For the first time, the PCA had granted its seal to a film that obviously was not family entertainment. *A Streetcar Named Desire* broke a substantial barrier. It went on to win three Academy Awards in the year 1951. Its brooding star, Marlon Brando, also rose to the peak of stardom. His behavior projected an arrogant independence that appealed specifically to the non-conformist generation of teenagers in those early years of the Fifties. However, Brando's controversial personality has continued through the years. In 1973, he stunned the Academy by rejecting their Oscar for Best Actor in *The Godfather*. He sent an Apache woman to reject his Oscar on Awards night by saying that he was turning down this Oscar because of America's treatment of the Indians. Recently, he condemned the Hollywood "Jews" on the *Larry King Show*. His comments raised a storm of protests.

In the year 1915, the Supreme Court had made a decision that classified movies as the product of a "business pure and simple"[22] and were therefore not eligible for constitutional protection. However, the year 1952 witnessed the Supreme Court reversing its own decision. An Italian film by Roberto Rossellini entitled *The Miracle* had been banned in the state of New York on the grounds that it was sacrilegious. The Italian film is about a peasant girl who is seduced and impregnated by a shepherd. The girl believes the man to be St. Joseph and that her child was as immaculately conceived as was Mary's child, Jesus. When a distributor brought *The Miracle* to one of New York's art houses, Cardinal Spellman was outraged at the movie's content. The film was picketed by 1,000 Catholics and New York's Commissioner of Licenses, Edward McCaffrey, threatened to take away the license of any theater who showed the movie. McCaffrey found the film "to be a blasphemous affront to many of our fellow citizens."[23] He made good on his threat and yanked the theaters' licenses.

The angry distributor took his case all the way to the Supreme Court. It became a censorship test case for the highest court in America. The Supreme Court opened the door for Hollywood. America today lives with the consequences of that decision.

"It cannot be doubted that motion pictures are a significant medium for the communication of ideas like newspaper and radio. Motion pictures are included in the press whose freedom is guaranteed by the First Amendment."

Supreme Court Justice,
William Douglas[24]

Chapter 2

Contempt for Morality

After the Supreme Court Ruling

The year 1953 witnessed a central turning point for Hollywood as it started wearing its new garment of protection under the First Amendment. Harry Cohn of Columbia Pictures had carefully watched the battle between *A Streetcar Named Desire* and the Hays Office. He was ready to produce *From Here to Eternity* from the controversial book about World War II. Yet this time, it would be the Hays Office getting its back pushed up against a wall. Cohn was ready to see how far he could go under the new Supreme Court ruling. The studio head had accomplished his purpose by breaking through another PCA barrier. Columbia succeeded in filming Burt Lancaster and Deborah Kerr and their celebrated kiss on Waikiki Beach. Although *Life* magazine called the film, *From Here to Obscenity*, the movie went on to win six Oscars that year.

Joe Breen failed in his efforts to get the studio to at least wrap the married woman and her soldier lover in beach robes. Still yet today, Hollywood rejoices to flash the infamous beach kiss between Lancaster and Kerr as one of Tinsel Town's legendary scenes. This scene is a salivating memory for Hollywood because it represented a major victory for them in their never-ending battle with the Hays Office. The kiss may appear rather mild, even phony, to our worldly-wise society of today. Yet when the ocean wave swept over the swimsuit-clad, sand-covered lovers embraced in their passionate kiss, Hollywood knew that the wraps had come off more than the two lovers.

Hollywood prided itself as simply gaining further creative ground. Because they could not see the silent hand of Satan working on the back lot of their studios, the hallucination haven rejoiced in their victory of being handed approval for what they believed to be only the reality of their art. They ignorantly believed they were simply reflecting a realistic picture of America to her citizens. After all, the Kinsey Report had informed the country about the male attitude toward sex. Hollywood justified itself by contending that it was merely holding the mirror up for Americans to view themselves. However, Joe Breen believed that when Hollywood talked about realism, they were usually talking about filth.

Furthermore, the Supreme Court opened the year of 1953 by continuing to widen the arena of freedom of filmmakers. New York's ban on a movie because of "immorality"[1] and Ohio's prohibition of a film because it could "incite crime"[2] were both thrown out by the supreme justices in January of 1953. *The Supreme Court did not say, however, that films could never be censored.*

By October 1953, Joe Breen of the Hays Office had grown tired of repeating himself. His words had begun to ring hollow. Joe Breen, the administrator of the Production Code since 1934, retired. The following year Will H. Hays died. Christianity began its slow retreat from the trenches of its influence within Tinsel Town. The era of restraining immorality ended. A close study of the Hays office will reveal some of its hypocrisies and inconsistencies, yet its regulations restrained filmmakers from offending the moral consciousness of Americans. Perhaps the restraining arm of the PCA had also been instrumental in painting Hollywood's canvas that became known as "The Golden Age." Indeed, the Code had placed specific restrictions on sex, violence, obscene language, religious ridicule, ethnic insults and other offensive elements. However, it cannot be denied that the PCA's presence dominated over the films produced during those years that Hollywood itself calls its *Golden Age.*

Possibly the one person that fanned the fires of change for Hollywood the most during the Fifties was Marilyn Monroe.

Unlike former stars who had been exposed for posing in the nude, the public willingly forgave Marilyn Monroe when her nude body pictured on a calendar was brought forth. The public's first reaction to Marilyn's "I was hungry"[3] turned their heart in sympathetic understanding. Their second reaction proved just how much they had forgiven her when a million copies of the calendar sold. The public once again closed its ears when a film was produced showing the younger Marilyn, nude once again, sensuously caressing her own breasts in front of a camera. Upon the public release of the film, Marilyn turned to pills to help her live in the reality of the image Hollywood had built for her. Tinsel Town's sex object ended up as one more tragic suicide statistic. Even today, over two decades later, Hollywood parades her before the world as a legend and exalts her as an ideal role model.

In 1956, the movie industry eased the restrictive Production Code. It permitted *references* to drugs, abortion, prostitution and kidnapping. The Code also strengthened its ban on racial epithets. This was the first major revising of the Code since Joe Breen became the Hays Office administrator in 1934.

Under this new freedom, Elia Kazan directed another controversial movie called *Baby Doll* in 1956. Kazan ignored the blatant condemnation that came from more than a few quarters. *Time* magazine wrote, "*Baby Doll* is just probably the dirtiest American motion picture that has ever been legally exhibited."[4] Cardinal Spellman made a rare appearance in the pulpit at St Patrick's Cathedral and warned Catholics that they would be committing a sin if they went to the film. The National League of Decency had already condemned the picture. Despite the condemnation, theaters booked the film anyway. For the first time, the theaters ignored the Legion of Decency.

For the benefit premiere of *Baby Doll*, Elia Kazan had Marilyn Monroe and Marlon Brando as ushers at the Victoria Theater in New York. Kazan ordered the longest movie billboard in history to be displayed in Times Square. The billboard stretched for a block above the Victoria and Astor Theaters. It was 135 feet long. The billboard showed *Baby Doll's* star, Carroll Baker, lying in a crib, sucking her thumb. In the film, Carroll Baker played the role of a teenage bride who refused to consummate her marriage with her aged Southern husband. Her husband eased his frustration by peeping through a hole in the wall, watching his child bride in her bedroom. In the movie, she chided her husband but fell under the sensual spell of another man's pursuit of her.

By the time the Sixties arrived, the land of the free was beginning to lose its way. Beatniks made art houses fashionable and most of the movies they watched were foreign. Foreign movies meant sex. The French star, Brigitte Bardot, exploded onto the international film scene in a movie called *And God Created Woman*. This new French sex symbol was notoriously uninhibited and Hollywood flaunted what they called her innocent sexuality before America. They likened her to a playful kitten whose supreme command was love. Pictures flooded the country of Bardot's nudity that was either tangled in bed sheets or sun-splashed in a tiny bikini. This new sensual child of nature with her thick mane of hair proved Hollywood's ability to fuel the nation's imagination. Slowly, Americans accepted and expected more freedom in all areas of its films.

It is interesting to note that America took her first notable step away from the LORD in 1962 with the Supreme Court ruling that prayer be removed from our public schools. A definite correlation lies between America's direction in 1962 and all that has followed in the aftermath of that one decision to remove prayer. Christianity dropped the ball in 1962. We should have gone on the offensive *then*. The year 1962 is when Satan dropped his first nuclear bomb on this country because he obviously knew the importance of prayer more than the Body of Christ. Prayer is a direct expression of our dependency upon God. When we as a nation, allowed prayer to be taken out of our public arenas, we were opening the door for the enemy to enter. When America allowed her *dependence* upon the LORD to be dissolved by the Supreme Court, then He allowed her to reap the whirlwind of that *independence*. It is most notable that almost immediately after the 1962 Supreme Court ruling, the Production Code began its own inevitable downward slide.

Shortly after Bardot hit the American scene, the Production Code was changed at the beginning of the Sixties to permit the portrayal of *sexual aberration*. That is,

Hollywood could now produce films on homosexuality as long as it was done in good taste. It was during this time that the sexual revolution exploded upon America. Hollywood instantly began shattering one taboo after another in its films.

Shortly after the assassination of John Kennedy in Dallas, America changed her vocabulary. Trust, virtue and integrity fell into the dead language of the nation's founding fathers. New words of First Amendment rights, individual freedom and radical rebellion against the establishment carved their way into the nation's psyche. Then America became entangled in a war that she could not win, a war that would scar her soul for decades. With the bitter taste of the Vietnam War souring on the taste buds of our youth, America entered into a legally uninhibited era of film making.

The radical and rebellious Sixties changed more than the landscape of Hollywood. The Baby Boomers flexed their muscles of influence as they uprooted old traditions and rejected the archaic conventions of their parents. They proved to themselves and America that their generation had the power to radically change things. Under their banner of "Don't trust anyone over thirty," they flourished by the sheer strength of their numbers. Swaggering around in their hip-huggers and bell-bottoms, they pledged to change the world as they crawled into the bed of rebellion against the establishment. Theirs was a posture of *anti*. They were anti-religion, anti-family, anti-business, anti-military, anti-establishment—just anti. Their attendance swelled the theaters after the release of *Easy Rider* in 1969. Their adopted religion became recreational sex and drugs brazenly manifested during their messianic mudfest at Woodstock. Unfortunately, they became frozen in their radical mindset. Baby boomers currently inflate the ranks of Hollywood, television and the music industry. They cannot escape their youthful compulsion to push their world view of the Sixties onto America through their films. One of Hollywood's most prominent Baby Boomer directors is Oliver Stone. Still trapped in the mindset of his youth, still determined to prove that his generation was right, Stone displays this through such films as *JFK*, *Nixon* and *Natural Born Killers*. Typical Baby Boomers remain trapped in their own warped time tunnel of the Sixties and Seventies.

The counterculture rebellion made itself felt in more than just the social and political arena. The entertainment industry especially opened its arms of welcome to this irreverent attitude of the Baby Boomers. It was during the Sixties that the Production Code issued its seal of approval for the first time on a movie, *The Pawnbroker*, that contained nudity. *Who's Afraid of Virginia Woolf* became the next victory for Hollywood when it received the Production Code seal despite the four-letter words sprinkled throughout the film. Although the Legion of Decency continued its attacks on Hollywood for its increasing number of morally objectionable films, the cries of outrage grew fainter in the ears of the studios.

Michael Medved comments on these years in *Hollywood Vs. America*: "At the time of the industry-wide upheaval that shook Hollywood in the late '60s, only one member of the old guard grasped the full scope of the revolution in values and accurately anticipated its hugely destructive impact on the business he loved. Frank Capra, three-time Oscar winner and creator of several of the best-loved motion pictures ever made, walked away from the business at age sixty-four because he refused to adjust to the cynicism of the new order. In his 1971 autobiography, *The Name Above the Title*, he wrote of the altered attitudes that made his continued participation impossible: The winds of change blew through the dream factories of make-believe, tore at its crinoline tatters....The hedonists, the homosexuals, the hemophilic bleeding heart, the God-haters, the quick-buck artists who substituted shock for talent, all cried: "Shake 'em! Rattle 'em! God is dead."[5]

The existence of the Hays Office and the Production Code Administration (PCA) ended in 1966 when Jack Valenti assumed leadership of the Motion Picture Association of America. Hollywood sighed with relief when Valenti finally cut the jugular vein of the Production Code. The Motion Picture Association of America is Hollywood's largest political lobby. Valenti had been an aide to President Lyndon Johnson and he moved with ease in Washington's lobby arena. He still heads the MPAA today. The new code still called for restraint in portraying violence and for no undue exposure of the human body.

Valenti responded to these accusations that violence and nudity were running rampant in films by announcing his own creation of a *standardized system* that would become known as the Rating System. Before Valenti's rating system, they rated movies by dozens of local communities and religious councils. However, in 1968, Valenti met with the major studios and theater owners and presented his national ratings system with its four designations of G (general audiences), M (mature audiences), R (under 16 not admitted without a parent or guardian), and X (under 17 not admitted). Within two years of its initialization, the MPAA began to make changes in its alphabet soup. They changed the M (suggested for mature audiences) to GP for "general audience, parent guidance suggested." Then a year later, they changed it to PG for "parental guidance." Then in 1984, *Indiana Jones and the Temple of Doom* caused such an uproar that a new rating was again created. PG-13 is introduced as the rating for "parental guidance suggested for children under 13." In 1990, the MPAA gives us a replacement for the unfavorable "X" rating. The new rating, NC-17 (no children under 17), replaces X. NC-17 sounds much more respectable than "X." As more than three decades have proven, Valenti's standardized system has been anything but standard. But with the extinction of the old Production Code, Hollywood was in control. Nothing would be barred to its *artistic creations* now.

"According to the Hollywood Reporter, fifty percent of films earning Production Code seals in the first two months of the year (1968) are 'suggested for mature audiences,' compared with fifteen percent for the same period last year."

— Movie Time

Jack Nicholson got his breakthrough role when he starred in the film *Easy Rider*, the road film that became a metaphor for the Sixties. In that same year of 1969, *Bob & Carol & Ted & Alice* was released. The ads promoted the film with the slogan of "Consider the possibilities."[7] The *possibilities* proposed wife swapping. The film is about two married couples. One couple persuades the second couple to participate with them in wife swapping. The familiar landscape of Hollywood became almost unrecognizable. J. Edgar Hoover told a government commission that was investigating violence in America, that "seemingly limitless excess of sex, sadism, degeneracy and violence is only too apparent in the offerings of the motion picture industry."[8] Yet the worse was still to come.

Again, Michael Medved writes regarding the closure of the Hays Office and the failing box office sales of Hollywood: "In 1967, the first year in which Hollywood found itself finally free to appeal to the public without the 'paralyzing' restrictions of the old Production Code, American pictures drew an average weekly audience of only 17.8 million—compared to the weekly average of 38 million who had gone to the theaters just one year before! In a single twelve-month period, more than half the movie audience disappeared—*by far* the largest one-year decline in the history of the motion picture business.

"There is no way to test the extent to which these appalling numbers represent a direct response to the closure of the Hays Office, but the statistics nonetheless definitively deflate the notion that liberating the industry from its established standards would help it to win a huge new audience. The suspension of the Production Code may have contributed to some extent to the alienation of the public, but it seems unlikely that it constituted a primary cause of the crisis."[9]

In the years that followed the closure of the Hays Office, some filmmakers ecstatically produced films under their newly-given artistic freedom. Yet an overall comparison of the *quality* of motion pictures between Hollywood's Golden Age in the Thirties and Forties and those of the Eighties and Nineties should verify that the former decades would come out on top. Unquestionably, *technical superiority* exists in today's films, but the *quality* award goes to Golden Age films. The Production Code is included in Appendix A. Most of us would agree that its rules appear antiquated by today's standards, yet there can be no denial that Hollywood produced some of its greatest masterpieces under the Code.

The beginning of Hollywood was once viewed by Americans as a place populated by beautiful, talented, rich and famous movie stars. As the years passed, however, the country began to see that a split vision existed in Hollywood.

In private life, some of Tinsel Town's stars were hopelessly insecure people menaced by suicidal longings. These same stars of Hollywood have been our national role models for decades. From the beginning, America and Hollywood entered into a marriage with a no-divorce clause in the relationship. Hollywood is not vacating its home in America. It has taken up permanent residence here. However, domestic violence has become rampant in this relationship between Hollywood and America. America, unfortunately, has been on the receiving end of all this ruthlessness. She has been morally battered and beaten half to death by Hollywood.

Remember

▶ Hollywood began with the long shadow of Babylon's influence cast over it.

▶ Many of Hollywood's *stars*, who are paraded by the media as role models for our youth, seem to always be entangled in a web of wickedness and immorality.

▶ Hollywood has made praiseworthy films of righteousness and inspiration in the past and is capable of doing so again.

Callie sat hushed and quiet as the movie began. The featured film on this opening night was to be a re-run of the 1982 film, "An Officer and a Gentleman." The movie opened with a scene of a naked man lying in bed with two naked women. Sitting in the dark theater, young nine-year-old Callie gasped suddenly and automatically at the shameless nudity. Without hesitation, her first instinctive response was to cover her eyes. Her little heart thumped loudly against her chest wall. Then timidly, she peeked out from between her fingers. She looked around her to see the response of those sitting near her. All eyes were focused on the picture before them. She felt shame at her reaction since it apparently did not affect the others. She looked back toward the screen in time to see a young American boy a few years older than herself. The young boy walked down a cluttered, dirty street in the company of three other dark-haired boys. Quickly, one swarthy skinned boy swung around and kicked the American boy with his foot, knocking him to the ground. The next image showed the stunned, young American boy with a bashed–in bloody nose, sitting in the echo of the three boys' laughter as they ran off with his money.

Callie relaxed once she saw the young man Richard Gere look at himself in the bathroom mirror. Even as young as she was, Callie realized that the scene of the young boy was Richard Gere's memory of himself as a child. In a flashback, he was remembering the time he had been brutalized by the other three boys. Almost immediately, Richard's drunken film father staggered onto the screen. Callie grimaced when she heard a horrid sound of retching vomit as the father leaned over a toilet in a dirty bathroom. Richard Gere's screen father slouched before Callie. He stood in only his boxer shorts with the fly open. His beer belly drooped over the elastic of his underwear.

"How gross," thought Callie. She was repulsed by the sight of his father and she realized now that he had been the nude man lying in bed with the two nude women.

Callie glanced up at Aunt Heather. There was no outward reaction by Aunt Heather. Nothing seemed to be out of the ordinary for her sophisticated aunt, but Callie felt uneasy watching the images in front of her. It took several more moments of hearing the thumping of her heart and squelching her feelings of guilt before Callie truly relaxed. Yet as she watched Richard Gere get on his motorcycle and ride onto the naval base, she pushed the nudity, the bloody nose and the sound of vomiting out of her conscious thinking. Soon she was swept away with the tension of this young man's story. An attractive, dark–haired young woman soon appeared on the screen. Callie liked this part. Callie was certain that this pretty woman who worked in a factory would soon meet Richard Gere. She leaned over to Aunt Heather and whispered:

"Isn't she pretty?"

Aunt Heather patiently acknowledged Callie's comment with an affectionate smile, patted her on the hand and then looked immediately to the screen again.

Once or twice during the unfolding of the story, Callie thought back on the opening scene of nudity with the two women sprawled out in a drunken stupor. At the same time, her mind flitted quickly back to the image of the young boy's bloody nose. Yet the images flashing across the large screen in front of her pulled her back to the present moment of action.

Callie's innocence kept her from knowing what was about to happen when the handsome young officer candidate took his pretty factory woman to a hotel room. Without prior warning, Callie saw the attractive couple in larger-than-life nudity before her. The lovely lady from the factory was lying on top of Richard Gere entirely naked. This time, Aunt Heather leaned over to Callie and whispered for her to cover her eyes. She instantly obeyed. Yet it was a moment too late. Her eyes had already taken in the image that now burned as a technicolor picture in her brain. Their nudity still sizzled before her in her mind's eye as she sat obediently in the dark theater covering her eyes with her small hands. Callie covered her eyes, yet her ears transmitted to her brain the heavy breathing and low, animal-like moans surrounding her in stereophonic sound. She instinctively realized that those sounds were somehow connected with their nudity.

Several more times, Callie covered her eyes when nudity came onto the screen. People sitting around her were not covering their eyes at all and she had begun to sense how young she was when the others nonchalantly watched what she sensed was wrong to view. Guilt pointed two different arrows at her. She felt guilty if she looked at the nudity, yet felt ashamed because the others watched it with no noticeable shock at all. She felt almost like a grownup because she was not as startled at one particular scene. A young blond woman walked across the screen in skimpy bikini panties. Sneaking a quick glance to the right and left of her, she noticed that the other people in the dark theater did not cover their eyes either. Quickly, she made the decision not to cover her eyes. She felt rather mature—yet guilty.

The worst nudity was yet to come. In a scene of unexpected horror, she saw Richard Gere's good friend, chalky white, limp, and grievously nude, swinging lifelessly with his belt around his neck in a shower.

"Oh no!" she moaned spontaneously. In an instinctive response, she covered her eyes just as Aunt Heather put her arm around her and whispered, "Don't look, honey."

On the drive to the restaurant that night, Callie kept remembering how happy she had felt when Richard Gere walked into the factory at the end of the movie and carried his lovely lady away to the make-believe land of everlasting happiness. However, the conversation drifted to other topics in Aunt Heather's Mercedes-Benz. Callie bubbled over in a conversation about the new boy, Brett, who had recently moved into town from California.

Everybody's talking about them, Aunt Heather. His father is some physi. . . phizcyst? Yeah, that's what he is. Granny says he's got to be one smart man to be a physi. . . to do that kind of work. His daddy is going to be in charge of the lab. Yeah! The nukleer—the big one just outside of town. There was a picture of them in the newspaper. . . front page. The whole family. Brett was wearing a suit. Oh, you saw that picture? I told you he was cute. You can tell he's from California. His face is still tan. Corey says he was over at Brett's house and he's got shelves of trophies for all kinds of sports and surfin'. Brett's mother is prettier than Richard Gere's girlfriend. I heard Mama and some of the ladies at church saying she looks about ten or fifteen years younger than his daddy. All of 'em were all talking about how pretty she is. Guess that's why Brett is so nice looking. He's smart, too. David says he's the smartest boy in class with math. 'Cause if anybody can beat David in his times tables, then he's smart. Darla and Laura try to sit by him every day at lunch. I watched him last week to see what he'd do. He's nice to them. But still. . . I think he thinks they're silly, though. Tiffany and Jamie are always saying he likes me. I told 'em he **did not**. *All the girls think he's so cute! Jamie says if he doesn't like me then he sure does pick me to be on his team first. . . before he even picks one of the boys. I don't why he picks me. Oh, Aunt Heather! You always say that. Mom says you're predjust. She says if everybody gave me as much as you do, I'd be spoiled rotten. I don't think I'm as good as Tiffany or Jamie. Do you think so? But you always think I'm prettier than everyone, Aunt Heather. But Tiffany and Jamie run faster than me. I don't know why he doesn't pick them first. I think he's the teacher's pet. She always lets him be captain. David says it's* because he's the fastest runner and the best kicker. Corey says it's 'cause the teacher grew up in California like Brett. I don't know. Laura says it's because he's so smart. See where that white car is pulling out. We got here at the perfect time. How neat! We got here just in time. It's right up front so we don't have to walk all the way 'cross the parking lot. If Granny was with us, she'd say the LORD saved this parking space just for us. Maybe He did. I hope they have our special table upstairs, Aunt Heather. Remember how we used to come here all the time before you moved away? I wish you didn't have to live so far away. Do you think he picks me for his team because I'm prettier? Oh, Aunt Heather, no wonder you're my favorite aunt. Mom says you do spoil me rotten and if you weren't her twin sister, she wouldn't let you do so much for me. Do you think I'm rotten, Aunt Heather? Mom says it's cause I look more like you even though you are twins. Granny says I remind her more of you, too. I'm just like you when you were little, she says, 'cept for our hair being different colors. As Callie walked through the door into the restaurant, the scene flashed before her about Richard Gere carrying his lovely lady out of the factory in the movie.

Following the hostess to the table, she giggled to herself about the scene on the playground last week. Some bully had purposely bumped into her and caused her to drop the ball. It happened so quickly that Callie would have missed it if she had blinked her eyes. Brett shoved the bully down and then dared him to pick on someone—like him, Brett—who was more his size. The bully snarled something incomprehensible and stood to his feet. Glaring at Brett, the bully turned on his heels and swaggered away. For the rest of that week, the bully avoided Callie like the plague.

For the next hour, Aunt Heather giggled and gossiped about their family, friends and church members as if she were only a nine-year-old like Callie. Together, they feasted on raspberry tea, Caesar salad and chicken fettucinè.

But later that night, Callie dreamed of chalky white bodies and empty black eyes staring down at her. Throughout the night, bodies dangled lifelessly at the end of ropes. She woke up screaming when one of them reached out and slipped the rope around her neck.

Part II
The Crisis

"Television is perfect. You turn a few knobs . . . and lean back and drain your mind of all thought . . . . You don't have to concentrate. You don't have to react. You don't have to remember. You don't miss your brain because you don't need it. Your heart and liver and lungs continue to function normally. Apart from that, all is peace and quiet. You are in the poor man's nirvana."

—Raymond Chandler,
written in 1950

Chapter 3

Catastrophe of the Sexual Revolution

Friday Afternoon — Spring 1993

Thirteen-year-old Callie dawdled on the front steps that led up to the middle school. Her best friends, Tiffany and Jamie were there with her. A lively conversation about a few of the latest movies circulated among them. Brett was inside the school gym talking to the Coach. Callie was waiting for him so they could ride their bikes to Granny's that afternoon. As long as Brett rode with her, Callie's parents had approved of their weekly bicycle ride to Granny's house. This was Granny's day for baking. She insisted that Brett visit her every week, along with Callie, and take a loaf of her freshly-baked bread for himself.

"I don't see how anyone could sit through Silence of the Lambs twice! That was a freaky movie! It scared me to death!" screeched Tiffany with as much dramatic flair as any Hollywood actress.

"Tiffany, you're so dramatic. Why do you go to movies if you hide your eyes?" scoffed Jamie. "You're the one who talked us into going to that crazy thing. Then you sit there with your eyes covered. That's one trashy movie, Callie. Ought to be glad you didn't go. . . you went also? When did you go? Oh. . . bunch of cannibals, wasn't it? That is all that movie was about. Weird, man—I'm talkin' weird!"

"It was a dollar movie, Jamie. Who cares about a dollar?

45

Besides, the only reason I went was because I like Jody Foster. I don't care what you say. She's a good actress," Tiffany stated flatly, ignoring Jamie's rolling eyes. With a girlish giggle, she added, "I looked over once and even Corey had his hands over his eyes. It was so neat, you guys! You should've been there, Callie. Cracked me up. I'm never lettin' him live that one down. You know Mr. Star Wars himself who always says, 'It's just a movie, Tiffany!' and then tells me how they do everything with special effects. Oh, no. . . no, listen Jamie. I forgot this part! Just about the time they're showing that gross corpse, David comes walking in with some popcorn and coke—this was so funny!—and he stumbles over Corey's feet. . .spills his coke on the lady sitting in front of us! She was so mad. We laughed until I thought we were gonna be thrown out. . . ."

". . . ever-body hushing us. You know how David is—he stands up and says, 'Hey, we're sorry, man! sorry. . .with that corpse on the screen, we thought you needed to lighten up a bit. Okay? Sorry.' Then ever-body cracked up laughin'. I loved Sister Act. If it shows at the dollar movie, I'm going again. Girrrrl, don't even talk to me about missing that show. Uh-huh! No way! Wha' you talkin' 'bout, girl. I am **not** missing that movie. Jes' give me my ticket and git otta my way, honey!" said Jamie.

Callie and Tiffany's laughter split the afternoon air.

"You are so good at that, Jamie. You sound just like Whoopi Goldberg," smiled Callie.

"Good?! Honey, I'm better'n good! I can imitate her perfect. Listen to this. 'No sex. No booze. No men. No way!' I got that line down perfect. Whoopi is soooooo funny! I loved that movie."

Several minutes passed as Jamie performed another monologue, imitating Whoopi Goldberg. Callie and Tiffany watched, amused, occasionally bursting out with laughter. Then momentarily, a horn blared half way down the block as it came toward the girls.

"Come on, Jamie. There's Mother. I've got voice lessons today and I can't be late," said Tiffany.

"Callie, tell Granny I'm comin' with you guys next week," said Jamie as she scrambled down the steps. "Tell her to make me some of those Jewish cookies! I love those. Call me. Tiffany, hush up. I'm right behind you. Your Mother hasn't even stopped yet."

Callie watched Tiffany and Jamie, first cousins, fussing at one another as they departed. She plopped happily down on the school steps to wait for Brett. Her thoughts stayed on the different times she and her friends had gone to the dollar movies on Saturday afternoons. She began remembering some of the movies they had watched together. Chuckling to herself about Jamie's imitation of Whoopi Goldberg, Callie's thoughts took a turn to the left as she thought about another black culture film by director Spike Lee— Jungle Fever. It had starred the black actor Wesley Snipes who had an affair with a white woman in the movie. Callie had been a little embarrassed during the explicit sex scene between Wesley Snipes and Annabella Sciorra since Brett, David and Corey had gone with her and Tiffany and Jamie. Yet at another movie, they had all roared with laughter during City Slickers. Corey wanted to go buy a baby calf afterwards. David walked around imitating Jack Palance as well as Jamie did Whoopi Goldberg.

[Billy Crystal]   "Hey Curly! Kill anybody today?"
[Jack Palance]   "Day ain't over yet."

Callie watched all kinds of movies with her friends— comedies, adventure films, scary movies, romances. The girls loved the romances. She and Brett both agreed, however, that she best loved the movies that made her cry. A small bubble of joy surfaced inside her sitting on the school steps when she thought of how Brett lightly, but lovingly, teased her when she cried. Sometimes, they cried together at the movies.

It depends on the movie, Callie thought. There are different degrees of sadness in movies. I can just blink a couple of times during some movies and the tears don't come out. Or maybe pretend to swipe the hair back from off my face. Who wants your friends to know that you get tears in your eyes when it's not a really sad—shed tears—kind of movie? Then there's the one-tear-trickle-down-the-face kind of movie. I kind of like those. Usually Tiffany and Jamie start crying the same time I do. Darla and Laura are always a few minutes behind. It must be because they're older—almost three months older— than us.

We all agree that the best kind of movies are the ones that we have to pull out the Kleenex. We don't care if anybody sees

*us crying at those movies. Most everybody in the theater is cry-
ing with us anyway. I just cry and cry for the people in the
movies who get hurt. I don't care if anyone hears me. Jamie
usually blows her nose when she starts crying. She sits there
and bellows out, "This is so sad." And Tiffany gets quiet
when she cries. Me? I can't help it. I make everyone stay with
me until the credits have finished rolling at the end. I'm sobbing so much that I can't leave. The stories are so real. Tears
probably sell more tickets for the movies than anything else.*

*"Hey!" said Brett as he sat down next to Callie and looked
at her. "Have you been crying?"*

*"No," answered Callie, brushing a tear off her cheek with
embarrassment.*

"You have, too. What's wrong?"

*"Nothing—really! I was remembering the part in Steel
Magnolias when Sally Fields was walking up the sidewalk to
get her grandson. That was so sad."*

"That was sad," agreed Brett.

*For a moment, the two of them sat in silence on the school
steps. Both of their minds were replaying the scene of an auto-
mobile driving down a highway with an early morning sun-
rise behind it. . . passing a service station. . . pulling up in
front of a house. . . weary-looking in a baggy brown sweater,
Sally Fields stepping out and walking up the sidewalk. . .her
blond-haired toddling grandson, still in his red and white
pajamas, stretching out his arms toward her. . .Sally Fields
has just left the hospital where his mother, her daughter, had
died. . . .*

*"It's the music that makes it so sad," murmured Callie to
Brett.*

*"Yeah. . .we'd better go. Granny will send an all-points
bulletin out to the FBI if we're more than thirty minutes late,"
he said.*

*Brett placed their books in his back pack before straddling
his bike.*

"Callie . . . ."

"What?"

"Oh, nothing . . . ."

"What is it? What's wrong, Brett? Something's wrong."

"I promised I wouldn't tell."

*"Tell me, Brett. I **won't** tell."*

"Mom wants to leave Dad and move back to California. She made me promise not to tell Dad. They've been arguing so much lately. I think they might get divorced. They say it doesn't have anything to do with me, Callie, but I can't help wondering."

"Of course, it doesn't have anything to do with you, Brett. Just because your Mom and Dad don't love each other anymore doesn't mean they don't love you."

Callie stood motionless, holding onto her bike. Then she saw moisture glisten in Brett's eyes. Although they were both thirteen years old, Brett had grown at least five inches taller than her this past year and she sometimes had to raise her chin to even look into his eyes. Brett rambled on, almost to himself as the two of them stood straddling their bikes in front of the school.

"I can't help wondering. Maybe if I didn't play football and basketball or if I stayed at home more with Mom. She never has liked it out here. Always talking about how much she misses California . . . she hasn't made any friends except with the wives of the other men at Dad's work. They're all a bunch of old grandmas. Maybe she'd still love Dad if I'd spent more time with her. We used to do more things together. . . when we lived out in California. Other kids tell me it's not so bad when your parents get a divorce—Dad says that's out of the question. He'll never give her a divorce. He loves her too much.

Mom doesn't want to do things with us anymore, but at least we're all still together. Mom cried yesterday when she told me she wanted to go home to California. She made me promise not to tell Dad. I started crying when she said she didn't want Dad to move with us. She doesn't love Dad anymore. That's what she told me. All he does is work. He's no fun anymore, she said. She used to love him, but now she doesn't. Now she's decided we'll move back to California. It'll be better she says. Better for who? Not for me or Dad, that's for certain.

I wonder if she'd still love Dad if I hadn't been born. She never wanted more kids after me. She's always told me that. I used to ask her for a little brother when I was young. I don't anymore. Maybe she never wanted me. I don't know. Maybe if I hadn't been born, Mom would still love Dad. She used to tell me how much fun they had when they were first married.

I just can't choose between them. How can you pick between your Mom and Dad when you love both of them? I can't even imagine my life without both Mom and Dad. I keep thinking something will change. Maybe Mom doesn't love Dad anymore, but I still love him. What fun would it be to play football without Dad up there in the bleachers yelling for me? Nobody realizes he's a nuclear physicist when he's up there screaming his lungs out for me when I make a touchdown. And the worst part of all is seeing Mom cry. It rips my guts out. That's the trouble. Mom cries. Dad cries. I cry. Why can't things just be the way they used to be when we were all so happy. . . Callie, what if I have to move back to California with my Mom?"

Callie's face turned a sudden white.

"That won't happen," she said softly.

"It might."

"No, it won't. We'll tell Granny and she'll pray. The LORD won't make you go back to California."

"Then tell Granny to have Him make my Mom love my Dad again. We can't tell Granny. I promised my Mom I wouldn't tell anyone. I wasn't supposed to tell you."

"Then I'll pray. The LORD won't make you go back to California. I know He won't. "

Callie and Brett rode to Granny's house in silence that late Friday afternoon.

On Sunday when Brett returned home from church, he opened a pink envelope that had been placed on the pillow of his bed. He would not be moving back to California. His mother deserted both him and his Dad. Brett picked up the telephone to call his father at work. Dad's at work. Always at work. Mom's on a plane to California. He felt his world crumbling around him when he placed the receiver back into its cradle. He wept by himself, all alone, in the city's largest house, owned by the family most envied by the local people.

Then several weeks later, in the kitchen, with fresh bread saturating the air, Granny started talking about Jesus. He and Callie had stopped by on their weekly visit. Callie was on the telephone in the living room, having a three-way conversation with Tiffany and Jamie about their English homework. Quite unexpectedly, Granny started the conversation as casually as if she were describing to Brett how her bread tasted so good. Tears filled Brett's face when he realized the truth of why this Jewish Man had been nailed to a Roman cross. Without saying a word, Granny reached over and picked up a Bible with a leather binding that was faded and worn. Brett could barely see the words on the page because of his tears as Granny used her finger to point at each verse. Then the words of the thief who had been crucified on Jesus' right side fairly jumped off the page to him: "... but this Man hath done nothing amiss." Suddenly, Brett understood. It was not what men had done to Jesus. It was that God allowed Jesus, this Man Who had done "nothing amiss," to be punished on that cross for what he—Brett—had done wrong. Jesus had been crucified in Brett's place. Guilt and heaviness settled in his heart. In that instant, Brett felt as if he were more guilty than the soldier who had pounded that huge spike into Jesus' hand.

"—He died for me?"

The only answer Brett received was a warm smile and a gray-haired nod.

Callie entered the room minutes after he and Granny finished their private prayer meeting. She squealed with delight upon hearing what had just occurred. Then she doubled her fist and gave Brett a mock slug on the shoulder.

"Why didn't you call me?"

"You were talkin' on the phone. . . ."

"You should've called me," she answered with a pretend pout.

Brett not only gave his heart to Jesus that day—he gave it to Granny as well. She replaced his lost mother. At times Brett was not certain what Granny did the most. . . pray for those whom she loved or bake them loaves of bread and prize-winning pies.

The Big Three

Christianity focuses most of its concern toward the "big three" of Hollywood—sex, violence and profanity. However, Hollywood's value system includes more than these three subjects. Its morbid messages, dark distortions, preference for the perverse, destruction of human dignity and other startling subjects can be as poisonous for our children as sex, violence and profanity. The limitations of this book, however, hinders us from covering violence and profanity in particular. For our purposes, we will focus primarily upon the sex promoted through movies, television, music and the computer.

For too long, America has feasted upon the contaminated banquet set before her by Hollywood. Her skirts are polluted. She now stands disgraced before the LORD. However, as surely as our ancestors fought and won battles for us, we must fight. It is essential that we win this battle for our children. It is essential that we re-establish the principles of the Word of God upon which our nation was founded. We must return to our foundation as "One Nation Under God." It will take each of us to join ranks and to face the enemy as a fiercely united army. We must pick up the baton of civic responsibility handed down to us by our Founding Fathers.

Hollywood's Smutty Saloons of Sex

Keeping in mind that the devil is the true director of Hollywood's value system, let us *belly on up to the bar* and observe the decadent drinks he offers our children through the medium of movies and television sitcoms. We might reel a bit at the taste of it, as though we ourselves were inebriated. For in looking at sex through Hollywood's eyes, we will be viewing it from the bottom of the gutter. Our gaze will be directed toward the sewers of depraved debauchery. America's modern entertainment industry goes out of its way to insult the traditional and Biblical view of sex as given to a husband and wife by God. Most movies openly endorse sexual affairs between strangers, married people or single people. Rarely does a movie exhibit any context of condemnation for sex outside marriage.

Hollywood views faithful, married couples or celibate, single people as boring and wearisome. Michael Medved's controversial book, *Hollywood Vs. America*, tells how they increasingly emphasize extramarital sex in today's prime-time shows on television: ". . . researchers for the American Family Association logged a total of 615 instances of sexual activity depicted or discussed on prime-time shows. By a margin of *thirteen to one* (571 to 44) these references favored sex outside marriage over intimate relations between life partners."[1]

Hollywood still produces an abundance of sexually-explicit

movies, but it now believes that it needs to stretch its horizons beyond mere sex. Its latest project may be the task of enlightening us and our children about the world of pornography. The adult theaters in Times Square may be shut down in New York, but sex and pornography stubbornly hang onto America's mainstream culture.

Hollywood intends to shove this *hot* topic down America's throat. They will release five movies regarding pornography. During the writing of this book, Columbia Pictures released *The People Vs. Larry Flynt*. The picture follows the notorious publisher of the pornographic magazine *Hustler*. The story takes the blue-collar porno king from the backwoods of Kentucky to the courtrooms of Washington as he fights the First Amendment for his right to degrade women. The picture presents Flynt as a hero of the First Amendment. It never reveals the violence with which Flynt portrays women in his porno magazine. The magazine, *Hustler*, shows acts of torture, murder and sexual degradation toward women. Milos Forman, the producer of the film, has bragged about his having never looked at a *Hustler* magazine. Such an admission suggests that Hollywood is content to remain blind in what it defends. Flynt's own daughter appeared on the Charles Rose Show on PBS television in opposition to the film shortly after its release. She believes that the film is a "dangerous message"[2] to people who have been abused. She declared that her father Flynt does not care about free speech—he cares only about his money and protecting his assets. She said that if we "start looking to Larry Flynt as a hero, we're in serious trouble."[3]

Flynt's battle with Jerry Falwell ended in the Supreme Court. Falwell had sued Flynt for a *Hustler* magazine ad. The ad was typical of some of the twisted, perverted material promoted in *Hustler* magazine—it portrayed Falwell as having an incestuous relationship with his then 82-year-old mother. Woody Harrelson, who plays Flynt, wears a prosthetic beer belly in his portrayal of the porno magazine king who married a junkie stripper. The person who portrays Flynt's wife in the movie is Courtney Love. She is the quarrelsome rocker who pretends to perform oral sex on teenage boys at concerts and has a well-reported history of heroin in her own life. In real life, Flynt's wife later died of AIDS. Early previews suggest that Flynt will be presented in a favorable light to draw the audiences sympathy. In the movie, they actually portray him as a hero of the First Amendment. To bash the LORD again, the film is certain to highlight Flynt's supposed conversion to fundamental Christianity. Milos Forman, the director of *Flynt*, enthusiastically promotes the film as having all the same ingredients of *Forrest Gump*. The following conversation occurred between the female producer of *Flynt* and Sony's lawyer who had read the script: "Okay, if you see an erect [male genitalia] for a second, it's okay, but if you're *dwelling* on it . . . ."4 In view of that conversation, *The People Vs. Larry Flynt* does not appear to resemble *Forrest Gump* at all. Hollywood certainly could not describe the film as family entertainment. The producers of the *Flynt* movie are not showing what the movie actually contains. However, the reviews are telling people to get ready to view raw footage.

Some controversy surrounding the film, however, has already begun to surface. More than a few people have condemned the porno-king for being portrayed as some sort of hero. In reality, Flynt uses his magazine to degrade and humiliate women by showing violent, sadistic portrayals of them in a sexual context. Flynt's own daughter has condemned the movie and its portrayal of her father as a folk-hero.

With its customary habit of dragging morality down to the pits of perversion, Hollywood has fervently taken on the orgies of the previously secret industry of pornography. Since the movie industry believes it no longer shocks people with its parade of nudity, it now probes into the dark world of pornography. Another soon-to-be-released movie with pornography as its theme is *Boogie Nights*. It is about a young nightclub employee lured into the porn industry. The script calls for full-frontal nudity of both male and female. *Good Vibrations,* yet another porn movie, vividly exposes the sex-toy business. The movie advertises itself as a comedy about the sex industry.

From experience, we understand how Hollywood always introduces its *forbidden subjects* under the guise of comedies. It is a known psychological fact that our defenses are down more when we are laughing. How often have we covered the truth in a stinging remark of sarcasm by laughing as we make the statement? Remember when the fabrication factory wanted to dispense its approval of wife swapping in the Sixties? It produced the *comedy* of *Bob & Carol & Ted & Alice.* When it wanted to slip in the back door with an authentic-looking portrait of a sturdy, gay marriage, it produced *The Birdcage* under the hilarious cover of Robin Williams. Of course, the released timing of the picture harmonized perfectly with the national fury over same-sex marriages. Some Hollywood *purists*, who demand their art be presented the way they created it, complained that American filmmakers had cleaned up *The Birdcage* so much that it was not recognizable as being adapted from the French original, *La Cage aux Folles.*

The trend of Hollywood always filters down to the small screen. After *The Birdcage*, television writers rushed to their keyboards to throw out scripts that exalted "drag" and promoted the transvestite. ABC bragged about how *The Drew Carey Show* received its highest rating when Drew Carey cross-dressed as his co-worker. NBC followed with its version by having the veteran transvestite, Dave Foley, from his *Kids in the Hall* days strap on his bra for *News Radio*'s costume party.

In the same company with the homosexual issue is something called *ménage à trois* that Hollywood promotes. However, they carefully introduce this taboo subject to us only after we are laughing. The extremely popular television program, *Seinfeld*, has Jerry and his good friend George, who is always good for a laugh, acquaint the audience with *ménage à trois* in an amusing situation. By our laughing, our attention is directed toward the comical predicament in which Jerry finds himself rather than on the immoral perversion of *three people having sex together*. Television also used the *comedy* sitcom of *Roseanne* to air one episode of a gay marriage. ABC graciously moved the episode to an hour and a half later in the evening to limit the number of young viewers. They justified the episode as having *adult humor* that *might* not be appropriate for children. When we laugh, our defenses collapse. Filmmakers know this, as do television writers.

Most of us as children instinctively recognize the power of laughter. My brother David and I knew that if we could get our mother to laugh when she had caught us doing something wrong, our punishment would be lighter. If we succeeded in making her really laugh, we knew that she might not punish us at all. I was the lieutenant, but my younger brother David was the undisputed champion of our laughter squad. As young boys, we instinctively knew that laughter would not allow our mother to be so discriminating in her judgment of us.

Those who write Hollywood's scripts also understand this. They recognize that once we are laughing during a movie, we do not make good analytical observations. Our laughter overrides the ultimate message of the story. The goal of any writer is that people perceive the world as they do. Most of the time Hollywood writers and producers want us to accept some socially-forbidden taboo that they have accepted. The world's laughter covers up the devil's intent to lure us away from holiness into sin. We do not take seriously anything that we laugh at in life. The laughter causes the seriousness of the subject to lose its power. While we are laughing, we do not *seriously* consider homosexuality or group sex.

By my writing the above, do not think that I lack a sense of humor. I believe that God not only gave us a gift when He gave us stories, but He likewise gave us our sense of humor. My brother David has a God-given gift of humor. Even in some of the most devastating times through which our family has moved, David's humor had the ability to raise the spirits of those around him. Yet there are different forms of humor and amusement.

One form of crude humor makes up a great deal of the television comedy, *The Drew Carey Show*. Sex jokes flooded one episode as women used coarse language and graphic body language to describe what they would like to do to Carey's genitals. Men and women on *L. A. Firefighters* crack jokes about male genitals and sex. They liberally sprinkle episodes of *Friends* with crass genital jokes. Humor can be clean or it can be crude. Naturally, humor amuses us, but it can be employed to either celebrate our humanness or to mock people. Humor can be used at our own expense or at the expense of others.

Yet from the devil's viewpoint, humor is a great weapon in his arsenal of diversionary power. Satan can only imitate or pervert what God has created. The devil perverts our sense of humor by slipping in his dark distortions under the cover of our own laughter. Hollywood has labeled this dark humor as *adult humor*. Of course, this kind of fun is just for *adults*! It is not suitable for children to view. Not yet, that is! Once the devil can get adults laughing so he can bludgeon their senses with his perversion, his next battle plan will be to conquer our children. We must not deceive ourselves in the enemy's strategic plan. He knows that what one generation fights, the next generation accepts. If we fight our children watching *adult humor* in this generation, our children of the next generation will accept it. So we must understand that the devil is not so foolish as to thrust blatant sexual immorality such as *ménage à trois* before us without its being mixed with humor—at this point in time anyway. He first diverts our moral discrimination by getting us to laugh so much that our guard is down.

French Twist is another film adapted from a French version of *ménage à trois*. The movie tells the story about another gay nuptial *comedy*. Only this time, the comedy involves a butch lesbian interloper who seeks to turn a husband and wife into a *ménage à trois,* which will naturally include her. Critics again complain because they have sanitized *French Twist* from its French version, starting with the original film title that was *Gazon Maudit*. Why not leave the original title on the film? After all, what person would be curious enough to track down the idiomatic translation that means *accursed lawn*? Does *accursed lawn* make any sense for the title of a movie? Only if we understand that it is slang for a woman's private parts.

In *Bulletproof,* Hollywood again disguises the true message of the story by marketing it as a truly platonic friendship between a black and a white male. This buddy-buddy story leaves its unsuspecting audience of mostly teenage boys laughing. Consciously, the teenagers might miss the true message of this movie about the love between the black man and white man. They tucked this taboo love safely away behind violence and comedy. The *buddies* adore each other with a passion, in spite of their homophobic jokes to the contrary. Most of the teens roar with laughter when the naked Adam Sandler attempts an escape through a window only to have Damon Wayans shove a gun up his backside with the subliminal message of homosexual penetration. Talk between the two men throughout the movie is saturated with *tush-fixated* remarks.

Not wanting to be accused of sexual prejudice, however, Hollywood produces movies about lesbians as well. The movie, *Bound*, develops a lesbian relationship between two provocative women who concoct a plan to steal two million dollars from the Mafia. The movie forcefully pushes its sexual agenda onto the screen with a strong flesh-on-flesh naked scene between the two women.

Movie studios seem unconcerned about the commercial failures that usually follow in the wake of a sexually-explicit film. In their obsessive desire to please only themselves, the financial outcome of their celluloid projects apparently does not drive most filmmakers. Previews of *Striptease* did their best to lure audiences and they failed dismally on the domestic scene. However, it proved to be a box office success overseas. Demi Moore played the leading role in *Striptease*. She is a star because they tell us she is—not because of anything she has performed on the screen. The most she can show us on the screen is her ability to graphically perform oral sex on Michael Douglas with the intent of destroying his career in *Disclosure*. Also, in the pointless flop *Striptease*, the unharnessed Demi showed us what she does best. She defiantly parades her nudity. Again, the dream factory served America the same old plate of rubbish under the guise of a nutritious entertainment diet. Columbia must have had a different goal other than earning money with *Striptease*. Their budget for the film was forty million dollars and it grossed only thirty-five million at the box office.[5] Most of America's gross sales, 30.2 million, was earned during the first several weeks after the film's national premiere. Stop and think what that means. It means that after the first several weeks of the release of the highly-publicized film, word-of-mouth spread the news that the movie was as fake as Demi's fur costume was in *Striptease*. The grassroots of middle-class America still holds more power within its grasp than does Hollywood or the news media.

Another sexually-implicit movie that bombed at the box office was *Showgirls*. The story about topless Vegas hookers was reviled by critics and ignored by the public. The moviemakers intended that the sex-crazed, psycho-sluts in the movie would portray the ultimate female fantasy role for men; instead, it crashed and burned.

Since filmmakers are no longer saddled with the stifling presence of the Hays Office and the Production Code, these creative artists have their license to pursue any topic. Their guiding star is realism. They defensively proclaim that their art is merely *imitating life* as we know it in America. *Bastard Out of Carolina* is the title of one movie made for television. As of the publication of this book, the movie *Bastard Out of Carolina* has mercifully been shelved. Yet this movie that is a tense depiction of sexual child abuse will one day doubtlessly gain its way onto the television screens in our living rooms. Many who watched the first preview of this film were visibly shaken at the graphic scenes of child molestation. One gritty scene, a long and intense rape scene, shows the stepfather punching his adolescent stepdaughter in the face. He then rapes her as blood trickles down her face. Following their historical pattern of perseverance, filmmakers will not give up until this graphic raping of children becomes common on the screens in our living rooms. They know child abuse will be strongly resisted at first, but experience has also taught them that repetition of a subject soon loses its ability to shock us. No doubt, those who wish to broadcast *Bastard* on television will win their battle and will probably air the movie even before the production of this book.[6]

Another bizarre film, *Crash,* has been postponed in its American showing—at least until the Spring of 1997. The movie is about people who get sexually aroused by re-creating car wrecks like the one that killed James Dean and Jayne Mansfield, both stars of the late Fifties. The movie shows endless "ambi-sexual couplings" and parades one more sexual perversion as the norm.

As reported in *Entertainment Weekly,* the surprise person behind the shelving of these two films is Ted Turner of Time Warner. In response to a reporter's question about *Crash,* Turner replied:

"I yanked it off the schedule. It bothered me. . . . The people with warped minds are gonna like it, though. I mean, it's really weird . . . . Imagine the first teenager who decides to have sex while driving a hundred miles an hour, and probably the movie will get 'em to do that."[7]

According to the article, Turner is not backing down from his civil war with Hollywood in the "long-smoldering debate between artistic license and restraint on sexuality and violence in entertainment."[8] One of the stars of *Crash* furiously attacked Turner for being "reminiscent of Jesse Helms . . . .

Turner's moral fascism has no place in the entertainment industry."[9]

To those who have heard Ted Turner make such comments as: "Christianity is a religion for losers" and that Christians are "bozos," the above comment by the star of *Crash* appears rather contradictory.

However, I have purposely included these two conflicting sides of Ted Turner. It appears as if those in the entertainment business view Turner as a moral fascist while Christianity has taken the opposing view. Perhaps it is time to place Ted Turner high on our prayer list if he continues to manifest the courage and honesty to face critics who want to peddle their immorality in movies and on television. Is he antagonistic toward Christianity? Past evidence points in that direction. Yet, prayer can move mountains. Later in the book, we discuss the importance of prayer. Remember Ted Turner when we examine the power of prayer and its ability to turn wrong into right. One vital component of saying "no" to Hollywood is prayer. Ted Turner is a perfect example. Evidently, from past comments, Ted Turner scorns Christianity; however, if he takes a stand for morality then we should by all means pray for him. God still answers prayer.

Sex-drenched Soap Operas

Although sexually-explicit movies may fail at the box office, television's sex-drenched soap operas boast about decades of popularity with its viewers. Since the first black and white television made its debut in American living rooms almost a half century ago, the tube has had a profound, if not hypnotic effect on its audiences. Nowhere is that more true than in the daytime soap operas. The problem arises in what they are teaching us through these daytime dramas. The producers and writers of these soap operas generally trace Hollywood's footsteps by stating that their *art* merely imitates life in America. They justify what they produce as vehicles for dispersing information and they believe they are educating their viewers. With pride, they speak of how their story lines are socially relevant. Some writers brag that their well-developed characters help people to solve their own problems. These writers and producers delude themselves when they think that by creating characters who are involved in such bad things as date rape, abortion, homosexuality, business scams, demonic cults and infidelity, that these role model characters somehow set good examples for their viewers. Still, others shun the responsibility of their characters' actions. They believe their job does not entail making moral judgments and they are not responsible for promoting a higher level of ethics. Unlike Hollywood that denies having any influence on our children regarding sex and violence, however, soap operas often boast about their influence. They believe their soap opera characters are the communicators of the world. Everyone wants to do what they see on television. A synopsis from the movie guide reveals some things that soap opera characters teach us.

All My Children: Dimitri and Erica make love, yet later Dimitri confides to Peggy that he is tormented by another woman (Maria) with whom he recently made love. While trapped in a wine cellar, Maria and Edmund talk through their problems, but Maria does not mention her night of passion with Dimitri. Skye confides to Janet that she saw Dimitri making love to Maria. While Liza was having an affair with Jonathan, she left Skye for dead. Brad and Michael plan a date. Mateo and Hayley win the gold medal in the hot couples category. They now share living quarters.

Another World: Fearful that Sofia and Nick may marry, Maggie tells Sofia about making love to Nick in the barn. Maggie pretends she is getting an abortion. Maggie lies and says she is going to leave town to have her baby. Nick feels pressured and relents to marry her. After moving into their apartment, Nick leaves Maggie one night to go get drunk. He tries to pick up a woman. The relationship between Grant and Sharlene is definitely the hot couple in training for this month.

As the World Turns: Cal asks Connor for a divorce. Connor pleads with Cal not to get a divorce, but he insists their marriage is over. Mark confides to Ben that he may never get over Connor, although he had an affair with Agent Jones. Mark learns that a distressed Connor is all alone and he rushes to her. Connor pushes Mark away, but then changes her mind and races off to find him. She finds him in a hot embrace with another woman. Ryder and Nikki share their first kiss. Dani pretends to forgive Nikki for "stealing" Ryder, but secretly vows revenge. Later, Dani follows Nikki and Ryder and jealously watches the happy couple on a date.

Bold & Beautiful: Grant who dates Michael (female) shares a kiss with Brooke who dates Ridge (male). Later, Brooke is upset when Ridge passes on her offer for them to have a romantic interlude during the work day. Meanwhile, Grant confesses to Michael (female) that he kissed Brooke. He promises that he and Brooke are finished. Dylan (male) gives a final command performance before he retires his G-string. Sly takes out Jasmine's trash and he stashes a black mask and gloves into the bag—just like the ones worn by Jessica's rapist. The nurse Sheila confesses that she pumped Stephanie full of poisonous mercury pills.

The City: Zoey shows up at Richard's door clad only in her birthday suit. They *finally* give in to temptation and make love. The couple had a good thing going. It's a shame. They are half brother and sister. Zoey advises her friend Molly to seduce Danny. Molly acts on the tip and takes Danny to the rooftop, where she does an impromptu striptease for him. Sydney hopes to rekindle her affair with Danny.

Days of Our Lives: Bo arrives at a hotel and finds his fiancée, Hope, in bed with Franco. Rachel runs into DiMera and pulls a gun on him. He warns her that if she shoots, there will be an explosion because gas is leaking through the rubble. Undaunted, Rachel pulls the trigger and the tunnel explodes. Daniel Scott (who worked with Peter to drive Laura crazy) decides to return to Salem and extort money from Peter. Marlena warns Kristen that she will lose John once he learns about her deception.

General Hospital: Jason and Robin fall asleep at the Quartermaine boathouse. They are discovered the next morning wrapped in each other's arms. Later, Jason encourages Robin to share her feelings about Stone, sex and her HIV status. After their revealing conversation, Jason and Robin finally make love. The next day, the two spend some more romantic time together on the beach. Tom and Felicia try to mend their damaged relationship by making love. Ned and Lois decide to extend the "Eddie Maine" tour and move to Los Angeles. They celebrate by making love.

Guiding Light: Rachel hands over the cocaine to Drew. Rachel also explains that she is upset about the revelation that Nora had an affair. Todd walks unnoticed into the room and is stunned to see his wife about to make love to the man for whom he took a bullet. Marty goes out drinking and dancing and then lies to Dylan about what she had done. Maggie accepts Max's offer of ten million dollars to help him pull off his "miracle water" scam. Lucy is shocked when her husband says that he made a deal with the devil.

Young & Restless: Jill contemplates whether she wants John Silva to be her lover or her lawyer. Phyllis, the psycho redhead, plants a dead octopus in Chris and Paul's honeymoon bed. Later, Phyllis crawls into bed with Paul, who is heavily medicated. Paul begins kissing Phyllis. Chris enters the room. She pulls back the covers and finds Phyllis—naked—and in bed with her new husband. Victoria goes skinny-dipping and dares Ryan (who is not her husband) to join her.

Chapter 4

Corrosion of Our Culture

In the Beginning—Music

From the beginning of our world, God engaged music. One account of the LORD's personal testimony of His creation is found in the last chapters of the book of Job. God demands that Job "Gird up now thy loins like a man; for I will demand of thee, and answer thou me."[1] However, it is quite noticeable that God Himself does most of the speaking. The theme of His speech to Job is His power in creation. During this discourse, God tells what was happening as He laid the foundations of the world. In Job 38:7, the Bible paints a picture of a heavenly chorus of angels who sang as the LORD created the universe. "When the morning stars sang together, and all the sons of God shouted for joy." According to Job, the drama of the creation of the world had its own angelic soundtrack.

Then again, God displays His music appreciation by creating it within some of His angels. Ezekiel 28:13 tells about God creating Lucifer with this symphonic capacity. "The workmanship of thy tabrets and of thy pipes was prepared in thee in the day that thou wast created." Accordingly, many believe that before his fall, Lucifer was heaven's director of music. This would account for the devil's intense interest in music. Constantly, he attempts to pervert music from its God-intended use. The enemy persists in his invasion of our senses with his raging, destructive, poisonous lyrics.

In a primal sense, the truth of music's power is evidenced within our own physical bodies. Physicians teach us that our bodies are a musical score within themselves as we daily move in rhythmic, metered melodies. Our bodies produce their own biological symphony. Our internal pulsations, the rhythmic beats of our hearts, the crescendo and decrescendo of our lungs all serve to keep us physically alive. When we listen to a piece of music, the rhythms, beat and pulse of the music arouses our own internal rhythms. Music awakens the beating and the pulsations of our own physical bodies. As we listen to music, physiological changes in our bodies can be measured through elements such as blood pressure, galvanic skin response and hormone levels. Scientists have proven that sound waves give shape to the physical matter of our cells, tissues and organs. They have also proven that music greatly influences our state of health.

Music shapes our sensory behaviors and responses. Listening to music is a psycho-physical event. As it is heard and processed through our senses, music can powerfully affect our physical bodies and our emotions. This is evidenced as we watch a movie. It is the accompanying music that makes us feel frightened when we see an actor enter into a darkened room—not just the action of watching someone enter a room. Our emotions are aroused during a chase scene by the music—not by the sight of horses racing across the screen. The vibrations of music reach us not only through the ears, but also through our skin, bones and viscera (internal organs as the heart, liver, intestines). Music has such a strong impact on us because it works unseen on our nervous system and emotions. During elevated moments of experiencing the music, a *natural high* can occur. Music excites peptides, which are agents in the brain, that release endorphins that in turn produce this natural high or a state of euphoria.

Scientific research uncovered the above neurological effects that music has on the brain and the body. There is growing evidence that music can be successfully used as a natural healing agent and in place of the psychiatrist's couch. With the knowledge that God gave music as a gift to man, it would appear that such discoveries regarding music's healing ability may have substantial validity.

Further research on how music affects the mind and emotions has been done regarding infants. Inside the womb, the fetus hears only the steady, pulsating beats of its mother's heart. Researchers recorded these human sounds of a mother's body. They then played these *mother sounds* back to a nursery filled with newborn infants. They quickly discovered that even if the infants were crying as a result of being either hungry or irritable, they would immediately hush at the sound of their mother's body music. The newborns became almost instantly silent once they heard the *music* they had been accustomed to hearing inside their mother's body. Medical technicians observed the physical behaviors such as blood-oxygen levels, heart rates and blood pressure during the moments when the infants were agitated. Then the technicians subsequently observed the infants when the tape of mother's musical body sounds played. Tests showed a significant increase in oxygen levels, which is a good sign, in all of the infants. Grateful mothers all over the world now welcome these musical pacifiers because they have proven so effective in hushing their crying babies.

If God intended music for the good of man, then the devil, who has been hanging around imitating God for centuries, assuredly has his own label of music. The devil knows that he cannot create. He can only imitate God. He therefore takes what God created and does the exact opposite. God's intent was to bless man by giving him music to soothe, heal and inspire him. Satan's intent is to destroy man with his own perverted form of music.

In the beginning, God knew that music would have the capacity to evoke deep feeling responses. In His creation of us, He formed us so that music would profoundly affect us. Which of us has not been deeply affected by a love song, by a funeral dirge, or by patriotic anthems or marches? Music is used to worship God, to ignite sexual appetites, to arouse patriotism, to bury the dead and to marry the living. Music provokes the highest, and the most primitive, of emotional reactions. The power of music lies in its ability to touch us both emotionally and physically. When music vibrates our physical beings, we respond with our emotions. Music offers a great venue for power. The devil knows this truth and has acted upon it for centuries.

Music underwent a radical change during the Sixties and Seventies. Listeners of those songs could not have guessed that the young Baby Boomers were drug addicts, patients in mental institutions and suicides walking around waiting to happen. Musicians encouragingly escorted the Baby Boomers as they moved toward the free sex drug festival of Woodstock. Some musicians were shrieking acid rockers. Others hid behind the rundown world of drugs and cathedral hymns that condemned the mad, bad world their parents had built. The singing Baby Boomers rejected the discipline and tradition of their parents. Rage, bitterness and hallucinations became their hallmarks of reality. Counterculture singers led the nation in promoting Indian philosophy, hallucinogenic drugs, tribal ecstasy and all the other holy grails of the rock quest.

Dedicated rock fans blindly followed these disillusioned pied pipers on their destructive soul voyage. As years passed, however, the ravaged lives of the musicians started to loom larger than their buoyant music. These pathetic, misguided musicians became our youth's role models.

Throughout the world's history, music has been singled out for its inherent power to move man. It is the universal language of mankind given by God to His creation. His gift to man was a very powerful tool. He gave it for the good of man. The LORD never intended music to be the highway upon which our young people travel to drug addiction, sexual perversion or ultimate suicide.

Perverted Pied Pipers

As with anything given to man by God, it has the potential for good or bad. Used rightly, music can elevate the hungry soul toward God, raise goose bumps of patriotism, acknowledge true love and romance at weddings and honor memories of the dead at funerals. Music works invisibly, but surely, on our emotions and nervous systems. Studies prove that the effect of music can alone induce non-ordinary states. The LORD created music knowing its mysterious ability to awaken the psyche. As with all of God's creations, His intent was for good. When exploited for the wrong purposes, music stimulates lust, anger and rebellion. Our youth are daily exposed to a world of music that endlessly celebrates the raw power of lust. Boom boxes in our nation belch out obscene lyrics that describe rape, oral sex and feces. No one can escape this musical pounding. We hear it in schools, in malls, and in public parks. We cannot often drive more than a few blocks with our windows down except we hear a deafening blast of musical filth. Like an octopus, the music industry covers our country in the grip of its powerful life-sucking tentacles.

Before reading further, I believe it is necessary to warn my readers that some of the following may be offensive to their Christian sensibilities. During my research, I was frankly "blown away" in the most literal sense as I came to realize the depth of the slime pits into which our American culture has fallen. In writing this portion of the book, I found myself pulled between the boundaries of moral Christian decency and glaring cultural truth. How could I present the gravity of America's moral and cultural crisis without reproducing even a tiny portion of its filth and raunchiness? It was difficult. I recognize that the following material will offend the spirits of some. As I shared in the Introduction, my own pastor, Gary Coleman, stated that he felt as if he needed to "take a shower after reading the section where you took the mask off Hollywood." He was sympathetic in understanding my dilemma of presenting the truth, yet it made him personally feel unclean.

In seeking godly counsel from several sources, I struggled to find the middle ground between moral standards and yet faithfully present the unexaggerated truth regarding the crisis in which we now find ourselves. Because the terms "ass" and "hell" are used in the long-time trusted King James version of the Bible, I have likewise used them in the quotations below. However, I assuredly understand that their usage in the Bible is not intended to be vulgar and offensive as is the case in the following quotations. My intent is not to shock or offend. It is to sound the trumpet of alarm. *America must declare war on Hollywood's standards!* How can an army be sent forth to battle without a cause? How can we understand the true cause unless we have knowledge—although that knowledge is so utterly offensive to our sensibilities? How can we defeat the enemy if we are unaware of how desperately he needs to be destroyed?

My concern on how to present this material seems best answered by quoting Dr. James Dobson and Gary Bauer in their book, *Children at Risk*. These two well-respected authors found themselves faced with the same dilemma of how to truthfully expose some unsavory material: "I must alert you that the following materials are highly explicit. Read the next page or two only if you really want to know! If it offends you, how do you feel about your children reading similar concepts in class?"[2] We can choose to bury our heads as ostriches in the cultural sands of ignorance, but the crisis does not go away by our ignoring it. Whether we choose to believe it or not, every man and woman, every young person and child in America will be influenced by the hazardous chaos of our nation's culture.

To the best of my ability, I have *cleaned up* that which follows; however, let me be quite frank with you, dear reader. What is included in this book can best be described as Disney's classic version of *Cinderella* being compared to a pornographic film. The following examples are the *Cinderella* versions of what truly exists in America's culture today— which is dark, deviant, demonic, depraved, decadent, debauched, degenerate, distorted, deluded, demoralized, defrauded, desecrated, corrupt, adulterated, maniacal, masochistic, nymphomanical, sadistic, perverted, prostituted, psychopathic and pornographic. Get the picture? Yet in reality, those words fail miserably in their attempt to paint an authentic picture of how far our culture has fallen. To include some of the more explicit examples to which my research took me, I must truthfully admit, lies beyond the decency of this book's intent.

Music's sludge factory holds hands with Hollywood in the promotion of deviant sexual behavior. Music promoters today use an insistent beat that builds sensuality and directs the hormones of teenagers toward the bedroom. The powerful music industry targets its offensive and obscene content toward the youth of our nation. The psychedelic Beatles generation of several decades ago now often considers the music of today pornographic. Yet today's generation considers it music worthy of winning Grammy Awards. Death metal bands, rock groups and gangsta/porn rappers poison their listeners with their gritty, gutter language about sex.

In its *Young, Rich & Dangerous* album, the rap group called Kris Kross sings a recurring theme of having sex, sex and more sex. This is the group that influenced kids to wear their pants backwards. Now Kris Kross influences their adoring young fans with staggering suggestions of having casual sex with multiple partners. A female lead singer, Courtney Love, is with one of the "slut rock" girl groups. Incidentally, this lead singer also stars as the wife to porno-king Larry Flynt in a recent film that was discussed earlier. Her songs whine forth the testimony of how she turned tricks as a teenage whore. Bored with old vices, Meat Loaf searches for new ones in the album, *Welcome to the Neighborhood*. Utopia for Meat Loaf is to have casual sex without precautions or having to face the consequences of a tumble in the bed with a drunk Mexican prostitute.

Raunchy lyrics and obscene themes pepper the music of the late Tupac Shakur before the gangsta rapper was shot and killed in September 1996. Shakur's gangsta rap albums were produced by a recording company called Death Row—now that's a nice name for a company. Although Shakur was Death Row's biggest star, the recording studio is still reaping the financial benefits from Shakur's posthumous album. More than a million copies of *The Don Killuminati: The 7 Day Theory*, topped out on the *Billboard* charts at No. 1. The rap business generates phenomenal profits. Shakur's death has taken on the legendary proportions of a black "Elvis" and some of his fervent fans refuse to believe he is dead. The *heroic* (?) rapper, however, is indeed dead and lives only through his albums. Shakur's murder has boosted sales of his previous releases—for example, his *All Eyez on Me* has re-entered *Billboard*'s Top 10. The album inflates the themes of sexual braggadocio. Perversity saturates his lyrics with manifold uses of the "f" word. His smutty lyrics promote sex with minors, multiple partners, oral sex and anal sex in the 2Pac album.

The down-and-dirty lyrics and song titles of today's popular culture music hit us like a fist in the face. These cultural *artists* pride themselves on writing intellectually creepy titles such as: *Filthy Habits, Go to the Sugar (Cocaine) Altar, Titties & Beer, Phone Calls From the Dead*.[3]

Would you want your child to listen to songs with those titles? Yet these are the role models who are paraded in front of our young people. Many of these singers end up in hospitals to be treated for drug addiction. However, before and after they have been admitted to the psychiatric ward, they continue writing and singing their psycho babbling lyrics. A trade magazine reviews these lyrics in several songs, clearly show the mind set of people in the music industry.[4]

"...a working-class tough guy with a past that includes heroin addiction, alcoholism and jail time—is one haunted (expletive). Singing in a compassionate growl that fuses pain, anger, shame and courage, he's chased by memories he can't outrun. 'I've looked the devil in the face,' the singer . . . declares."

"...sound that is as mind-blowing as it is masturbatory. . . And it will work not only in those wee post-clubbing hours when you're out of Rohypnol but also on days when you just don't want to take your Lithium." [Author's note: *Rohypnol* is the illegal drug used by men to sedate women for the purpose of date rape. *Lithium* is a psychotropic drug used for treating manic-depressive illness. Patients must be closely monitored with respect to the possibility of suicide until *Lithium* has its effect. The writer is implying that this drug *Lithium* is commonly used among singers for their manic-depressive personalities. The writer is stating his case that the music affects a person in the same manner as a psychotropic drug.]

"These tales of low life and hard-luck women are free of the whining and petty sexual rage that some of today's female artists try to pass as signs of feminine empowerment."

Bear in mind, that the above was written about the musicians themselves, their characters or their lifestyles. Some of these musicians' actual lyrics go beyond the moral scope of this book. With each passing decade, musicians grind out their rotten-to-the-core lyrics with increasing audacity.

As children who were born to parents who started the sexual revolution of the Sixties cultures, today's singers openly flaunt their nasty and perverted viewpoint of sex. The now-declining rock star of the Eighties, Prince, helped to desensitize youth with his offensive lyrics that suggested incest and omnisexuality. One of his songs spoke of, "My sister never made love to anyone else but me/She's the reason for my sexuality." Some musicians glorify sexual voyeurism by standing on stage naked with only their guitars covering their genitals.

They strive to manifest the most bizarre, outrageous and offensive behavior possible when they are before the eyes of the public. Screaming crowds of young people cheer joyfully as the musicians walk on stage with hair dyed yellow and red, blue paint streaking down their faces and hands groping at their groins.

At times the singers shout foul statements to their audiences such as "You can lick my (expletive) ass." Mostly, today's death metal bands, rock groups and gangsta rappers just belch out their nasty lyrics of gross obscenity. Judge Jose A. Gonzalez of Florida ruled that the notorious album *As Nasty as They Wanna Be* by the rap group 2 Live Crew was legally obscene. The group's black lead singer protested about being condemned as a *creative black artist*. Some of the following lyrics are evidence of the group's creative ability as artists:

> Song: "Me So Horny"
> "I won't tell your momma if you don't tell your dad
> I know he'll be disgusted when he sees your (female genitalia) busted."

> Song: "The (expletive) F____ Shop"
> "Let me fill you up with somethin' milky and white
> 'Cause I'm gonna slay you rough and painful . . .
> I wanna see you bleed!"

The news media covered the story of the Florida judge's ruling against the group's album. One professor testified at the obscenity trial that the rap group "actually exemplified a long and honorable ghetto tradition." The professor compared the group's lyrics as in the same class as Chaucer and Shakespeare's bawdy language. He "insisted to the jury that lines such as 'suck this (male genitalia) d___, (expletive for female dog) b___, and make it puke' actually amounted to an imaginative use of metaphor."[5] However, other prominent black leaders protested against 2 Live Crew representing their culture. "We are particularly offended by their efforts to wrap the mantle of the black cultural experience around their performances by saying this is the way it is in the black community . . . cultural experience does not include debasing our women . . . (or)the promotion of deviant sexual behavior."[6] This rap group delights in singing lyrics that glorify the mutilation of female genitalia. They mockingly praise a preacher's daughter who "did the whole crew" and lets a "gang of niggers [sic]. . .rape her." At the same time, they flaunt their *"musical (?) metaphors (?)"* with graphic descriptions of oral sex such as: ". . . the dumb b____ licks out their asshole."

In Dr. James Dobson's book, *Children At Risk*, he and Gary Bauer list the words, descriptions and acts as recorded in the album, *As Nasty As They Wanna Be.*

- 226 uses of the F-word
- 117 explicit terms for male or female genitalia
- 87 descriptions of oral sex
- 163 uses of the word for female dog
- 15 uses of "ho" (slang for whore) when referring to women
- 81 uses of the vulgarity "s__t
- 42 uses of the word "ass"
- 9 descriptions of male ejaculations
- 6 references to erections
- 4 descriptions of group sex
- 3 mentions of rimming (oral/anal sex)
- 2 inclusions of urination or feces
- 1 reference to incest
- over a dozen illustrations of violent sex[7]

MTV's Lewd Lounge for Young People

The real demonic power behind music's appalling content today can be seen on Music Television—or MTV. This network advertises itself as a *cultural force* that has "affected the way an entire generation thinks, talks and buys." For twenty-four hours a day, young people can tune in to get their hormones ignited, their traditional values degraded, their fantasies applauded and their rebellion nurtured. MTV predominantly promotes sex, sex, sex. The videos graphically present hands self-stroking thighs and bellies. So much skin is shown in the videos that it borders on stark nudity, while couples suggestively cling to one another.

Without a doubt, musicians defile our youth's sense of hearing through their smutty lyrics. However, MTV gives youth a double workout. MTV's graphic sensuality and obscene lyrics assault young people's sense of sight and sense of hearing. The videos shown on MTV glamorize rape, exploit female genitalia and exalt any form of deviant sex. The rapper Coolio's video of "Too Hot" condemns abstinence. Coolio's video plays repeatedly on MTV and promotes his sexual philosophy:

> "Everybody and their mother is preachin' abstinence,
> but kids ain't checkin' for absti-sh_ _.
> Just put a condom in their hand and hope it don't bust."

Along with the music videos, MTV developed two of the most obnoxious characters in cartoon history. These two pyromaniacs, *Beavis and Butt-head* love "to burn stuff." This gross duo also loves making crude sexual jokes about everything from masturbation to sadomasochism. MTV flaunts their in-your-face attitude as they habitually talk about things that "suck."

MTV created their own version of a dating game called *Singled Out*. The game starts by selecting fifty guys from the studio audience that compete for the ideal mate of the opposite sex. Fifty girls are also selected. A process of elimination begins with questions such as:

"Sex—lights on or lights off?"

"You're on a nude beach—are you bare assed or embarrassed?"

Improvisation time begins once the crowd of fifty has been eliminated.

"We're rollin' hot 'n heavy under the sheet in my bedroom and all of a sudden my mother bursts through the door. What would you do?"

Co-host for *Singled Out* is Jenny McCarthy. This role model for young people has already posed for *Playboy* magazine. Sexual innuendos are constantly on her tongue. In an apparent effort to be amusing and cute, she twists and contorts her face in the most outlandish expressions in front of the television camera. On one of the episodes, McCarthy walks on stage with a woman slung over her shoulder. The woman's backside is toward the camera. In her customarily raunchy and offensive manner, McCarthy tells the contestants: "This is the new host." Then McCarthy holds the microphone next to the woman's backside and yells, "Carmen, say hi!" The media's fascination for the perverse has exalted McCarthy's offensive and ridiculous antics in front of the camera as being the vogue behavior for young people. Incidentally, the new host, Carmen, has also posed for *Playboy*. Apparently, it is a prerequisite to host *Singled Out*. Nice role models.

After a while, MTV thought the opposite sex dating game needed some spicing up and so it held the first nationally televised dating game for gays and lesbians. The network also began recruiting teenagers to play a role in its show: "Sex in the 90s: the Safest Sex of All." They ask that teens send in their sexual fantasies about their favorite rock stars. The program promotes itself as providing a "safe environment" for teenagers to discuss masturbation as an alternative for safe sex.

These are shocking revelations to most of us. Yet the March 1996 issue of *Plugged In*, (see Appendix B) produced by James Dobson's Focus on the Family, reveals that the youth in our churches are as influenced by MTV as the youth who do not attend church. If we believe that Christian teens are exempt from the influence of music videos like this, (Coolio's "Too Hot") think again. "The sad truth, statistician George Barna discovered, is that Christian teens were *more likely* to watch MTV (42%) than their non-Christian peers (33%). In his just-released book, *Generation Next*, Barna notes that the typical teen will allocate roughly one quarter of his or her TV attention—that's about 25 minutes a day—to MTV."[8]

Due to the brevity of this book, I have not listed more of the popular songs being listened to by our young people. These songs continue to regurgitate the same old offensive sexual lyrics over and over again. Shame for us as a nation haunted me regarding the perversion so prevalent in our country's music. The content of MTV should startle, even frighten, some of us who were unaware of the depth of its depravity. However, we need steadfastly to focus on the youth of our country. They are worth the battle! We ourselves need to repent of the unsavory diet upon which we have allowed our personal sense of sight and hearing to feast. There is a great need for Americans to return to the God of their founding fathers. We need to cry out for Him to cleanse us and our nation. I can assure you that He eagerly yearns for the repentance of America—repentance that will occur one citizen at a time.

Global Town Hall of Cybersex and Cyberporn

Even as Hollywood is not leaving our culture, another form of communication has firmly planted itself within our world—computers and the ability to talk in cyberspace. The computer has two sides to its coin as do most things in life— good or evil. Let us remember the beginning, however, and remind ourselves that the LORD has always known about the invention of computers.

"But thou, O Daniel, shut up the words, and seal the book, even to the time of the end: *many shall run to and fro, and knowledge shall be increased* . . . Many shall be purified, and made white, and tried; *but the wicked shall do wickedly: and none of the wicked shall understand; but the wise shall understand.*"[9]

The television show *20/20* recently aired an episode about the effect that TV has on children. At one point, it shows a mother having literally to drag her young daughter of about four or five years of age away from the computer. Even our very young children are becoming increasingly attached to the mind-boggling world of the computer. With as much ease as my grandfather's generation turned on the radio, and my father's generation habituated the drive-in theater, and my generation lounged in front of the television, my own son's generation will grow up in front of the computer.

Most of us should be aware of the tremendous good that computers offer our world. We can access the Internet to promote our businesses, find jobs, obtain knowledge and even make money. More than a few people have become long distance or even international friends by chatting via the Internet. Many testify of how their chats on the computer result in spiritual knowledge or even leading someone to the LORD. Computers stand in man's Hall of Fame regarding his inventions. That is the good side of the coin.

The evil side of the computer coin is alarming to those

who stand firmly in their moral values. There is easy accessibility to filth in the world today of our young people. Without diligently guarding our youth, they can enter an amphitheater of explicit and perverse sex on the computer in their own homes. Some conversations are outrageously perverse. Keep in mind, however, that the "shorthand version" *sex chat* quoted from *Rolling Stone* magazine is mild in comparison to what is normally found in the computer sex forums. Due to its explicit perversion, the entire conversation obviously will not be quoted in this book. Only the first few sentences are reproduced below:[10]

User 1: Hmm, make me nasty.
User 2: Spreading your legs that are hanging over the table
User 1: Opening up wider
User 2: Running my hands up and down the inside of your thighs.

This public, in-front-of-everybody conversation between two strangers continued in the *Rolling Stone* article with increasingly graphic sexual language. Anyone in the world with a computer could have accessed this conversation. Sexual perversion has gone beyond the films of Hollywood, the screens of television and the CDs of popular culture music. It is now available in the modems of computers.

The *Rolling Stone* article specifically targets America Online, whose name was chosen by its CEO for being ". . . a name that both Abbie Hoffman and Jerry Falwell could feel good about."[11] People talk sex on all cyberspace services, yet America Online is becoming known as host to "the swinger's lounge of Middle America, the place where Nike-wearing, Chevy-driving, Pepsi-guzzling adventurers are redefining their sexual selves in *open revolt against the repressive climate* of our times."[12] I find it ironic to read articles that view traditional morality as being *repressive*.

The six-page article continued to relate the story of a 36-year-old female school teacher whose friend talked about all "the wild stuff" that happened on America Online. The friend encouraged the school teacher to try it. This *"extraordinarily devoted (?) teacher,"* whom the article called Denise (not her real name) took her friend's advice and found her way into some of the sex chat rooms. At first, the sex talk stunned the teacher who had attended Catholic schools for twelve years. She became spellbound by this "faceless, anonymous environment," however, and lost all of her self-consciousness as America Online became her public bedroom for illicit pleasure. The article details the teacher's experience with cybersex until it ended in a real relationship with a total stranger.[13]

"...talking with a stranger in real time, one on one, in a private room, stoking [sic] each other to orgasm. One night she met a couple online who were looking for a woman to form an online threesome . . . Well, why not?

'I felt a reawakening of my sexual being,' she says quietly but confidently. 'I began to explore fantasies I didn't even know existed.' In private chat rooms, she discovered she was intrigued by bondage—something she had never tried but had always been fascinated with.

Before long, she did something that a few months earlier would have been unimaginable—she agreed to meet a man she had talked with on America Online. It turned out to be more like an interview than a date. They sat in a restaurant and talked openly for several hours about what kind of sex they liked and what kind they did not like. She then made a date with him. A few days later, they ended up at his house, where he tied her to the bed and spanked her.

'And that,' she says in her teacher's voice, 'was the beginning of my new life.'"[14]

Unfortunately, what Denise did not realize at this "*beginning of* (her) *new life*" is that she had opened a door for the Biblical lasciviousness to enter. Lasciviousness is unrestrained sexuality and no shame because of that unrestraint. While reading an article on the pornography industry in America, I was given a perfect example of lasciviousness. The article was written by a worldly-wise reporter who, during his research, entered a warehouse that was the studio for making pornography films. When he was ushered into the business office, he was shocked at what greeted him. A sexual orgy between two men and two women, all four of them connected together in some form of sexual activity, assaulted his sensibilities. This was a *business* office? Not one participant stopped what they were doing. One man greeted him with: "Sorry, I can't shake your hand," and then asked the reporter to have a seat. "We're not filming right now, but we'll be finished momentarily." The boss' casual attitude jolted even the worldly-wise reporter.

No shame. No restraint. This is lasciviousness. It runs rampant in America.

It is chilling to consider the possibility that an *enlightened* (?) teacher such as "Denise" could be guiding our fifth and sixth graders—especially in sex education. Yet this story of the teacher could be indicative of thousands of other citizens who can freely access the sex chat rooms on their computers. The article discusses America Online's belief "that instead of trying to censor the medium ourselves, we'll give the users the power to make those decisions for themselves."[15]

This sexual base of America Online's customers has brought it much criticism, although the CEO states that "The majority of our users don't use AOL for that purpose."[16]

However, the article continues: "But to say that sex is just an incidental part of AOL's business—the equivalent of a juke joint on the wrong side of a town's railroad tracks—is not accurate, either. More accurately, sex is the bedrock, the foundation of the city and the profit center that has allowed AOL to finance other programming. AOL's usage records demonstrate this. During May 1996, there were a total of 26,377,881 hours of connect time. Of that, 26 percent of the total— 6,950,171 hours—came from chat. . . Clearly, chat is huge. Of those 7 million hours, how much was devoted to sex—however it's defined—is impossible to estimate . . . On a busy night, there are sometimes 8,000 public and private chat rooms humming at the same time."[17]

The news media reported recently that users of the service are beginning to pull away from AOL and not just because of the lewd communication that is so prevalent. Users are frustrated because they hear nothing but "busy signals" when they try to access someone through AOL. America Online has seemingly built its reputation on quicksand and even the secular world recognizes it as a purveyor of pornography and promoter of moral decline.

The article concludes by stating: "'Sexuality is a part of our lives,' says AOL's David Gang. 'A frank discussion of it is a good, healthy thing. The public has to understand that. And we have to understand that as a company.' And when the crusaders rant about how the world is going to hell in a hand basket because of AOL, the best reply may be to point to Denise, who is still teaching *fifth* and *sixth* grade. One of the benefits of her time exploring on AOL, besides discovering the pleasures of wrist restraints, is that she has become a better teacher—in some subjects, anyway."[18]

"'Teaching sex ed now is a breeze,' Denise says. 'My students always try to embarrass me by asking the crudest questions they can come up with, like, 'How long is a vagina?' 'How big is a (male genitalia) d____?' And I always tell them, 'You're not going to embarrass me. It's just not going to happen.'"[19]

It is astounding that fifth and sixth graders are permitted to use such coarse street language in our nation's classrooms. With each succeeding generation, our children tragically enter the evil of this world at younger ages.

Technology Turned On Us

The intent of including the above quotations from *Rolling Stone* was to *jar* our adult sensibilities—not to offend you or to condemn AOL. We included the above excerpts from *Rolling Stone* that focused entirely on AOL; however, we recognize that other online services can be equally used in an evil sense. We need to sound the wake-up call for ourselves, for our children and for our nation. We must spiritually inoculate our children regarding the computer. In spite of the potential evil side of the computer coin, it remains our responsibility as parents and spiritual leaders to equip our children regarding the latest technology. In the same sense that sex has been perverted from its intended God-given purpose, computers have likewise been prostituted. We and our youth need to drive skillfully down their generation's electronic highway of computer technology, fiber optics, cellular telephones or any other upcoming invention. Yet we must forewarn them about the dangers lurking on the sides of that highway.

Most young people whom we have trained on computers at school are savvy enough to plug into a "sex" address that offers a whole range of *adult* pleasures. Young people can plug into any type of deviant sexual behavior such as bestiality (sex with animals), pedophilia (sex with children), multiple partners (*ménage à trois*), transvestites, gays or lesbians. If children should happen to get bored, they can access the "sounds of sex in stereo" that they play through their sound cards.

We purchase a computer to enhance our children's education and have unknowingly given them a possible passport into the sordid sex of cyberspace. With the click of a mouse, their young innocence can be eradicated. Online sites provide detailed explanations and illustrations on how to do almost anything. We can discover how to obtain illicit drugs, how to contact prostitutes in every major city in America, how to build bombs, how to commit suicide or how to indulge in every bizarre and deviate form of sex. The news abounds with stories and statistics of children being lured online and getting into situations where they become victims of sexual predators. Some of these sexual stalkers persuaded their unsuspecting victims to personally meet with them. They consequently battered, raped or killed their victims.

The technology of computers is not in itself evil. Neither telephones, televisions nor VCRs are evil. Yet our own technology, the creation of our own hands, has turned on us. It devours us like a ravaging beast. It gorges itself upon our senses. It consumes us with its insatiable appetite. Both we and our nation lie in the path of its destruction. America stands at a critical point in this cultural crisis. We cannot afford to ignore the warning signs of imminent destruction.

Remember

▶ God created our universe with music. God gave man music for the good of man, not for purposes of evil. He created our bodies with an internal, biological symphony.

▶ Music arouses the beating and pulsations of our physical bodies. Music greatly affects us.

▶ As the universal language, music works invisibly, but definitely, on our emotions and our nervous systems.

▶ The music for today's popular youth culture is the Perverse Pied Piper who leads our young people into

▶ Today's lyrics are often smutty and corrupt with obscene themes. The lifestyles of most singers are as undesirable as their raunchy lyrics. They rarely qualify to become our young people's role models.

▶ MTV packs twice the punch on the senses of our young people. It bombards both the eyes and the ears with crude and explicit sexuality.

▶ Cyperspace sex on the computer poses great threats for our young people. Its lurking, hidden dangers seek to ensnare our children as readily as the movies, television and music feed upon their senses.

▶ Our technology has turned on us, devouring us with its debauchery because we have allowed it to be used for evil rather than good.

Summer 1996

Callie!"

Callie turned toward the sound of her mother's voice as she walked toward her car in the church parking lot. Callie moaned inwardly. Instinctively, she knew the exact direction of any conversation with her mother.

"Where are you going?" asked her mother as they came closer to each other.

"Out to eat," replied Callie, restraining her impatience.

"Who is going?"

"Some of us from the youth...." Callie stopped in the middle of her sentence. She knew she would have to give her mother all the details. "Darla, Laura, Tiffany and Jamie."

"Just you girls?"

"No, Corey and David are going to meet us there after they finish helping the pastor move the new chairs into the youth department—and Brett is meeting us there."

"Meeting you where?"

"Wendy's, Mom. I need to go or I'll be late."

"Why has Brett stopped coming to church, Callie?"

"How many times have we had this conversation, Mother? He stopped months ago. He doesn't come back because people. . . ." Callie ignored the frown creasing her mother's brow. ". . .nobody likes him around here, Mom. Just because his Dad stopped coming with him. It's not his imagination. I've seen it. So has Granny. Corey and David are the only ones who talk to him anymore. I need to go, Mom. Everyone will be finished eating by the time I get there."

"Callie, you are only 16-years old and—"

Callie sighed heavily but her mother did not notice. She would never make it to Wendy's on time now. Her mind traveled to Wendy's and the salad bar. She visualized all the others sitting down already, eating, laughing . . . .

". . .what about me. Think this is easy on me? You bet it isn't! I work to try and give you nice things. Your father is so busy at work. . . all he can do is come home, prop his feet up in front of the TV and watch the evening news. He works hard. I work hard. Heaven knows, he's doing the best he can teaching that Sunday School class. Attending the deacon's meeting. Maybe he needs to give up being a deacon. I do my best, Callie. Not every girl has her own car—oh, I know—Heather bought your car, but I worked like a dog to buy that television set for your bedroom. I never had my own TV until I was married to your father! You get a lot of things to be a 16-year-old, young lady. I don't mind that you want to be with your friends. . .they're all good kids. I know that. Even Brett. You couldn't ask for a better kid. Comes over and mows the yard for me. I am not saying he's a bad kid. But Callie—it's embarrassing when the preacher asks me why he doesn't come to church anymore. Everyone asks me about it all the time. LORD knows we've never been able to get his father involved in church. Think he'd be more willing since that happened to his wife. Terrible! Murdered in her own bedroom by some live-in boyfriend. Your sins will find you out the Bible says. Poor thing. Can't help feeling badly about that, even if she did run off and leave Brett and his Dad. I know what you're thinking, Callie, but people just want what's right for Brett. LORD knows we've tried to help him since his mother deserted him. You look just like Heather when you frown at me like that. All right! Run on, but—be careful. I can't believe Brett is even meeting you kids—he refuses to go anywhere on Sundays anymore

without his Dad. I've never seen a kid love his Dad as much as Brett loves his."

Callie glanced in the rear view mirror as she pulled out of the church parking lot. Her mother remained on the sidewalk, Bible in hand, furrow in brow. Driving away, Callie observed her mother watching her departure.

Mother—Mother! Why can't you just let me grow up, thought Callie. She loved her mother and did not want to be disrespectful, but her mother simply did not understand. It was different now than when her mother was young. *Why can't she remember what it's like to be young,* thought Callie, remembering the picture of her mother as a laughing teenager in her hip-hugger pants and knit shirt.

She reached over and turned the radio up to about 90 decibels. The music magically transferred her thoughts from mother to Brett. A tremor of excitement charged through her at the thought of seeing Brett. Although they had known each other since grammar school, Callie still shivered inwardly when she first saw the strong, handsome features of Brett's face. She thrilled to see his athletic ease as he walked toward her down the hallway of their high school. In spite of the disapproval of the church members, Callie inwardly admired Brett for refusing to take out his earring. All the guys on the football team wore earrings. With his tousled blond hair, Brett looked like a Roman gladiator to Callie. His facial features looked as if they had been sculpted to perfection by a Greek artisan. Brett's T-shirt and jeans made a futile attempt to cover the defined hardness of his muscles. Brett had become Callie's security blanket. She felt lost without him. Always, he had been there for her, silent, like a majestic lion, guarding, watching over her—even when they were children.

She glanced at herself in the rear view mirror. A smile crept onto her face. People were always telling her what a perfect couple she and Brett made. Two exact opposites. Brett the imperial blond of the sun, and Callie, the melancholy dark of the moon. In Callie flowed the gentleness of the wind song and the rhythmic beauty of the pounding surf. She had grown up hearing people brag about her porcelain skin and dark hair, whispering among themselves that hers was the classic beauty that could launch a thousand ships like Helen of Troy. Yet to Callie, her mirror reflected no such legendary beauty. She could see only excitement dancing in her eyes when she thought of winning Brett's approval. Soon she would see that reflected approval swimming in Brett's eyes once he saw her. Only with Brett did Callie sparkle as brilliantly as the evening star.

No wonder people always tell me I'd be lost without him. I guess I would be, she mused to herself. Callie pressed her foot down onto the gas pedal with anticipation. She reached over and turned the music up to 120 decibels. Off to her right, she saw a billboard advertising Hollywood's summer release of **Striptease**. Callie had gone with Tiffany and Jamie. People at church said it was trashy, but Callie rather enjoyed it. She thought about the movie and its star, Demi Moore, who was notorious for exhibiting her nudity. Callie wondered if the rumor about Demi Moore's having silicone breasts was true. They looked silicone to Callie.

A few blocks from Wendy's Hamburgers, Callie's thoughts switched from Demi Moore's breasts to her own. She wondered if Brett could feel her breasts when they kissed. She thought on these things until she turned into the parking lot at Wendy's.

Part III
The Consequences

"...television is not the truth!...we are in the boredom killing business! If you want the truth, go to God, go to your guru, go to yourself because that's the only place you'll ever find any real truth! But man, you're never going to get any truth from us. We'll tell you anything you want to hear. We lie like hell! We'll tell you Kojak always gets the killer, and nobody ever gets cancer in Archie Bunker's house...we'll tell you any [expletive] thing you want to hear! We deal in illusion, man! None of it's true! But you people sit there-all of you-day after day, night after night...we're all you know. You're beginning to believe the illusion we're spinning here."

— Actor Peter Finch as Howard Beale,
in his speech as the "mad prophet
of the airways" in *Network*

Chapter 5

Consequences of Our Action

Fall 1996

    Callie sprawled across her bed, picked up the remote control and clicked on her VCR. The theme song of General Hospital came onto the television screen. For years, she had taped her favorite soap opera so that she could watch it immediately upon arriving home after school. This time alone, in the quiet of her own bedroom, relaxed, peaceful, was one of her favorite moments of the day. It was her transitional time from school to home, from social to solitude. Callie watched Robin as she shared her feelings about having HIV with Jason in their motel room. Robin and Jason were okay, but Callie's favorites on General Hospital had always been Luke and Laura—but the old Luke and Laura, the hot couple whose steamy romance had finally culminated in a television marriage. Moments later, Callie rolled over and snuggled up to her pillow as she watched the two soap opera stars, Robin and Jason, make love for the first time. Callie's body shivered involuntarily as she watched the couple, completely unaware that she was awakening her body through her sense of sight. Her eyes saw Robin and Jason on the television screen, but Callie's thoughts turned toward her and Brett.

    When the credits began to roll at the end, Callie clicked the remote to stop the VCR and then changed the television channel to MTV. She pushed herself up off the pillow and went to get her habitual apple and glass of milk between General Hospital and MTV—all part of her Monday through Friday routine.

Skimpily-clad black female bodies moved seductively across Callie's television screen when she returned from the kitchen crunching her first bite of the apple. A close-up shot showed the dancer's hands move enticingly across her naked thigh and almost-bare breasts. The tempo of the black rap song increased behind the dancer. The semi-hypnotic, suggestive movements of the sleek dancer pulled Callie's imagination into the scene before her eyes. Yet in her mind, it was she who danced on the television screen. . . for Brett. Sitting on the edge of the bed, she imitated a few of the seductive shoulder movements of the MTV dancer.

Callie continued to watch MTV until she grew bored. For several minutes, she surfed through the channels, pausing occasionally to see if anything piqued her interest. When a woman dressed in the costume of about the 1800s using sign language appeared on the screen, she stopped surfing. HBO. This must be "The Piano" that Darla and Laura had told her they had watched the other night. Callie plumped her two pillows up and leaned back onto them, comfortable, ready to be entertained. Glancing at the clock on her nightstand, she knew she'd have enough time to watch the movie before her mother got home from work. Not that her mother would object since she did not oversee what Callie viewed. She was allowed to watch almost anything—still yet, Jamie had told Callie there were some fairly suggestive scenes in the movie. Not much nudity though. Jamie, the movie monitor for the group, warned Callie not to be watching it. Yet Callie sensed that this might be a movie she wanted to watch—in private, however, without an adult around to supervise or regulate. Yes. There was enough time. Maybe even enough time to get her homework finished—well, at least start the homework.

Since the movie was a third of the way finished, it took Callie a while to get the plot straight. What is going on here? That native guy is blackmailing her into doing perverted things with him just so she can play the piano. Oh! The Piano...that's why they are calling it The Piano. Stupid husband...it's all his fault. He should have realized how much she loved that piano. After she experienced the trouble of bringing it over on the ship. . . and he won't let her have it! What a weirdo that native guy is! Sitting under the piano touching her legs while she plays. Gross! I don't blame her for stopping—that guy is a pervert. Who wants to play the piano with him under there doing that?

Callie was interrupted several times during the movie with phone calls from her friends. She missed some of the actors' conversations, yet she never took her eyes off the screen. With her eyes, she followed the plot, snatching an occasional word here and there.

"Oh my goodness, Tiffany! She is getting into bed with that guy now. They don't do anything? Well, he's being nicer to her than her dumb husband. Gotta hand it to that native guy. At least he realizes how much she loves that piano. I know. . . that's where he's smarter than her husband. Look at him! Oh, I'm sorry. Don't get smart—I know you can't see through the telephone, but her husband is outside that native guy's house peeping in at them. This is the part Jamie warned me about? Tiffany, why do you say that? I'm not doing anything wrong. You watched it, didn't you? That's worse than what the native guy was doing. How can that husband stand there and watch his wife doing that? That is gross! He is spying on them! Yeah, okay. Yeah—talk to you later."

Callie pressed the volume button twice. Moments later, she felt a rush of heat cover her face as she saw the native man lift the woman's long black skirt and disappear beneath its folds. She vacuumed in a gasp of air as she watched the expression on the woman's face. In that suspended moment of time, everything within Callie told her she should quickly turn the channel and yet she did not. Guilt mingled with curiosity. *Tiffany and Jamie had both tried warning her not to watch it. Well crumb! They watched it, didn't they? She wasn't doing anything wrong. . .besides, it's just a movie.* She felt a strange stirring inside her body. Taking one of her pillows she pulled it close and pressed her body into it. Unconsciously, a sigh escaped her. She liked watching this.

Outside her bedroom window, she heard the sound of a car door slam. *Mother! What is she doing home so early?!* A sudden pounding in her heart almost choked her as she scrambled toward her backpack, turning the TV off as she went. She grabbed notebook, pencil and English book and *dashed to the kitchen table. Her mother's steps entered the kitchen just as Callie placed pencil on paper and pretended to be writing.*

"Hi, Mom. . . what're you doing home so early?" she asked, nonchalantly, keeping her head bowed in mock study.

"Got another migraine. Did you realize you're parked in Dad's spot in the drive. . . are you sick, Callie? Your face is as flushed as I've ever seen it. You don't feel feverish? Are you sure you're not feeling badly? No? Well, you look as if you've got a fever. Just the same. Don't worry about doing that now. You can finish your homework later. I hope you're not coming down with something."

Callie sighed inwardly with relief that she had not been caught watching the movie. Yet she knew that her mother and father watched those kind of movies all the time when she was not in the living room with them. Her mind burned each time the scene played again about the native man disappearing beneath the woman skirts. It was as if the frontal lobes of her brain had been branded with a hot searing iron. When Brett called after dinner, she tried to sound casual when she asked him if he had ever seen the movie. He answered with an uninterested no and moved to another subject. She followed his lead and did not mention the movie again, but she wanted to share that particular scene with him. It had stirred a strange excitement in her.

For several moments, they exchanged information about their geometry class. Callie moaned to Brett about the test that was coming up next week. She chided him when he showed no sympathy.

"It's easy for you, smart guy! Just because you've got your father's brain."

Brett did not answer. Callie turned the conversation toward one of the singing groups that had appeared on MTV that afternoon.

"Did you hear about Tha Dogg Pound who wrote about God on their Dogg Food album, Brett?"

"Yeah—I'm still not impressed with them," answered Brett.

"But they read what they'd written on the album on MTV today. One of them said, 'I'd like to thank the Lord Jesus Christ, King of my Life.' I saw it on TV."

"You're so naive, Callie. What about the one that wrote 'I wanna first give thanks to God, who made all this sh_ _ possible?'"

"Brett!"

"Brett! You better say Tha Dogg Pound. They're the ones who wrote that—not me."

"But I don't like to hear you say things like that," Callie answered. "My grandfather said that in front of my grandmother once and you know what she told him?"

An amused laugh came from the other end of the telephone. Callie smiled in spite of herself. She loved the sound of Brett's laughter.

"What'd Granny say?"

"She said, 'George William! I wouldn't have in my hand what you just had in your mouth!'"

A volley of laughter erupted in the telephone. It splashed upon Callie's ears like warm waves of pleasure.

"Your Granny! I love her almost as much as I love you," said Brett.

"Well, she wouldn't love hearing what you just said," answered Callie with phony seriousness, wanting their conversation to continue.

"Granny would be ashamed that you can't see through Dogg Pound's phony show of self-righteousness," answered Brett. "They try to look like Peter out there walking on the water with the LORD on their album cover—then they write lyrics that sound like the devil. How can you go to church as often as you do and not see these things?"

"You sound like a preacher," said Callie.

"You sound like Granny."

"Granny thinks you're special to the LORD. That's all she ever talks about."

Nothing but silence answered Callie.

"Brett?"

"Gotta go. I need to finish my English report."

"Brett—"

"See ya tomorrow. Meet me at the Coke machine in the cafeteria."

The Lesson of Phineas Gage

Most of us have never heard of Phineas Gage, but to some scientists he is one of the most interesting people to have ever lived.[1] His story is a haunting reminder of the delicacy of God's creation. Phineas Gage was a man traumatically changed from saint to sinner. During the year 1848, the young man Phineas Gage was in charge of a crew of men who were building a road in Vermont. One tool that Phineas used was a long, heavy iron rod that weighed thirteen pounds and was more than an inch thick. An explosion happened and turned the iron rod into a three and a half foot long bullet. The rod rocketed upward into his cheek, smashed through the front part of his brain and then tore out through the top of his head. The rod was moving so fast that it continued its flight high into the air and landed thirty meters away.

People working with Phineas were horrified when they saw what the accident had done to him. The fact that the rod did not kill him astounded them even more. He did not even appear to be hurt that badly because he talked to the people who rushed immediately to his side. Momentarily, he got up and walked to a nearby ox cart. Then he rode by himself to wait for the doctor to arrive at his lodgings. After his physical wound healed, Phineas moved and talked without difficulty. His memory was just fine. He continued to work. His mental faculties had not diminished at all.

Yet Phineas Gage changed. The man people had known before the accident had been kind. Indeed, he had always been favored among his co-workers. They considered him a smart businessman. He was all these things—hard worker, well-liked, devoted family man, cheerful and sensible. However, after the accident, Phineas became obstinate, willful, lazy and inconsiderate. He lost his temper easily and swore a lot. Alcohol became his constant drink. He no longer wanted to work and so consequently, he lost his job. For a while he earned his living by exhibiting himself with Barnum's Museum, telling his story to people who had come to see the freaks. Always, Phineas carried with him the iron rod that had turned him into a different person. For a short period, he lived in South America. He returned to the United States in poor health and then died in 1860, twelve years after his accident.

Phineas' story is important to scientists who study the

human brain. His famous iron rod remains on display in a museum at Harvard University, along with models of his damaged head and brain. The accident of Phineas Gage helped scientists begin to understand that various parts of the brain have different purposes. His terrible accident destroyed a large part of his brain. Nevertheless, he walked, talked, ate and worked as everyone else. Yet the accident turned him into a very different kind of person.

When the iron rod drove a huge hole into the front part of Phineas' brain, it changed the thing we call character or personality. Initially, scientists who were interested in the brain thought the fact that Phineas survived for so long meant that part of his brain was not very important. Later, when they understood how the accident affected his behavior, Phineas' injuries became part of the evidence that helped convince scientists of the central role of the front part of the brain. This part of the human brain is much bigger than in almost any other animal. This area, scientists discovered, did not relate to the basic functions of life, such as breathing and moving around and eating. *Instead, it was the location of the human personality. What happened to Phineas Gage demonstrated that our sense of right and wrong, of moral restraint and societal convention, also originates from the brain, or, more specifically, from the human frontal lobes.*

The extreme example of Phineas Gage teaches us an invaluable lesson. Although a three and a half foot rod may not have ruptured our brains, still yet something assaults our brains and it affects us in the location of our human personality. In Chapter Eight, we discuss the natural law of our senses. The devil utilizes this natural law to constantly fracture the frontal lobes of our brains with offensive, trashy images or perverse, filthy language. Over time, the steady onslaught of these twisted cultural messages cripples our ability to distinguish between right and wrong. An immediate change might not be as pronounced as it was with Phineas Gage, yet there is mounting evidence that the images we view and the words that we hear are changing the personalities of both children and adults in our American society.

We must ask ourselves: why has the moral restraint of our country plummeted to the depths of degradation? Have the social practices of our nation fallen so low that it is now commonplace to see Hollywood's top-paid stars vomit, defecate or urinate on the screen?

How have the lyrics of sadomasochism, masturbation, rage and murder embedded themselves as a prevalent attitude in our youth's culture? What caused America's national personality to change from saint to sinner? Who knew that four decades of having America's senses bombarded with horrific images and trashy words could endow our country with such a drastic change in her personality? The devil knew this. Satan knew God's natural law of how the brain, the mind and the senses operate under this natural law. For centuries, the devil has employed these natural laws to capture and then ultimately destroy us. *No human being walking around on the face of the earth is an exception to these natural laws!* With the rise of Hollywood, the devil organized his forces of darkness to produce a constant invasion onto the frontal lobes of America. His goal of such depravity was to pulverize our nation's personality. His goal of deception was to try and convince us that this prostituted perversion coming through most movies is ***art!*** With the provocative power of the movies, television and popular music, he has seduced America's senses. The effect in the mental and spiritual realm is that we have had an iron rod thrust up through our frontal lobes and it can potentially change our personalities as much as that of Phineas Gage.

To control us, Satan *must control our senses*. For our senses, as explained in Chapter Eight, are the only messengers allowed to enter our brains. Without a doubt, the greatest chance for an outside source to cheapen, to rape and to prostitute our senses in these latter days comes through the mass communication and entertainment industry. Like Phineas Gage, we still walk, talk and eat as always, yet we are gradually eroding the fibers of our personalities.

Reaping the Whirlwind

In the book of Hosea, the prophet writes that God's people "have sown the wind, and they shall reap the whirlwind. . ."[2] Wind varies in force from a slight breeze to a strong gale. To reap a whirlwind is to suffer disastrous consequences as a result of recklessness or folly.

America is reaping a physical whirlwind. The tragedy is that most adults have been captured through the natural law of their senses. They are incapable of helping their children to do anything other than to move into that same captivity. The youth of America have inherited a social nightmare not of their own making. They are raised in a society with low sexual standards and where technology sits on the throne.

Before most of them can walk, our children are introduced to their most reliable baby-sitter. This faithful "Nanny" never stops talking to them. Unlike Mom and Dad, Nanny TV is never too busy, too frustrated or too involved in the adult world to give young children her undivided attention. While they are still quite young, she patiently teaches them all about *her values*. She instructs them in *her standards*. When the "real mama" is busy chatting on the telephone or cleaning house, this one-eyed Nanny TV faithfully entertains them. She is willing to keep them constant company. "Sure!" she exclaims in silence, "I promise—you can run on outside and play for a while. I'll be right here when you return. I won't move an inch. I promise." Unlike parents, Nanny TV never fails to keep her promise. She is always there, constant and true, unconditional and faithful. Children never fear that she will leave them. They may leave her company for a while, but she never leaves them. Children grow to passionately love their one-eyed Nanny TV. Through her cheerful and colorful commercials, she advises them on the best kind of toys to purchase. May mercy and grace follow parents up and down the aisles of the toy department if Mom or Dad ever dare suggest a toy other than the one recommended by *their "Nanny TV!"* Their loyalty to her is excessive and they adhere closely to her instructions in purchasing certain products. Have you ever been in the same aisle when a parents dares to choose a box of cereal that is more nourishing than the one that *their Nanny TV* told them about during Saturday morning cartoons. Wow! Talk about temper tantrum time at Tom Thumb's Super Market! Soon, the children cling to their Nanny TV's skirt tail and protest vigorously if they are forced to be separated from her. Just one more cartoon? Mom, please! Pleeeeeze! Why do children react so strongly? Why not? This Nanny TV has become their constant friend and companion. She never scolds them. Never has she forced them to eat their vegetables. Yuk! If they are naughty, she never offers a word of reproach to them. Johnny can bang Susie over the head with a baseball bat and yet she never yells at him. She certainly never punishes him. The next time he sits down with Nanny TV, she will be as comforting and entertaining for him as if Susie did not need to have twenty stitches in her head.

In a tragically true sense, television is the security blanket for America's children. The consequence of our children being raised by their Nanny TV is that they have been *conditioned* to accept the fact that life is lived in front of the television. And again, I ask, and why not? Why not spend hours in front of a television as an adult? They did as a child. Television is the only parent and companion that several generations have ever known.

As they grew older, our children were gradually weaned from the solitary breast of national television. They were introduced to solid food—the movies and the music of their popular youth culture. The process of changing their thinking is so gradual and so subtle that they are not even aware what is happening to them. Studies have proven that when people watch pornography and other sexual content repeatedly, the viewers begin to see rape and other sexual crimes as less offensive. Research studies give approximations about what the average person views regarding sex: "9,230 sex acts, or implied sex acts, a year on television. Of that sexual activity, 81 percent is outside the commitment of marriage. This means that if the average young person, watching ten years of television from age eight to eighteen, watched 93,000 scenes of suggested sexual intercourse, 72,900 of those scenes would have been pre- or extramarital. What kind of impression does that make on young people. . . ."[3]

The physical consequence of our country's open sexuality is undeniable. Naturally, Hollywood alone is not the sole contributor to the following physical consequences. Yet Hollywood most assuredly cannot escape its blame—although one of Hollywood's favorite phrase is: "Don't blame us!" Who are the individuals that produce this steady diet of perverse promiscuity? The soul of Hollywood's *elite* community was revealed in a study in the early 1980s by Linda and Robert Lichter and Stanley Rothman.[4] It reveals a disturbing difference between the *elite* community who controls Hollywood versus mainstream America.

The movers and shakers in Hollywood are composed of 98% white males. Out of that category, 82% are from a metropolitan area and 56% from the northeastern part of the United States. Almost two-thirds reported an earned family income of over $200,000; one in four reported a family income over half a million dollars a year; only 4% reported incomes of less than $75,000 a year.

The study reported that 93% of Hollywood's elite had a religious upbringing with 59% of them being raised in the Jewish faith. Those raised with a Protestant background were 25% and Catholics came last with 12%. However, 45% now claim no religious affiliation whatsoever, in spite of their religious backgrounds in childhood. In fact, 92% stated that they seldom or never attend any religious service. Three-fourths of them admitted that they are liberal and lean toward the left. In the study, the Hollywood elite stressed that religion and the military should have the least amount of influence on our culture.

The husband and wife team of Lichter and their co-author Stanley Rothman reported the most striking discovery of their study: ". . . two out of three believe that TV entertainment should be a major force for social reform. This is perhaps the most striking finding in our study. According to television's creators, they are not in it just for the money. They also seek to move their audience toward their own vision of the good society."[5]

Hollywood's vision of their "good society" has resulted in some devastating consequences. An issue of *Newsweek* magazine also comments on the elite in an article entitled "The Elite and How to Avoid It."[6] The data quoted in the article was gathered by a Washington-based group called The Center for Media and Public Affairs which is Richter and Rothman's. The article contrasts the differences between what the media industry thinks and feels about certain issues in comparison to what the average American thinks and feels about the same issues. This 1991 survey reveals the great gap between the average American and media's elite.

▶ 85% of Americans still believe that adultery is wrong.
▶ Less than 50% of Hollywood executives believe that adultery is wrong.

▶ Over 76% of American believe that homosexuality is wrong.
▶ Only 20% of Hollywood executives believe that homosexuality is wrong.
▶ Less than 60% of Americans believe that abortion is right.
▶ Almost 97% of Hollywood executives believe that abortion is right.

The *Newsweek* article stated: "There is a genuine culture war going on in American society—in education, the arts, religion, law, politics—and the entertainment media are only its most visible battleground."[7]

Some of the following facts and statistics are overwhelming. The entertainment industry can continue to change its *alphabet soup* of ratings; however, the cure is not to be found in adding yet another letter to the "PG, R, PG13, and NC17" rating code. The cure is in the content of that which is produced and promoted by the media elite and the entertainments industry. Hollywood and television's films and the music industry's lyrics have been instrumental in destroying the moral fiber of our nation and youth.

America has allowed the "soft-core" pornography of *Playboy*, first published in 1953, to give rise to "hard-core" pornography. The FBI now estimates that over 5,000 murders occur annually because killers feed themselves on a diet of pornography. America now has over 1.5 million missing children. Many have been kidnapped and forced to perform crude sexual acts before cameras and most are then brutally murdered in what the industry calls snuff films. Forty-one percent of all sex crimes are directly related to the use of pornography. Rape has increased by 700% over the past 30 years and it is estimated that one out of every four young girls who are now under twelve years of age will be sexually assaulted at some time in their lives. Ninety percent of child molesters admit they first saw what they did modeled in a pornographic magazine or movie. Many believe that for every reported case of child abuse, nine may go unreported. This means the problem could be ten times larger than statistics reveal.[8]

Pornography is one of the largest industries in our nation—reaping profits in excess of eight billion dollars annually. *U. S. News & World Report* wrote extensively regarding the financial profits generated by pornography in the United States.[9] Random excerpts from that article document the out-of-control expansion of pornography in America.

"Critics of the sex industry have long attacked it for being 'un-American'—and yet there is something quintessentially American about it: the heady mix of sex and money, the fortunes quickly made and lost, the new identities assumed and then discarded, the public condemnations of a private obsession...the number of hard-core video rentals rose from 75 million in 1985 to 490 million in 1996....

"Last year Americans spent more than $8 billion on hard-core videos, peep shows, live sex acts, adult cable programming, sexual devices, computer porn, and sex magazines—an amount much larger than Hollywood's domestic box office receipts and larger than all the revenues generated by rock and country music recordings. Americans now spend more money at strip clubs than at Broadway, off-Broadway, regional and nonprofit theaters; at the opera, the ballet and jazz and classical music performances—combined...

"Twenty-five years ago, a federal study of pornography estimated that the total retail value of all the hard-core porn in the United States was no more than $10 million and perhaps less than $5 million...1980s, the advent of adult movies on video-cassette and on cable television, as well as the huge growth in telephone sex services, shifted the consumption of porn from seedy movie theaters and bookstores into the home...most of the profits being generated by porn today are being earned by businesses not traditionally associated with the sex industry—by mom and pop video stores; by long-distance carriers like AT&T; by cable companies like Time Warner and Tele-Communications, Inc; and by hotel chains like Marriott, Hyatt, and Holiday Inn that now reportedly earn millions of dollars each year supplying adult films to their guests... America's porn has become one more of its cultural exports, dominating overseas markets. Despite having some of the toughest restrictions on sexually explicit materials of any Western industrialized nation, the United States is now by far the world's leading producer of porn, churning out hard-core videos at the astonishing rate of about 150 new titles a week . . . San Fernando Valley of Southern California, near Universal City and the Warner Bros. back lot, an X-rated movie industry has emerged, an adult dream factory, with its own studios, talent agencies, and stars, its own fan clubs and film critics. . . .

"A movie videotape may cost the retailer $60 or more per tape and rent for $3 a night. A new hard-core release by comparison may cost $20 per tape and rent for $4 a night. Some mom and pop video stores now derive a third of their income from porn . . . approximately 25,000 video stores that rent and sell hard-core films—almost 20 times the number of adult bookstores. The spread of hardcore videos into mainstream channels of distribution has fueled a tremendous rise in the production of porn. Since 1991 the number of new hard-core titles released each year has increased by 500 percent. . . in 1978, perhaps 100 hard-core feature films were produced, at a typical cost in today's dollars of about $350,000. Last year, nearly 8,000 new hard-core videos were released, some costing just a few thousand dollars to produce...

"Hard-core videos now cater to almost every conceivable predilection—and to some that are difficult to imagine. . .gay videos and straight videos; bondage videos and spanking videos; tickling videos, interracial videos. . .'she-male' videos featuring transsexuals and 'cat fighting' videos in which naked women wrestle one another or join forces to beat up naked men... videos for senior citizens, for sadomasochists, for people fond of verbal abuse. . . .

"Redbook magazine readers regularly watch pornographic movies in the privacy of their homes...Great Western Litho, which prints the box covers for hard-core videos, is now one of the town's largest employers, along with Hewlett-Packard and Anheuser-Busch, The Mid-Valley Chamber of

Commerce never mentions in its community guide that hard-core videos are one of the area's major exports. . .last year, Americans spent more than $150 million ordering adult movies on pay-per-view...money earned by the nation's major cable companies: Time Warner, Continental Cablevision, Cablevision Systems Corp., and TeleCommunications, Inc. . . . AdultVision porn service and its main competitor, the Spice Channel, often attract more viewers than channels offering Hollywood movies. . .these are cable companies that rank in the Fortune 500 that now earn money through the sale of love oils and lingerie. . .last year guests spent about $175 million to view porn in their rooms at major hotel chains such as Sheraton, Hilton, Hyatt and Holiday Inn. Few hotels have refused to carry adult material on their pay-per-view systems. When a guest orders an adult movie through pay-per-view, the hotel gets a cut of up to 20 percent. . .the number of strip clubs in the United States roughly doubled between 1987 and 1992. Today there are about 2,500 of these clubs nationwide, with annual revenues ranging from $500,000 to more than $5 million at a well-run gentleman's club. . . .

"Telephone sex considered simply one more form of 'audiotext' by executives in the trade—became a huge business in the 1980s despite government efforts at regulation. . . perhaps a quarter of a million Americans pick up the phone and dial a number for commercial phone sex. The average call lasts six to eight minutes, and the charges range from 89 cents to $4 a minute. . .most are answered by "actresses"— bank tellers, accountants, secretaries and housewives earning a little extra money. . .interactive quality of phone sex explain its commercial success and its relevance to the future of the Internet. Last year Americans spent between $750 million and $1 billion on telephone sex. . .AT&T is one of the biggest carriers of phone sex."

How does Hollywood treat this horrifying malignancy of pornography that has attached itself to our society? It honors those such as Larry Flynt by portraying him as a defending hero of the First Amendment as discussed in Chapter Three. Then it goes on to produce several more movies revolving around the pornographic industry. All of them are slanted to seduce the audience into being sympathetic.

The consequences of some of Hollywood's influence is seen in the statistics below. These consequences were primarily taken from David Barton's book, *America: To Pray or Not To Pray*. That book contains the chilling documentation of when America took a decisive change of direction. That pivotal moment occurred on June 25, 1962 when the United States Supreme Court ruled through the case of *Engel v. Vitale* that prayer in the public arena of our schools was no longer constitutional. Barton lays the foundation of how our nation was conceived and birthed in prayer and then proves through countless statistics how the foundations began to crumble after the year 1962. Needless to say, it was of great interest to me that the Production Code of Hollywood was eliminated in 1966, just four years after the Supreme Court decision. When we, as a nation, allowed prayer to be taken from our public arenas then it affected all areas of our society—one of which was the entertainment industry.

Information on Student Activity [10]

- Two-thirds of America's 11 million teenage boys say they have had sex with a girl...By the time they are 18, on the average, boys have had sex with five girls.
- Most boys had their first sexual experience at 14 and girls at age 15.
- Of those students who have gone through a comprehensive sex education program, 65 percent are sexually active, a percentage almost twice as high as those who have *not* completed a sex education Curriculum. . .
- According to the Sex Information and Education Council of the U. S. (SIECUS), one out of every two boys and one of every three girls between the age of 15 and 17 have had sexual intercourse.

A survey conducted by the Rhode Island Rape Crisis Center revealed some rather shocking results. In different schools across the state, over seventeen hundred students between the sixth and ninth grade attended adolescent assault awareness classes. The students were asked if a man had the right to *force* a woman to have sexual intercourse with her if he had spent money on her. The results of that survey are shocking.

"Nearly 25 percent of the boys and 16 percent of the girls said yes! Then 65 percent of the boys and 47 percent of the girls in seventh through ninth grades said it is okay for a man to force a woman to have sex with him if they have dated for six months or longer. And 51 percent of the boys and 41 percent of the girls said a man has a right to force a woman to kiss him if he spent 'a lot of money on her'—which was defined by twelve-year-olds as $10 to $15."[11]

Information on Teen Pregnancy[12]

- The United States has the highest incidence of teenager motherhood of any Western country.
- Each year, 1 million adolescent girls become pregnant. Of those who give birth, half are not yet 18.
- 80 percent of pregnant teenage girls are unmarried.
- The birth rate for unmarried teens rose an additional 14 percent from 1980 to 1985, following an increase of 18 percent during the 1970s.
- Teenage motherhood among school students is so prevalent that a Dallas *high school* established a 15-bed nursery for students with children and Houston dedicated two entire high schools for the same purpose.

The impact of teen pregnancies in educational and economic areas is substantial:

- In 1985 alone, $16.65 billion was paid through welfare to women who gave birth as teenagers. In 1990, the cost had risen to $20.6 billion. Of those families headed by a mother age 14-25, two-thirds live below poverty level.

▶ Of the 1.3 million children of teenage mothers, 804,000 are currently in need of day care.

▶ Only half of those who give birth before age 18 complete high school (as compared with 96 percent of those who postpone childbearing), they earn half as much money, and are far more likely to be dependent on welfare (71 percent of women under 30 who receive aid had their first child as a teenager, i.e., during the late 60s and early-to-mid 70s).

Sexually Transmitted Disease[13]

Sexually transmitted infections now cause more long-term damage in chronic ill health, sterility and tubal pregnancies than ever before, despite antibiotics.

▶ Sexually transmitted diseases are no longer reserved for prostitutes or wayward GIs in foreign countries. They are infecting people from all economic and social strata at the rate of 33,000 people a day in the U.S. alone.

▶ That means 12 million cases a year, up from 4 million in 1980. At this rate, one in four Americans between ages fifteen and fifty-five eventually will acquire an STD.

▶ *Anyone* who has sex outside of marriage is at risk. STDs do not recognize a person's religious or moral beliefs, only his or her actions. As one researcher said, "Unless you're monogamous for a lifetime, with a monogamous partner, you're at risk. And the more partners you have, the greater the risk."

▶ The Minnesota Institute of Public Health warns that "there are twenty sexually transmitted diseases which are not prevented by contraception." They emphasize that fifteen million people now get a sexual disease each year.

▶ Dr. Edward Weismeir, director of the UCLA Student Health Center, warns students that, "Even an honest answer to an intimate question is no guarantee that a person is safe. While dormant in one person, an STD can be transmitted to another." He admonishes then that "one chance encounter can infect a person with as many as five different diseases."

▶ Until recent years, public-health experts counted barely five types of sexually transmitted diseases. Now, they know that more than twenty-seven exist. Research shows that the number-one concern of women—ahead of even war and peace—is sexually transmitted infection. Causing the most concern is AIDS.

AIDS has become this century's number-one health menace. "It is estimated that 1 to 1.5 million Americans are currently infected with the virus . . . It will probably prove to be the plague of the millennium. 'If you were the devil,' says Dr. Alvin Friedman-Kier, AIDS researcher at New York University, 'you couldn't conceive of a disease that would be more disruptive and disturbing than this one, a sexually transmitted disease that kills within a short period and for which there is no treatment.'"[14]

I met Bobby "Keith" Revis shortly before he died of AIDS. The following is a condensed version of his testimony that he shared with me.

"I don't mean to start with such a sad note, but I am dying. I am dying of a disease I am so ashamed of—AIDS. You reap what you sow and your sins will find you out, the Bible says. I am a prime example of that verse.

But I would like to tell you a little bit about my childhood. I grew up out in the country. I had a wonderful Mom and Dad. We attended a good church with a pastor who preached the Bible. We had a good life. Then they diagnosed my Dad with cancer. He went in and out of the hospital for about two years. He was only thirty-five years old.

It was snowing one day and so we were going to get out of school early. Excited about early dismissal from school, we rode the bus home, jumping up and down and acting crazy. My two sisters and I stayed with the preacher and his wife a lot while Mama was gone to the hospital. We were there and playing at one end of the house when I heard an awful scream. I knew at that moment that my Daddy had died. A man from church came and talked to me and told me that Daddy was no longer in pain, he was in a better place now. But I was mad. I got so mad at my Daddy because he had left us. How could he leave us? My Mama had never worked. She had always stayed home with us. She did not even have a driver's license. What were we going to do? I got mad at God. 'It's not fair! I had a good Daddy. Why did You take my Daddy? Why didn't you take some drunkard or another Daddy that wasn't any good? Why did you take mine?' Resentment welled up inside me.

On top of all this, I began having feelings and tendencies that I did not understand and that I could not control. But I thought I was just going through a stage and it would go away.

Later, my Mom remarried and when I turned sixteen, I left home. I was so unhappy. I started hanging out with the wrong crowd and started drinking. I began doing things I knew were wrong, but I did them anyway.

A few years later, I met a girl whom I ended up marrying. We had a little girl, a precious little girl, a beautiful little girl with big blue eyes. I was so proud of her. I was so happy! After several years, however, my wife and I could not get along and so we separated. We shared custody of our little girl, however.

I began to think maybe I needed to find out about these feelings that had never gone away. One night, I got up the nerve to go to this bar. What I saw scared me and shocked me. But if the devil can get you somewhere once, he can get you to go back a second time. I started going more often and eventually became relaxed. Once I tried changing and going back to church. I was trying to change myself. You cannot do it yourself. God has to do it for you. The devil told me that I had been born like this and I needed just to be honest and accept it. That is what I tried to do. I tried to make the best of it.

Years passed. One day I decided to get a bigger life insurance policy and so they routinely took blood tests. Before I received the result of the tests though, my stepbrother and his wife visited me. He pastored a church in Kansas. He asked why I wasn't in church. I told him I didn't know. But deep inside I knew. It was my lifestyle that kept me out of church.

Shortly after my stepbrother's visit, I received a letter from the insurance company stating they had denied my request for a life insurance policy. They also said that I needed to see a doctor. Although, I considered cancer since it ran in my family, but AIDS never entered my thoughts.

I began taking a New Testament with me to work and I read and read it. I knew the plan of salvation, yet the more I read the Bible, the more it convicted me about my sins. One evening, I began crying and was so upset that I called the pastor at church and asked him to come over to talk with me. I was so relieved after hanging up the telephone. The pastor came and we talked about the plan of salvation. I asked God to forgive me for all of the terrible sins that I had committed. I had lived a sinful life—a life that the Bible says is an abomination to the LORD. But God forgave me and He came into my heart. Things changed for me. The bondage that I thought would never be removed from me was taken away. God took it away. I started attending church and got baptized.

Then I got very sick and was in the hospital for six weeks. But the LORD has been with me. He has been so good to me and carried me through this. There are two things that I would like to express to you. One is that my Mama never stopped praying for me through all these years. If you have a loved one that you want to see saved, don't give up. Keep on praying. God answers prayers. The other thing is to those who are in bondage. I want you to know—whatever kind of bondage you are in—Jesus can bring you out and set you free. Jesus took my bondage away. He can do the same for anyone. He has been so good to me. This has been very difficult for me because I am so ashamed, but God has been with me. Christ is all we need. This is very true. Thank you."

Keith has died and is now home with the LORD. He was a victim of AIDS; however, that dreadful disease is not the only STD that causes the medical profession concern. Physicians regularly see patients who have contacted Chlamydia, gonorrhea, genital herpes, trichomoniasis, venereal warts, syphilis and pelvic inflammatory disease or PID. "One of the most striking characteristics of the current crop of STDs is that, with the notable exception of AIDS, their most severe consequences are visited upon women and babies."[15]

Teen pregnancy and STDs are not the only physical

consequences or physical risks involved in premarital sex, although these are some lesser-known consequences. "The earlier a girl begins having intercourse, for example, the higher her risk of developing cervical cancer as an adult. Cancer specialist, Dr. Hugh R. K. Barber, director of obstetrics-gynecology of New York's Lenox Hill Hospital, believes that the trend toward earlier intercourse is too new to know what other physical risks may turn up. 'We know a fair amount about females,' he says, 'but I suspect that boys aren't going to get off scot-free, physically . . . There's no data, but I wouldn't be surprised if boys eventually get cancer of the prostate at an earlier age than now.'"[16]

Physicians and researchers can offer little in the way of preventing STDs. Therefore, many experts are beginning to point people to look back at the monogamous relationship as the only answer for safe sex. One concludes, "Young people must be told the truth—that the best way to avoid AIDS is to refrain from sexual activity until as adults they are ready to establish a mutually faithful monogamous relationship."[17] The escalation of STDs may ultimately help close the door to an era of mindless promiscuity.

One of the most devastating physical consequences is abortion. "In the United States, an abortion is performed every twenty-two seconds; that is more than 4000 a day. In many states, a thirteen-year-old girl cannot receive aspirin from the school nurse without parental consent, yet the same girl can receive an excused absence from school officials to have an abortion performed without her parents' knowledge . . ."[18]

In speaking of the Roe v. Wade decision, President Ronald Reagan said, "Our nationwide policy of abortion-on-demand through all nine months of pregnancy was neither voted for by our people nor enacted by our legislators—not a single state had such unrestricted abortion before the Supreme Court decreed it to be a national policy in 1973. But the consequences of the judicial decision are now obvious: Since 1973, more than 15 million unborn children have had their lives snuffed out by legalized abortions. This is over ten times the number of Americans lost in all our nation's wars."[19]

The physical consequence of America's sexual promiscuity has been great. The emotional consequence in premarital sex is just as devastating. They can almost guarantee emotional damage from premarital sex:

"In 1965, perhaps a little too soon to reflect the changing attitudes about sex, there were 21,560 suicides in the United States, with a rate per hundred thousand members of the popular of 11.6. In 1977, twelve years later, 28,5000 people committed suicide with the rate of 12.6. Even if we cannot equate the rise in suicide with sexual activity, it is obvious there has been no decrease in the rate as a result of the sexual revolution. Surely the expert opinion has not proved that only the celibate or sexually denied are committing suicide. The suicide rate has increased in one age group that has become increasingly sexually active as the pregnancy, abortion and venereal disease statistics indicate. In the last twenty-five years the rate of teenage suicides has doubled. We are not suggesting, of course, that sexual promiscuity is the only factor operating in the teenage suicide picture, but it is certainly one factor, and the therapeutic effect of sexual liberation on the suicide rate is not apparent."[20]

The emotional consequence that follows sexual immorality is fear and anxiety. The fear of getting caught are enough to traumatize any young person involved in premarital sex. We can trace our fearfulness and anxiety back to the fall in the Garden of Eden, but it becomes supercharged in our emotional lives when sexual immorality comes into the picture. Fear does not need to be the bottom-line emotion in any young person's relationship or activity; however, it usually ends up being just the case if there is sex outside the bounds of marriage. Even if the couple eventually marry one another, studies prove that they damaged the trust factor between them. Although a young person's body may be physically ready for sex, there is still too great a chance for suffering emotional damage. If one partner leaves, or "dumps" the other, then the one left suffers not only from fear and anxiety, but also from feelings of hurt, anger and rejection

Another emotional byproduct of sexual immorality is shame and guilt. Hollywood and the entertainment industry has done its best to eliminate this factor, yet it still remains. God created us with a conscience that is programmed to feel shame and guilt. The problem came when Tinsel Town tried to convince us otherwise through the philosophy of its films.

Then when shame was erased from the blackboard of our nation's conscience, it left us with a society that went on a rampage of sexual immorality. Hollywood sold us the lie that it was "only being human" to have sex, even multiple sex partners, before marriage. What Hollywood did not show is the wake of damaged emotions that followed such a wave of immorality. Fear, guilt, shame, self- deprecation still accompanies premarital sex. If it does not come immediately, it will certainly come in later years. The LORD's word does not return to Him void. He tells us to: "Be not deceived; God is not mocked: for whatsoever a man soweth, that shall he also reap."[21]

Perhaps the pinnacle of emotional damage comes to those who have had an abortion. Abortion resolves one situation for the moment, but it never resolves the guilt or breaks the bond between a mother and her baby . . . these statistics by Anne Catherine Speckhard, Ph.D., of the University of Minnesota, on the long-term manifestations of stress from abortions (five to ten years after):

▶ "Eighty-one percent reported *preoccupation* with the aborted child.
▶ Seventy-three percent reported *flashbacks* of the abortion experience.
▶ Sixty-nine percent reported feelings of *"craziness"* after the abortion.
▶ Fifty-four percent recalled *nightmares* related to the abortion.
▶ Thirty-five percent had perceived *visitations* from the aborted child.
▶ Twenty-three percent reported *hallucinations* related to the abortion."[22]

The physical and emotional consequences have piled up on us as a nation until we stagger beneath the load. Most of us in the Body of Christ have a sense of urgency that we must do something to reverse the current tide of sexual promiscuity in our nation. With a renewed passion, we must reclaim the timeless values that our ancestors held so dear.

Remember

▶ The lesson of Phineas Gage

▶ The personality of America has changed because the individual personalities of her citizens have undergone radical transformations—just as Phineas Gage.

▶ The devil employs the natural law of our senses in order to change the fibers of our personalities.

▶ To control us, the enemy **must control our senses**.

▶ America has reaped the whirlwind in physical consequences because of uncontrolled sexuality.

▶ America has reaped the whirlwind in emotional consequences because of uncontrolled sexuality.

Later that night, Brett involuntarily smiled to himself several times as he worked at his computer. For Callie to be so smart, she was so dumb in certain things. Tha Dogg Pound! She thinks they're spiritual giants because they talk about Jesus. Anybody can talk about Him. Different story when it comes to walking it out. His habitual urge to protect Callie from any real or imagined danger surfaced instantly in Brett's heart. His fingers drummed lightly on the keyboard without actually typing as he thought about Callie. He had sensed her trusting innocence from the first day he saw her in grammar school, back when he was still the new kid in town.Once his thoughts were on Callie, it was always difficult for him to pull them back to history—or to any other subject.

Dad says it's easy to interpret the Constitution, Brett thought, once he began to concentrate. That's easy for him to say. He's written twenty papers on it. Don't know why I get so nervous working on this. So important to him, I guess. I've never flunked a test in my life, but it feels like flunking if I make a B. There. All right! That's a brilliant way to phrase *that. Dad, you are going to appreciate that little insight. Guarantee it! Bet you never considered it from that angle. You'll have to lay this concept on all the intelligentsia at your Thursday night Round Table. All you **saviors** of the Constitution. Saviors—what a joke.*

Shortly after eleven o'clock, he stretched his arms out to his sides. The back of his neck and shoulders still ached slightly from the blow to the head and shoulders that his father had given him several days ago. As he scanned over the last paragraph he had just typed, he subconsciously pulled his shoulder blades together in an attempt to alleviate the sharp pain across his shoulders.

Dad, what has happened to you? I miss Mom as much as you do, but you're going off the deep end on this. Maybe you should have signed those divorce papers. Then she wouldn't have started living with so many different men. She got lonely. That's all it was. But you've got to get hold of yourself, though, Dad. Chief physicist at the nuclear lab. . . you start acting as strange at work as you do at home, they'll send you to a psychiatrist. Go berserk over any small thing anymore. Maybe it's a late reaction to Mom's death. It's been two years since that guy murdered her. Some boyfriend, eh? She picked the wrong guy to get mixed up with that time. I thought you'd work yourself to death right after it happened.

Twelve. Fourteen hours a day. You'd still be doing it if you hadn't collapsed at work that night. Maybe that was when it all started happening—buying that computer to do more work at home. Keeping yourself locked up in the bedroom for days. Worried about you, Dad. I saw Thelma Lou putting all that liquor up in the cabinet the other day. When I asked her about it, she said it was the second time that week you'd sent her to the store. She's worried about you, too. Never eat the food she cooks for you. You don't brag on her anymore about what a good job she does. She works hard keeping the house clean for us. Ironing our clothes. She said you don't even seem to notice the nice starch job on your shirts anymore.

Do my best, Dad. I do. Try to make you proud of me. Tellin' you one thing though, big Daddy. You better never come at me again swingin' that baseball bat around like some drunken maniac. What has happened to you?! LORD Jesus! I don't even know my own Dad anymore. No siree, buddy. Dad or not, I won't take anymore of those poundings. You can put that in your pipe and smoke it at your Constitution Convention of perverted old cronies every Thursday night. Probably old Judge Gerald who showed you how to tap into that filth on your computer. Or that filthy-talking lawyer who thinks he's the final expert on Constitutional law.

Try to spend time with you every Sunday, Dad. I stopped going to church so we can try and be a family—like we used to be; you know when we did things together before Mom left us. Remember how we always did things on Sundays? Every Sunday. Now I'm afraid to leave you on Sundays because all you do is sit at the computer and drink bourbon. Don't like leaving you on Sundays. I'm afraid I might come home from church and see you've left like Mom. What has happened to you? You never used to get so angry at me. Now you yell at any small thing. It's what you're doing on that computer. If you'd let me help you. We could go do things together like we used to—you've got to quit foolin' around on that computer, Dad!

When Brett heard his father fumbling with his key at the door latch, his muscles tensed automatically. He had hoped to be in bed asleep when his father came home. Their encounters always ended in arguments lately. Brett quickly turned his light off in the bedroom first so his father would not realize he was still awake. In the dark, he turned off his computer, undressed quickly and slipped into bed. He heard his father's footsteps pause outside his bedroom door and then walk away.

The problem between father and son began the night that Brett had accidentally discovered why his father had insisted on locking the door to the master bedroom as he sat for hours before the computer. It was after the purchase of the computer that his father's personality had undergone such a drastic change. Brett could never remember his father missing one day at work. Yet at the beginning of Brett's junior year, his father began staying home on the days after he spent most of the night in front of the computer. Thelma Lou, the housekeeper, told Brett that his father was often still in bed when she left in the afternoons. The serious, dignified physicist had gradually turned into an explosive, unstable stranger. His former mild manners erupted with volcanic force at any small incident that involved Brett. When Brett had first questioned his father about his late hours, an explosion followed.

"*Dad—I just asked what you were working on that kept you up so late.*"

"*It's highly confidential! Stay away from my computer— do you hear me? You've got your own.*"

Months later, Brett discovered the reason for his father's obsession with the computer. When Brett's printer ran out of toner one evening, he saved his work on a disk and loaded it onto his father's computer to print it. The first thing Brett saw on the computer screen was his mother's name on the incoming mail. He immediately clicked on the icon to open the mailbox. After reading the first few lines, Brett sat paralyzed in front of the words addressed to his father. Obscene words arranged in smutty sentences and lewd language filled the screen. Tie him up and do what?! The message was vile and vulgar. Brett's heart suffered a sudden concussion. He was so numb from shock that he did not hear his father enter the room several minutes later. Like a wounded animal, deranged, demented, his father lunged at Brett and hurled him against the wall. Even as he felt the colliding force of his father's body against him, somewhere deep within Brett he wondered where this sudden strength had originated. It was almost demonic in force.

In the weeks that followed that ugly scene, Brett tried hard to push its memory out of his mind. Anger, shouting, cursing, pounding fists—they had all drowned out Brett's questions of what was going on. . . why was some woman using his mother's name to write such filth to him? That evening became the first of many explosions when Brett experienced his father's irrational anger. Silence began to live between father and son. It was only when a cloud of bourbon floated around his father that Brett heard his voice. What had happened to his father? Who was this stranger who sat across the table from him now? How had his dignified father, the respected nuclear physicist, turned into such a perverted recluse?

The recollection of James Dobson's interview with Ted Bundy, only hours before his execution, began creeping into Brett's thoughts at different times. Brett and Callie had watched the taped interview together on one of their visits to Granny's house. At the time, Brett found it hard to believe that Bundy's perverted lifestyle—that resulted in his killing over twenty-four females in sex-related crimes—had all begun in a seemingly innocent pursuit of soft core pornography. Bundy's preoccupation with pornography had progressed to such hard-core pornography that it eventually led him into the brutal, demonic killing of women.

Brett never told anyone—not even Callie—what he had discovered about his father. He mumbled some excuse when she quizzed him why they never spent time with his father anymore. His constitutional urge to always protect Callie surfaced immediately. In his heart, Brett knew he could never again allow Callie to be alone with his father. He felt such inward shame. Yet it was a shame too deep to be spoken—even to Callie—especially not to Callie.

Part IV
The Church

"I sought for the key to the greatness and genius of America. Not until I went into the churches of America and heard her pulpits flame with right-eousness did I understand the secret of her... power"

— French historian Alexis de Tocqueville who toured America in the 1800s and then recorded his impressions in *Democracy in America*

Chapter 6

Call of the Church

Thanksgiving Vacation 1996

Granny squirmed again in the church pew. There needs to be a law somewhere stating that dead, boring sermons ought to be excuse enough for stoning the preacher. . .'specially if they last more than ten minutes. Fifteen maximum. Be easier on the preacher and us too if he'd try spending some time alone with the LORD instead of visiting the old folks home every day of the week. Old folks home?! The old folks home is sitting right here on these pews every Sunday. This church died twenty years ago and they don't even realize it. Nothing but old folks sitting on the pews, trying to hold onto their "form of godliness and denying the power thereof." Look at Callie. And Corey! Both of them up there nodding off. Callie, my Callie. Precious grandchild. You come to church and never even realize that there is no life here—nothing but dead, religious ritualism. I'm about to fall asleep myself. Need to watch doing that in here. If somebody sees me they might think I've died and call the ambulance—like they had to do when old man Johnson died in the church vestibule last Sunday! LORD, help us! People dying right here in the middle of church. At church, LORD! Fell down deader 'n a door knob like George used to say. Right there in the vestibule. Right there in front of everybody. We're so deaf we can't hear "wisdom cryin' out in the streets" no matter how loud You shout at us. Don't they see *we're all **dead** around here?*

*Us old folks are dyin' off and the stench of our lukewarm-ness is killin' our young people. Oops! There goes Brother Bosher again. Every Sunday. Same old show. Nodding and bobbing around like an apple in a tub o' water. There goes his head. Dependable as Big Ben over in London. . .every Sunday, as faithful as clock work. Droops to the right. Further down, Brother Bosher, further. . . further. There you go. Rest on your shoulder for a minute. That's right. One minute, two minutes, three minutes. Whoops! There it comes. Faithful jerk of the head and ole Brother Clark Bosher's eyes fly open. Looks around like a sheepish school boy to see if anybody notices. Happens so smoothly every Sunday. After all these years, I'm not sure if Corey pokes his Papa in the ribs every Sunday or if Brother Bosher wakes himself up. By the grin on Corey's face every Sunday, I'd say he gives his Papa a secret nudge in the ribs when he thinks no one is watching. Corey is an expert at it. Gotta give Corey ten points, cause I never see him move if he does poke Brother Bosher. Look at Corey grinning. He knows the preacher has about five more minutes of his Papa's atten-tion before he nods off again. After all these years, Brother Bosher has that down to a fine art. Bob, bob, bob, rest—little jerk, big jerk! Bob, bob, bob, rest—little jerk, big jerk! Can't help but love old Brother Bosher. Countin' his bobs is the only thing that helps me endure these sermons that taste like three-day old, leftover chicken soup. If Brother Bosher was still in charge of the young people, maybe they'd get a little more excit-ed about serving the LORD. He built the biggest youth depart-ment we've ever had here. Him and my George. Couldn't stop those two young men in those days. Course, we were all lots younger then. O George, George, what are you and the LORD talkin' 'bout up there? George, go tell Him. . .we're dying down here and I can't get anybody to listen to me about these young'ns. What's to happen to them, George? They don't even know the LORD? O LORD—help us! How can I leave your work to a generation that doesn't even **know** You. They know about You, but they don't **know** you. How are they ever to expe-rience Your fullness in these catacombs? They don't realize how wonderful You are. And look at us—the great spiritual know-it-alls. We worry more about saving money for our retirement. Or planning a trip to Florida to keep warm in the* *wintertime. We want to stay warm in our old age, but we don't care if there's a fire burning for You in our kids' hearts. We're all livin' on a bunch of memories of how it used to be around here.*

Times I wonder why I even bother to show up anymore. For the kids, I guess. Can't give up on these children. LORD, You gotta do something! God Almighty, these children are dying like us old folks! You gotta do something. Send somebody to help 'em fall in love with You. Just give 'em one glimpse of Your glory!—that's all it'll take, LORD. Just one. The only glimpses they get nowadays is that filthy trash comin' out of Hollywood. Or through the trash on TV. Grimy, dirty trash. I try tellin' 'em but when their parents let 'em sit and watch that junk. . . what can I do, LORD? Grouchy old Granny. What do I know? I know how You made our brains and how Satan would like to control the way we think—that's what this old Granny knows!

What's to happen to these kids, LORD? If You don't step in and do something, we're gonna lose 'em. I know these kids, LORD. They can turn this city upside down for You. But they need some help. Somebody needs to help 'em. Look at them! They're bored to death right now. Whispering. Writing notes. Countin' the different pieces of stained glass on the windows. I can save 'em the trouble—there's 645 in the first window by the organ and 632 in the second window. O LORD, we come to church and count the organ pipes because we're so bored listening to empty sermons that have no life in them. There's no love for You. No wonder we lose our young people to the devil. He entertains them better through TV than we can preach to them through our lukewarm lives and boring sermons. No wonder You say You'll spew us out of Your mouth. Mercy, LORD. Have mercy on the children. Look at them. Callie, Tiffany, Jamie, Darla, Laura, David, Corey—they can be great warriors for You. And Brett—he doesn't even attempt to come anymore. Who can blame him? O LORD, I'm worried about that child. Somethin' is bad wrong there. What's wrong? Why does he refuse to leave his house on Sundays? I know what he says, but something is wrong. What is it? Something's wrong. O LORD, our kids are headed for a crash course with hell if You don't step in and intervene somehow. Don't let them go through life swallowing all the filthy lies of the devil. And seeing nothin' but cold, dead religion all around 'em.

Thank you, Jesus! There goes Mary to the organ. Two choruses of "Just As I Am" and we can get out of this mausoleum. Sometimes I'd like to stand up and just shout in the middle of the sermon, "Fire! Fire! We need fire in our hearts for Jesus cause there's a fire in hell! If we're gonna fight hell, we need fire from heaven!" O LORD, if it would wake 'em up. Fire. . . there's a fire in hell, people! I'd embarrass my daughter two shades beyond scarlett red if I did that. But somebody needs to do something. 'Course, if I was to try that one Sunday, I do believe that David and Corey would probably jump up and join me. . . Jamie? Yeah, I can see Jamie standing up and helping me yell FIRE! Tiffany? She'd laugh aloud, but she might get embarrassed. Callie, O my Callie, you would not even participate. Old Brother Bosher—now, he'd yell fire with us. Now that's a thought! Maybe I will yell **fire** *one of these Sundays. If I let Brother Bosher in on it, he'd probably run around the auditorium like a fire engine if he thought it would help the young people. Maybe me and him need to have a prayer meetin' at the house with these kids. Bible study or something. We could do it on Thursdays. I could bake extra loaves of bread for everybody. Maybe bake a pie or two.*

Roman Colosseum and Boiling Frogs

Rome—the word reverberates like the boom of a great historical cannon. It summons images of tramping legions and triumphant generals parading through arches built for their victories. Rome was the city of magnificent temples with the smoke of incense rising from blood-splashed altars to the gods of the Eternal City. Rome gave history a vision of timeless grandeur, cruel and sublime. The builders of the Roman empire must have surely dwarfed the human mold. Romans believed that their city had been singled out by the gods for a special destiny. They spoke often about how their city had been divinely ordained to rule the world.

Christians have written much about the parallel between the ancient glory of Rome and America. For our purposes, however, we want to look only at Rome's Colosseum. Romans built the great theater for their national amusement. Like our nation, Rome both enjoyed and abused the advantages of wealth and luxury. Quite literally, Rome amused itself to death. Thousands of despairing souls, whose mortal agonies were staged to distract and amuse the Roman crowds, fell to their deaths inside the Colosseum. The deadly oval of Rome drenched the earth with human blood. The ancient world of Rome was cruel and human life was cheap. Few nations were more systematic about its cruelties, its floggings, tortures, burnings, crucifixions and massacres of prisoners than Rome. None openly enjoyed watching them as much as the Romans— that is, none until the American cinema unrolled its own visualizations of Technicolor cruelty and graphic violence.

A comparison between the two nations is unnerving when we comprehend the truth that America, like ancient Rome, is amusing herself to death. The horror of Rome was that they were murdering humans as a public spectacle for means of entertainment. As a civilized nation, we believe ourselves to be beyond such horrific violence. Yet our senses send messages of having witnessed ruthless violence to our brain as if we had witnessed the actual action. Our sense of sight makes no distinction between reality and make-believe when it sends messages to our brains. Our sense of sight transmits only the image itself. That image tells our brains the appalling message that it is witnessing bloody membranes splattering forth from a bullet wound to someone's head. Our sense messenger does not say, "Oh yes—there's an addendum. Don't pay any attention to this message because it is only make-believe." With lightening speed, our sense messenger tells our brains that it is witnessing the gleaming blade of a large knife slowly slicing across a person's throat. The brain instantly sees scarlet blood gushing out from the victim's throat. Our sense of sight makes no distinction that we are only watching some technical make-believe. These sights affect us as if they were the real thing and our sense of sight reports only what it viewed. It does not say, "Hey, now! Don't pay any attention to that—it's just a pretend scene in a movie. Okay?"

The film critic Michael Medved writes some graphic messages that Hollywood feeds our senses in the much-heralded epic, *The Cook, The Thief, His Wife and Her Lover*: "We see sex in a toilet stall, deep kisses and tender embraces administered to a bloody cadaver, a woman whose cheek is pierced with a fork, a shrieking and weeping nine-year-old boy whose navel is hideously carved from his body, a restaurant patron whose face is scalded by a tureen of vomit-colored soup, and an edifying vision of two naked, middle-aged lovers writhing ecstatically in the back of a truck filled with rotting, maggot-infested garbage. The grand finale of the film shows the main character slicing off—and swallowing—a piece of carefully seasoned, elegantly braised human corpse in the most graphic scene of cannibalism ever portrayed in motion pictures. There is, in short, unrelieved ugliness, horror, and depravity at every turn."[2] How can our brains not recoil with horror at such graphic scenes? Did the gladiators in Rome indulge in cannibalism? Or did they have sex before the crowds in a bed of maggots? History records no such atrocities. The abomination of America's entertainment far surpasses anything that might have occurred in the Colosseum at Rome.

Along with our sense of sight, our sense of hearing faithfully executes its created purpose by sending its own messages. It tells the brain it hears the loud explosion from a gun being fired, the terrified screams of a person, or the gurgling, gasping sounds as the victim struggles to breathe as the murderer slices his throat. Instantly, our emotions respond to these sense messages as though we had witnessed an actual murder on the streets of our hometown. The result of all this *viewing* is that the frontal lobes of our brain, which contain the seat of our personalities and our characters, become *callous* over time. Just as the Romans became more calloused over the years of watching their favorite form of entertainment, Americans have become desensitized—and most do not realize the extent of that desensitization.

Like our own motion picture entertainment, the "games" in the Colosseum began quite innocently with no death involved. They progressed, however, until the people developed an insatiable appetite for barbarous violence and an unquenchable thirst for flowing blood. As a matter of salvaging his reputation, each succeeding emperor felt he had to eclipse the spectacles provided for the people by his predecessor. This type of morbid competition goes on today with our American filmmakers. They constantly strive to extend themselves *artistically* until they surpass their fellow filmmakers. Once a year Hollywood's round table of cinematic creators gathers in hopes of obtaining an Oscar—their god.

Under the domain of these proud Roman emperors, it soon became routine for professional gladiators to duel to the death. What really filled the arena seats was something especially bloody or grotesque, such as Christians being torn to shreds by voracious lions. *Callousness* became the darkest aspect of pagan Rome. Emperor Caraealla once received some visiting citizens from Alexandria and invited them to a banquet. He then had them all murdered. The Romans continued to brutalize their own sensibilities by the daily spectacles in the Colosseum; yet, they argued that what they watched was not harmful to them. Cicero himself argued that these visual spectacles of cruelty only inspired a strong, manly disdain for suffering. We hear Cicero's echo in Hollywood today as it defends its own polluted river of sadistic violence that flows from the theater screens regularly. They argue that life does not imitate art. Instead, they argue that their *art* imitates life as it is in America. They refuse to admit that the youth of our nation will imitate the savagery depicted in the *art* of their films. Yet data from scientific studies in recent years affirms the definite connection between Hollywood's fabricated brutality and the reality of hostility in our society.

If we doubt the callousness that has invaded our country, we need to re-evaluate ourselves. The American Family Journal recorded the following article. It relates a true incident by the former National Endowment for the Humanities Chairman Lynne V. Cheney that occurred in 1994. The incident provides us a shocking revelation regarding our society:

"That summer Mohammed Jaberipour, 49, was working a route in south Philadelphia in a Mister Softee ice cream truck when a 16-year-old tried to extort money. Jaberipour refused, and the youth shot him. As the father of three lay dying, neighborhood teenagers laughed and mocked his agony in a rap song they composed on the spot: 'They killed Mr. Softee.'

'It wasn't human,' another ice cream truck driver, a friend of Jaberipour who came on the scene shortly after the shooting, told the *Philadelphia Daily News*. 'People were laughing and asking me for ice cream. I was crying. . . . They were acting as though a cat had died, not a human being.'

Mrs. Cheney quotes the conclusion of newspaper columnist Bob Greene: 'We have increasingly become a nation of citizens who watch anything and everything as if it is all a show.' She adds, 'But however it has come about, people who laugh at a dying man have no sense that a stranger can suffer as they do.'"[3]

We can lay a great deal of blame at the doorsteps of Hollywood and the entertainment world because of this callous reaction of those teenagers. Hollywood has fed them a steady diet of violence, mockery and rebellion through its films. Rap music has especially fed teenagers with lyrics of callous violence. When we read about the historical violence of ancient Rome, we often find it quite unbelievable that people would find amusement in watching Christians being devoured by lions. Yet American teenagers are now celebrating in song after witnessing a murder. There was a time when we asked ourselves, "How could the Romans have allowed their entertainment, their amusement to progress to such depths of depraved humanity?" However, ancient Rome can rise from its historical grave and rightly ask us, "How could American movies have progressed to such depths of degradation?" The answer might lie in the parable of the frog.

The parable about the frog in the boiling water contains a great truth. It reveals a favorite tactic of the devil in his attempt to sabotage our lives. If we wanted to boil a frog in water, we would not immediately throw the frog into a pot of scalding hot water. The blistering water would cause the frog to jump promptly out of the pot. Yet if we placed the frog into lukewarm water and began slowly simmering the water, the frog would gradually acclimate itself to the increasing temperature. By the time the water was boiling, the frog would have lost much of its strength. Probably, the frog would be unable to regain enough strength to jump out of the pot. The water would then boil the frog to death. Hollywood placed us in the lukewarm waters of sex, violence and foul language during the Fifties. We felt at ease in our lukewarm environment. America had just come through the war that was to end all wars—World War II. We basked in the security of our new economy. Our war-worn parents worked to give their children the material goods and education they had never known. We were neither in the hot of war nor the cold of depression.

America enjoyed this lull of lukewarmness. She did not realize that the intensity of her movies and entertainment would rise to such a state of boiling filth in the decades that followed.

As the wanton waters of our popular culture kept heating up all around us, we sat as passive, sleepy frogs, content in our lukewarm churches, unaware that we were gradually losing our moral and spiritual strength as the army of God. Each succeeding generation born into this world after the Fifties and the Sixties simply accepted the culture they had inherited as the norm. They had never known anything different. The foundation of our American culture bequeathed to our children began crumbling before they were old enough to distinguish between right and wrong. Now our nation is as "hooked" as the frog because we seemingly cannot muster the spiritual strength to jump out of the boiling pot of water.

Like the unsuspecting frog simmering in the lukewarm waters, America accepted its new entertainment environment with its Rating System. Few Americans were even aware that they had ousted the Production Code in Hollywood. When Jack Valenti initiated the Rating System in 1966, it appeared reasonable. We felt comfortable. The temperature of our cultural water heated up so gradually that few of us recognized that we were in a cultural pot that was going to boil our nation to her death. The churches in America need to regain their strength and jump out of Hollywood's steaming pot of sex, violence and foul language! There is still time—*if we act* upon that which we now know and understand.

National Consequences

We skimmed the surface on some physical and emotional consequences of how Hollywood's sexual immorality has helped to usher in the statistics of the last chapter. Yet our nation has suffered some devastating national consequences also. Like the frog, our churches have sat contentedly in our lukewarm waters of lethargy, gradually allowing the views of the world to saturate our nation until we lost our Biblical perspective.

The influence of Hollywood's philosophy on sin has crept into our living rooms, our schools and our church pews. Most of us are familiar with Matthew 13:24-26 about the parable of the wheat and the tares. An enemy comes into a field sown with good seed and scatters bad seed among the wheat. How did this happen? What allowed the enemy to damage the good seed? The answer is found in verse twenty-five: "But while men *slept*, his enemy came. . . . " The LORD clearly tells us that it is because men—we Christians—were sleeping. The church slept and the enemy slithered in unawares. Now America's fields produce more tares than good wheat.

It is my personal belief that the greatest nap that the American church ever took was in allowing prayer to be taken out of the public arena in 1962. By our own sleeping surrender, we abdicated our nation into the hand of the enemy. Prayer documents our dependency upon the LORD. Every time a teacher opened his class with prayer, children learned the unspoken lesson of dependency on God. When Congress convened with prayer, our national leaders acknowledged dependency on God. As a nation, we were "under God" through the acknowledgment of our public prayers. Then the United States Supreme Court challenged not only the wisdom of our forefathers in their documented and historical dependency upon the LORD, but they challenged God Himself. The Supreme Court stated in effect that they did not need God's principles in our public affairs.

Obviously, we did not personally sit on the bench that made that immoral decision. However, scripture affirms that the LORD deals with a nation according to its leaders' actions. The posture taken by the Supreme Court judges forced us to become accountable as a nation, despite our personal stance. The psalmist David wrote: "If the foundations be destroyed, what can the righteous do?"[4] The decision to take prayer out of America's public arena most assuredly was the first blow in destroying the foundation of our nation. The national consequences that we have suffered are astounding.

Our ancestors swaddled the birth of America in the fabric of prayer and Biblical principles. Our ancestors nurtured us as a young nation by their faith in God. During the Constitutional Convention of 1787, Benjamin Franklin issued a small rebuke to our founding fathers. When he perceived that the opposition among them stemmed from their lack of dependence upon the LORD, he told them:

"In the situation of this Assembly, groping, as it were, in the dark to find political truth, and scarce able to distinguish it when presented to us, how has it happened, Sir, that we have not hitherto once thought of humbly applying to the Father of lights to illuminate our understanding! In the beginning of the contest with Great Britain, when we were sensible of danger, we had daily prayer in this room for the Divine protection. Our prayers, Sir, were heard, and they were graciously answered. All of us who were engaged in the struggle must have observed frequent instances of a superintending Providence in our favor . . . And have we now forgotten this powerful Friend? Or do we imagine we no longer need His assistance? I have lived, Sir, a long time, and the longer I live, the more convincing proofs I see of this truth—that God governs in the affairs of men. And if a sparrow cannot fall to the ground without his notice, is it probable that an empire can rise without his aid? We have been assured, Sir, in the Sacred Writings, that except the LORD build the house, they labor in vain that build it. I firmly believe this; and I also believe that without His concurring aid, we shall succeed in this political building no better than the builders of Babel; we shall be divided by our little partial local interests; our projects will be confounded; and we ourselves shall become a reproach and a byword down to future ages . . . I therefore beg leave to move that henceforth, prayers imploring the assistance of Heaven and its blessings on our deliberation, be heard in this assembly every morning before we proceed to do business, and that one or more of the local clergy of this city, be requested to officiate in this service."[5]

After Benjamin Franklin's rebuke, the Constitutional Convention delegates declared a three-day recess. They fasted, prayed and invited local ministers to address the assembly and to pray for them. In that renewed frame of mind, our founding forebears framed our Constitution. Our ancestors exercised wisdom by depending upon the LORD *through their prayers*. Their dependency upon Him in prayer assured that their labor would not be in vain, that the LORD would be the builder of this great nation. I do not see that we can do anything less. Our founding fathers did not build a Babel—yet we have grievously allowed it to become one. As the builders of this nation, their projects were not confounded, they did not become a reproach and a byword to future ages. It is we who will be confounded and become a reproach and a byword to future generations if we do not return to prayer. We cannot let the wisdom of their experience fall to the ground. If they relied upon prayer to build this nation, then surely we must rely upon prayer to sustain it.

America was born a Christian nation! We must never forget this! American soil has always welcomed and even protected those of other faiths, but a close study of the intents of our founding fathers reveals that this was to be a **Christian** nation. The Word of God, the gospel of Jesus Christ and His principles governed the purpose of our founding fathers. Not only were we born a Christian nation, but we developed and matured into the most powerful nation on earth because of our religious principles. As we honored the LORD in our public affairs, He elevated us among the nations of the world in our reputation, in our accomplishments and in our productivity. We prospered because of the moral standards of our nation. He bestowed honor and blessings upon us. "Blessed is the nation whose God is the LORD; and the people whom He hath chosen for His own inheritance."[6] However, our exalted position among the nations crumbled in the wake of our lukewarmness and apathy. We still rank first among the nations; however, it is with embarrassment that America leads the way in such classifications as below. Again, David Barton's book on *America: To Pray Or Not To Pray* pinpoints these "number-one-in-the-world" categories as originating after prayer was taken from our schools:[7]

▶ Violent crime
▶ Divorce rates
▶ Teenage pregnancy rates (leader in the western world)
▶ Voluntary abortions
▶ Illegal drug use
▶ Illiteracy rates (highest among any industrial nation)
▶ Documented cases of AIDs

In his book, *The Myth of Separation*, Barton cites some cases of the Supreme Court that reversed some of America's longstanding national traditions.[8]

1962: A verbal prayer offered in a school is unconstitutional, even if it is both voluntary and denominationally neutral.

1965: Freedom of speech and press is guaranteed to students unless the topic is religious, at which time such speech becomes unconstitutional.

1965: If a student prays over his lunch, it is unconstitutional for him to pray aloud.

1967: It is unconstitutional for kindergarten students to recite: "We thank you for the flowers so sweet; We thank you for the food we eat; We thank you for the birds that sing; We thank you for everything." Even though the word "God" is not contained in it, someone might think it is a prayer.

1969: It is unconstitutional for a war memorial to be erected in the shape of a cross.

1970: It is unconstitutional for students to arrive at school early to hear a student volunteer read prayers which had been offered by the chaplains in the chambers of the United States House of Representatives and Senate, even though those prayers are contained in the public *Congressional Record* published by the U. S. Government.

1976: It is unconstitutional for a Board of Education to use or refer to the word "God" in any of its official writings.

1979: It is unconstitutional for a kindergarten class to ask during a school assembly whose birthday is celebrated by Christmas.

1981: It is unconstitutional for the Ten Commandments to hang on the walls of a classroom since the students might be led to read them, meditate upon them, respect them, or obey them.

1985: A bill becomes unconstitutional, even though the wording may be constitutionally acceptable, if the legislator who introduced the bill had a religious activity in his mind when he authored it.

1985: It is unconstitutional for a kindergarten class to recite: "God is great, God is good, let us thank Him for our food."

1986: It is unconstitutional for a school graduation ceremony to contain an opening or closing prayer.

The above decisions came from a Supreme Court which hypocritically opens its sessions with: "God save the United States and this honorable court." It seems astonishing that the highest court in our land can strike down a centuries-old tradition of public prayer and then declare that this God, to whom we will not allow our children to pray, to *save the United States and this honorable court!*" Barton documents many occasions exhibited by our founding fathers when they openly and publicly proved their dependence upon God by praying. How utterly foolish for a court to hand down decisions declaring public prayer is *unconstitutional!* The men who founded this country walked humbly in their dependence upon God for His wisdom and guidance. "Times of dedicated prayer was part and parcel of the men who guided the nation through the Revolution. Both the national and state congresses regularly called for days of prayer and fasting or prayer and thanksgiving."[9]

Chuck Colson shares a humorous moment regarding an incident between himself and a publisher. The publisher was involved in the removal of the Ten Commandments. *Citizen* records the incident in Colson's words.[10]

"The publisher of a major U. S. newspaper chain recently invited me to a luncheon with his syndicate's editorial board to discuss criminal justice. I recall that before the official program began, the publisher asked me privately, 'You're one of those fellows who carries a Bible around and believes in the Bible, aren't you?'

And I said. "Yes, I am."

He said, "I suppose you believe in hanging the Ten Commandments on classroom walls?"

"Yes, I do."

"Well, we ran a campaign in this city to take the Ten Commandments off of classroom walls."

"Why did you do that?" I asked. "The Jews believe in the Ten Commandments, the Muslims believe in the Ten Commandments, Christians believe in the Ten Commandments. How many Buddhists do you have in this city?"

"We want to be enlightened," the publisher replied.

"Enlightened? How about teaching them history?" I suggested. "Teach them that the Ten Commandments are the basis for our laws. That's why there's a portrait of Moses which looks down on the Speaker of the House in the U.S. House of Representatives."

"No. We're going to be enlightened in this country. We're not going to do that," he insisted.

Fifteen minutes later, right in the middle of the luncheon's first course, the publisher cited reports which showed that 50 percent of public-school kids are stealing from one another. "This is terrible," he said. "How do we stop it?"

I replied, "Maybe we should put a sign up on the wall that says, 'You shall not steal.'"

We have become a nation of fools. How can we campaign vigorously against crime among our young people and not see the foundational significance of the truths contained in the Ten Commandments?

Barton documents some startling statistics since the year 1962 when prayer was first taken out of the public affairs of America.[11]

▶ Average SAT scores for students have dropped by more than eighty points.
▶ Violent crime (as noted above) has increased to unprecedented levels and school violence has now become commonplace.
▶ At least 50% of marriages now end in divorce
▶ Private enterprise has declined at least 70%
▶ Abortions average more than 1.7 million annually
▶ One million high school students drop out of school yearly
▶ United States is the greatest debtor nation in the world

How can we continue to ignore the disaster of these national consequences? George Washington's farewell address warned us that we could not maintain morality apart from the religious principles of Christianity.

"And let us with caution indulge the supposition that morality may be maintained without religion. Whatever may be conceded to the influence of refined education on minds...reason and experience both forbid us to expect that national morality can prevail in exclusion of religious principle."[12]

Our forefathers chartered a Constitution on the assumption that Christians would remain in all arenas of this nation's leadership. Only under the spiritual leadership of godly men was the Constitution intended to protect and guard us. The church has deserted the sacred task handed down to us by our founding fathers. For years, we contented ourselves with taking care of the business within our church walls. The world could take care of the public arena. We erroneously thought that the Father's business did not involve protecting His scriptural principles outside the church building. As *American* Christians, however, we are not only born again but we are born into a nation that demands Christian participation in every public arena if we are to follow our founding fathers' vision for this country. Will we regain that which we have lost? Are we going to pass on the baton of a faltering nation that is on the verge of aborting itself to our children?

John Jay was one of our founding fathers whom George Washington selected as the first Chief Justice of the Supreme Court. He left no question regarding the participation of Christians in public affairs: "Providence has given to our people the choice of their rulers, and it is the duty as well as the privilege and interest of our Christian nation to select and prefer Christians for their rulers."[13]

Behind closed doors, the darkness of Callie's bedroom hugged up to her in its secret arms. Only a faint glow from the television screen illuminated the room. A scarlett flush colored Callie's face, her entire body stretched and yawned, tingling with excitement as it received the sense messages that urged it to wake up. Wake up! Wake up and satisfy me. I'm getting the message. I'm stirred and anxious for fulfillment. Callie pulled the pillow even closer into her body as she watched Demi Moore in the shadows of her bedroom. Mom and Dad had rented the video, "Scarlett Letter" and she was watching it now— all alone. Her parents had gone to meet another deacon and his wife for dinner.

Naked, unashamed, Demi Moore turned slowly and wantonly in front of a mirror on the television screen. As she inspected the nudity of her body, Callie instinctively realized that Demi Moore was thinking about the preacher in the movie. Immediately Callie's thoughts turned to Brett. It was all so romantic to Callie. Sensual. Seductive. Sinless—

*Throughout the movie, Callie substituted herself as Demi Moore. Brett was the preacher. Such a strong love! Such physical desire! Such passion—Callie felt Demi Moore's passion. Callie's eyes kept feeding her mind a sensuous meal of sex. Her ears served her mind hungry words of sexual cravings. It felt so glorious to Callie's body. Her body responded with breathtaking eagerness when the screen showed the consummation of first-time sex between Demi Moore and her preacher lover. It was so romantic. Different parts of their nude bodies merging together on the screen. Upon discovery of her pregnancy, Demi Moore defied the entire community. She would **not** name the father. Never! Callie viewed the actress' decision as being so heroic!*

When the movie was finished, Callie could not bear to let go of her television couple and their glorious love. She loved it. Theirs had been such a great love. So romantic. A thwarted sigh and a shrug of disappointment kept Callie glued to her pillow, clutched tightly to her body, until the video tape clicked off and began to rewind itself. She slipped off her bed and turned on the lamp next to her bed.

Slowly, in the soft glow of the lamp's light, and in imitation of Demi Moore, Callie let her nightgown fall to the floor and then she observed the nudity of her own body in the full-length mirror. Slowly. Turning. Observing. Only Callie did not think of Demi Moore's preacher. Callie concentrated on Brett and the look of approval she always saw reflected in his eyes.

Chapter 7

Commitment of the Clergy

Christmas Vacation 1996

The full-length mirror. It had almost become Callie's constant companion. Silently, she stood observing her slender, young body just before she slipped into her pajamas. A hot flush covered her cheeks when she remembered what had happened only hours ago between her and Brett. They had not planned it. She was not quite certain how—it had just happened. Yet she loved Brett so much. And he loved her! They had not sinned. They loved each other. Then a wave of guilt flooded her heart when she thought of her mother and father. And Granny! What would her grandmother think of her? It would break her heart. Aunt Heather? Her favorite aunt who had so generously given her a rather substantial cash gift for Christmas. Aunt Heather might be more understanding, but Callie knew what a disappointment she would be to her sophisticated aunt. They must never know. None of them.

It will not happen again, she promised herself, as she pulled her pajama top over her head. She and Brett had both promised each other that they would never let that happen again.

That night Callie dreamed she and Brett had discovered a vast amount of treasure, but it was taken from them. Callie had never stolen a thing in her life, but in the dream, she and Brett were stealing the treasure they had discovered together.

They reached out to take the treasure when it was suddenly, inexplicably, taken from them by some unseen force. She woke up several times during the night feeling as if she had lost something that would never again be returned to her.

In spite of their repeated promises that nothing would ever happen again, it did. They both tried hard to keep their promise to one another. They failed. When school opened again in January, they could not return to just holding hands and kissing each other good-night. Callie began to cling to Brett even more than usual. She cried herself to sleep one night when he failed to call. The boundaries of their relationship had suddenly changed. Instead of just enjoying Brett's company, she suddenly became insecure and possessive. If he spent time with David and Corey now, she felt threatened. This new-found possessiveness caused her to even feel jealous of her two best friends, Tiffany and Jamie. Brett was hers! She did not like him to even tease with them as he had always done in the past. A new power had been given to her to control and make demands on Brett, yet at the same time she felt more insecure about their relationship than she could have ever imagined. Well, he was hers!

One evening, Callie called his house until almost midnight, but she got only the answering machine. Feeling guilty, she hurriedly dialed Tiffany's phone number. Relief! Tiffany was doing her English homework. Jamie? Another wave of relief washed over Callie when she heard Jamie's familiar voice answer the telephone. Callie was so relieved she spent an hour talking to Jamie. Well, wherever he is—he is not with one of her best friends. For the first time since they had been children, Callie snapped at Brett the next day when they met at the Coke machine.

"Where were you last night!?"

"At basketball practice. What's wrong?" asked Brett.

"Until midnight?"

"Coach treated David, Corey and me to a hamburger after practice. He wanted to talk about the upcoming tournament. What's wrong, Callie?"

"You didn't call me," she answered with a tremulous pout.

"It was too late. Hey, I didn't realize the world was going to stop turning while I was eating a hamburger. I promise to stop right in the middle of shooting baskets and go call you

next time, okay?" he teased, then reached out to take her hand. "Come on, let's go eat lunch.

"It's not funny."

"I know—but you're funny."

"I am not."

"You are when you act like you're going to punch me out just because I didn't call you."

Brett squeezed her hand, leaned over and whispered lightly in her ear, "I promise I'll call you every night from now on—but you'll be the one who gets in trouble with your Mom and Dad if I call at midnight one of these times." When David and Corey approached them, Brett squeezed Callie's hand once more, then dropped it to give the high five to his two best friends.

Brett kept his promise about calling. Once when his car had a flat tire, he walked several blocks in sleeting rain to a nearby service station. It was almost eleven o'clock when he arrived at the service station. However he kept his promise. He called Callie minutes before he and the attendant left to fix his tire.

Hollywood Vs. Religion

There is undeniable evidence that the elimination of prayer in the public arena began the destruction of America's foundation. However, if the Supreme Court writes its decisions into the law books, Hollywood propagates that lawlessness to the hearts and minds of the American people through its films. The Supreme Court made it legal for Hollywood to pursue passionately its distorted ideas. Hollywood has therefore become the false prophet who presumes to speak for God. Some of Hollywood's favorite targets are those whom they call *right-wing extremists, religious bigots* or *judgmental fanatics*. The entertainment business is not content just to exploit sex, employ violence and exalt foul language. They endlessly produce films that tear down and destroy every area of American public and private life. Some filmmakers greatest contempt is aimed toward religion. They joyfully attack the Judaeo-Christian faith and undermine its value system.

In addition to his book, *Hollywood Vs. America*, Michael Medved produced a video entitled *Hollywood Vs. Religion*.[1] Dr. James Dobson introduces the video and has made it available through his ministry as listed in Appendix B. Medved specifically examines the religious content in fifty movies in the video in an attempt to educate the viewer on understanding Hollywood's hidden messages. A clip shown in the video is about a young woman sharing her faith with a man. His caustic reply stops her: "God is just a drug." It does not take a genius to realize that one of the film's messages is that God is no better for your life than a snort of cocaine. In *Agnes of God*, Jane Fonda followed the Mother Superior into a room and hurled accusations that "you and your order and your church have kept her ignorant because ignorance is next to virginity, right Mother? Poverty, chastity and ignorance are what you live by." Our senses carry these subtle messages into the frontal lobes of our brains. After hearing and seeing many such messages, people gradually view God as nothing more than a temporary high like cocaine and perceive Christians as *ignorant* because they believe in God.

Medved also states that it is "no accident when filmmakers show so many villains who happen to be religious." He shows several religious characters who ultimately end up being the villains or psychopaths in the film. In the movie, *A Few Good Men*, Medved states that one warning sign that a particular character will be the criminal is his statement: "I believe in God and His Son Jesus Christ." Those beliefs mark the character as a dangerous nut and a leader in a murder conspiracy. Again, in *Benefit of the Doubt*, Medved teaches us how to discover the child molester and the serial killer in the film. It is the character who says grace at the dinner table. *Jungle Fever* depicts "a retired clergyman, known as the good Reverend Doctor," who murders his own son. The black clergyman slowly enters a room and says, "I pray for you, my son. Father, I stretch my hands to Thee," fires the gun at his son and then calmly places his gun down on the open Bible. The camera then accusingly focuses on the gun and the open Bible long enough to horrify the audience with its subliminal message. A Bible-reading father kills his son? What kind of people are these Bible-readers anyway?

One of the most horrible portrayals of a Christian as "a

sadistic psychopath" is the role that won Kathy Bates an Oscar in *Misery*. Her Christian character finds James Caan injured from an accident on the side of the road. She brings him to her mountain cabin to nurse him. Then the film reveals that she is a "believer." She tells Caan that the LORD told her, "I delivered him unto you so that you can show him the way." She then takes a hatchet and cuts off different limbs of his body.

Next Medved takes his audience back to the Golden Age era when Hollywood respected the individual who represented the LORD in some films that were "downright inspiring." He showed clips from three movies, *Angels With Dirty Faces* [1938], *Boys Town* [1938] and *The Bells of St. Mary's* [1945] all with positive roles of a priest played respectively by Pat O'Brien, Spencer Tracy and Bing Crosby. Then Medved talks about some of these older films that Hollywood recently remade.

He shows us how those remakes have "elements [added] to the stories that never contained them in the first place." Filmmakers stretched the story line of these old films to get in their savage stereotypes. The 1962 film, *Cape Fear*, was scary enough with its original story line about an ex-convict (Robert Mitchum) who returns to torture and terrify a husband and his wife. In those days, Mitchum's ruthlessness was portrayed by his walking up some steps in the opening scene. He brushed by an innocent lady who is loaded down with books and caused her to drop one of those books. Without acknowledgment of his rudeness, the stone-faced Mitchum continued up the steps. He never stopped. He did not attempt to help the lady pick up the book. With an expression of stunned bewilderment that anyone could be so discourteous, the lady watched Mitchum ascend the stairs.

Director Martin Scorsese (*The Last Temptation of Christ*) recently remade the film, *Cape Fear*. The opening scene has the same music playing in the background. However, a Bible commentary on a shelf replaces the books in the lady's arms. Scorsese shows pictures on the wall. One picture shows a man with two swords thrust through his body. There is a large photograph of Stalin. Then thumbtacked to Stalin is a picture of General Robert E. Lee. Without Michael Medved coaching us, let us together work this subliminal puzzle produced for us by

Martin Scorsese—Bible commentary, Stalin, Robert E. Lee and swords through a human body. That should translate into Christian, a terrorizing dictator, a Southern symbol and human cruelty. Our senses have already interpreted the message for us whether we realize it or not. We are about to be introduced to a despotic tyrant (Stalin) who is a Christian (Bible commentary) from the South (Robert E. Lee), who will do anything for power (Stalin), and human cruelty (two swords in human body). However, Scorsese determines to get his message through to the audience. He is not content to remain subliminal.

The first view we see of Mitchum's replacement (Robert DeNiro) shows a close-up of his back, rising, then falling in front of the camera. The discerning viewer will immediately realize that the naked back with the cross is a subliminal depiction of Jesus Whose naked back bore the cross. However, Scorsese depicts his contempt for Christianity in the symbolic *rising and falling* of this naked back in front of the camera; that is, the *rising and falling* of Jesus and Christianity. DeNiro is doing push-ups. His back is completely tattooed almost entirely with a large, realistic-looking cross. One arm has "Vengeance is mine" with "N.T. Romans 12:19" tattooed on it. The camera skims quickly over the reference, but not quick enough that the senses miss the message and take it to the brain. The "N.T." tattoo—just in case there are ever any questions—documents that the New Testament is this man's problem. Of course, who does not realize that the New Testament is synonymous with Christianity? The other arm is similarly tattooed with "My time is at hand" and its "N.T. Matthew 26:18" reference. Again, in case the viewer does not realize that Jesus quoted these words," the New Testament precedes the reference.

The camera continues silently to focus on scriptures such as: "The Lord is the Avenger" and "I have put my trust in the Lord God, in Him will I trust." These scriptures are tattooed strategically on DeNiro's body. One tattoo is a graphically-illustrated clown with a tear coming down his cheek, a freshly-fired gun in one hand and a Bible in the other. This is director Martin Scorsese's method for instantly linking "Christian fanaticism" or "clowns of American society" with DeNiro's "homicidal tendencies." At one time, it shows

DeNiro tormenting the wife in the film in his Southern accent, slowly drawling out the question of: "Ready to be born again? Few minutes alone with me, dahlin', and you'll be speakin' in tongues."

Medved states that: "The real power of mass media is to define our ideas of what constitutes normal behavior. If you see some sort of weird extreme often enough, then it's not only accepted, eventually, it's expected. So if the audience sees enough stories showing villains who happen to be wearing clerical collars, isn't it just possible that they'll begin to think that anyone who wears one in real life is also some kind of dangerous character? If movie after movie features killer-Christians, won't people become more cynical about religious faith and more fearful of its influence?"

"Well, why does Hollywood do it? Now the entertainment industry loves to say, 'We just give the public what it wants. If you, the audience, don't like what you see, don't blame us, blame yourselves for going to these movies and making them hits.'"

Yet Medved continues by saying that their reasoning does not add up. Hollywood produced more than "three dozen films" which portrayed "crooked, corrupt or crazy clergymen" such as: *Agnes of God, Leap of Faith, The Handmaid's Tale, We're No Angels, At Play In The Fields of The Lord, The Rapture, Heaven Help Us, Nuns On The Run,* and *Monsignor.* He states these films each averaged a cost of twenty-five million dollars per picture, including "production and advertising and distribution." That would total "nearly one billion" and yet none of them made "significant profits at the box office." Some of us probably never even "heard of them because they proved so unsuccessful." Yet these box-office failures will show up repeatedly as rental videos or reruns on television. These films can stay before a viewing audience.

Then Medved posed the question: "Why does Hollywood make all of these antireligious films?" He stressed that it is important not to think that there is some kind of organized conspiracy in Hollywood that wants to destroy Christianity. Rather, he talked about a "tightly-knit creative community whose members happen to share some similar, unspoken values and biases. One of those biases involves sincere and deep-seated contempt for religion."

Throughout the remainder of the video, Medved masterfully proves Hollywood's contempt for religion—Catholics, evangelicals and religious Jews. He opens the portion on the Catholics by showing Al Pacino making a financial deal with the Vatican in his role in *The Godfather Part III*. Michael Medved's video is a viewing must for those interested in learning how to say *No!* to Hollywood and in teaching others how to recognize some hidden meanings in films. Michael Medved is a courageous forerunner who has exposed Hollywood's destructive patterns in producing films. America owes him a round of applause for his gallantry in taking such a heroic stance for righteousness.

The Devil, Demons and Darkness

If the public displays a passion for religion, then Hollywood counters any such romance by denouncing the object of the American people's affection. *Touched By An Angel* has definitely received its wings as a God-honoring program in the eyes of the America public. It hushed the skeptics who produce and promote only sex, violence and foul language for today's audiences. Not to be outdone, however, Hollywood quickly produced its own angelic narrative. Television will not outdo Cinema City. If television contents itself with the normal labor force of angels, Hollywood prides itself in presenting only the super stars. It consequently premiered the film *Michael*, starring none other than the archangel himself. Yet this celluloid archangel is a beer-guzzling angel with bad manners. The feathers from his wings float down, but then maybe that is because he has sex with human beings. Hollywood's personal prejudices go beyond believers or ministers of the gospel. Even the archangels are not exempt from Hollywood's blasphemy and irreverence.

While Hollywood punches religion in the face, it nevertheless exalts the occult. Hollywood delights to serve its viewing audience a banquet of flesh-crawling frights and ghoulish garbage. *The Craft* is a recent film that portrays four young women who are disgruntled with the world. Is your world rotten? Nobody understand you? The world against you because you are black? This movie hooks together the unhappy. Four young women straddle their broomsticks and become part of the sisterhood of witches in a coven in training. They start practicing their magic and casting spells on those who have scorned them. At once, they get an exalted sense of revenge. These "brats" want to get even with everyone who has ever hurt or offended them. The movie shows one of them being levitated while one of them has her physical scars disappear. Hollywood serves the usual hors d'oeuvres as the film's appetizers: A girl slits her wrists, one falls out a window to her death, a man is hit and killed by a car, a graphic scene of an operation and an attempted date rape. A nightmare features a plague of rats, snakes, and slithery maggots—enough to gag Indiana Jones. Then holding true to form, the film magnifies a bleeding Jesus on the crucifix hanging over the door of the Catholic school that the girls attend. Nevertheless, Hollywood sits back in pride thinking it has offered teenagers a moral lesson about not following the herd by messing with evil.

The preoccupation with the demonic comes through in another movie for teenagers entitled *Fear*. The story line revolves around a deranged young man whose sexual appetite gets out of control for a young girl. *Fear* depicts the possessed youth as he sexually arouses the innocent girl on a roller coaster. However, if we have learned anything from Michael Medved's video, we can almost count on seeing some kind of subliminal religious symbol. Aha! When the film shows the fiendish youth in the privacy of his bedroom, we get the message. There it is. Another large Jesus on a crucifix is on his wall. One critic, apparently taught by Medved, wrote: "Catholic symbols are a shorthand way of saying, 'Beware, cuckoos at work!'"[2]

It is chilling to observe the success being accorded to television's *X-Files*. The paranormal mystery series shows a fondness for gruesome killer crime scenes, UFOs, conspiracies and alien bugs. The chill factor comes from the fact that so many other shows have attempted to imitate the bleak, dark side of *X-Files'* success. The list continues to pile up with *X-File* imitations on television such as *Dark Skies, Millennium, The Pretender* and *Profiler*. American audiences are apparently promised more upcoming tales of insanity, murder and demonic possession. Hollywood openly flouts its nasty, insidious agenda of blood oaths, involvement in the occult and evil spirits.

The music industry cooks up the same ghoulish garbage. Michael Jackson has released a video entitled *Ghosts*. The magazine, *Entertainment Weekly*, also once counted thirteen times when the superstar held his crotch and once gave the simulated motions of masturbating. The magazine again reports on Jackson's latest activities. His latest "thriller" video places the twisted singer in a haunted house and he "cavorts with a chorus line of decaying aristocratic ghosts . . . he gets to elevate his weirdo/demonic/am-I-black-or white? iconography to new levels of video game dazzle."[3]

"In *Ghosts*, Jackson is hounded by local townsfolk who accuse him of being a 'freaky boy' . . . see Michael morph into a scaly demon! See Michael turn into a gyrating, pelvis-thrusting, moon-walking skeleton! . . . The creepy difference between the *Thriller* video and *Ghosts* is that what was once a living-dead tease has now become a shade too real for comfort. When Jackson transforms himself into a living skeleton, a bone-jangles who fragments right before our eyes, he seems to be winking at his own degeneration. The King of Pop? Michael Jackson . . . had a face once; now he has only a mask."[4]

As Michael Jackson gyrates his pelvis and clutches at his crotch, the satanic death-rock band called Marilyn Manson promotes its own formula for destroying Christianity. The group takes its name from the Hollywood idol who committed suicide, Marilyn Monroe, and convicted cult leader and murderer, Charles Manson. The lead singer of the group is a dedicated disciple of the Church of Satan. Anton LaVey, founder of the Church of Satan, supports the band in their hatred of Christianity and their attempt to abolish it. MTV features the band's video of *Sweet Dreams Are Made of This* with its dark, sinister music and message. With chalky-white faces painted like witch doctors, satanic tattoos, stringy hair and torn clothes, the band does more than sing. They mock religious materials, destroy Bibles, carry banners of "Kill God" and testify about their sexual sadism.

Our world has gone mad. Our culture gorges itself on perversion. Our artists and entertainers are captive champions for the devil himself. So much of our literature, music and movies originate from the abyss of hell. They publish and produce exquisite banquets of cannibal feasts on our nation's menu of entertainment. Millennial violence and perverted characters are modeled after Jeffrey Dahmer. They expect that we and our children will find amusement in watching or hearing about HIV-positive characters, bathed in blood, who "treat each other as gourmets treat food: lovingly, passionately, sentence after sentence, they savor, season, dismember, and eat each other, raw or fried."[5] We are spared none of the gory details. They cram our senses into unconsciousness.

When will we say *No!* to Hollywood and its pervading curse upon our society? Hollywood holds Christianity in such contempt because Tinsel Town knows its Waterloo. The strategic efforts of the Body of Christ must cripple Hollywood on the battlefields of a Waterloo.

Spiritual Consequences

Are there spiritual consequences from Hollywood's promotion of open promiscuity? Has the church changed its tolerance toward sin? The answers are both *yes* and *no*. Yes—we tolerate our own sins. No—we do not tolerate others' sins. Until we learn to walk in personal holiness, we are guilty of falling into the deception described by the LORD in Matthew 7:3: ". . . why beholdest thou the mote that is in thy brother's eye, but considerest not the beam that is in thine own eye?" We tolerate sin in our own lives, yet condemn others. Unfortunately, Hollywood knows about this defect between us and exploits it more than any other.

Stop and think for a moment. Name one sin that can be found in the world that has not been found in the pulpits of America. Homosexuality? It conceals itself in unknown, but refined clothing. Adultery and fornication? They rank among the highest. Pornography? It has captured more than a few. Incest, rape, lying, stealing, pride, murder, occultism, child abuse, wife swapping—they can all be found fortified within the lives of church leaders. Each of us can recount an incident involving a pastor, a deacon, a songleader or youth pastor who has fallen into sexual immorality, financial dishonesty, even murder. If we do not know them personally, the newspapers and evening news are more than happy to inform us.

In spite of our national failure, the LORD continues faithfully to correct us. The LORD lifted the skirts of American Christianity recently in some sex sandals that rocked our country. Despite denominational differences, we all suffered from those exposures. Did the LORD allow this to shame us? The answer to that is an unequivocal *yes*. "This is thy lot, the portion of thy measures from me, saith the LORD; because thou hast forgotten me, and trusted in falsehood. Therefore will I discover thy skirts upon thy face, that thy shame may appear."[6] He exposed the lukewarmness of the church's sin before the entire world. He did it to arouse us from our luke-warm state of apathy. He did not allow the public humiliation to fall upon Christianity so that one denomination could point a finger at another denomination. Rather, His ultimate goal was to bring us to repentance. He fulfilled the scripture, ". . . that judgment must begin at the house of God: and if it first begin at us, what shall the end be of them that obey not the gospel of God?"[7] God publicly judged some well-known leaders of the church for their hidden sins—and rightly so.

However, the jury is still out on us who do not have such notable, worldwide ministries and those of us who are not as much in the eyes of the public. Yet, we need to ask ourselves these questions. They will shed light on the condition of our hearts. Did we point our finger of criticism and condemnation at those leaders who failed even as we ignored our closet filled with personal skeletons of sin? Are we still hiding secret sins? Do we talk our talk as spiritual leaders in the pulpits and yet fail to walk a walk of true holiness? Do we give our money and continue to hide our appetite for pornography? Are we teaching Sunday School while harboring bitterness and unforgiveness toward others? Have we taken the advice of Gypsy Smith whom they once asked how to start a revival? Evangelists have often quoted Gypsy's formula for revival: Go home, lock yourself in your room. Then kneel down in the middle of your floor and draw a chalk mark all around yourself. Begin to ask God to start the revival inside that chalk mark. When He answers your prayer, then revival will have begun.

If you are a preacher, you have no doubt preached on 2 Chronicles 7:14. If you are a lay person, you have no doubt heard sermons on the same. However, in spite of the famil-iarity of the text, we obviously have not taken the proper steps or else we would have received a national visitation from the LORD. "If My people which are called by My name, shall humble themselves, and pray, and seek My face, and turn from their wicked ways; then will I hear from heaven, and will forgive their sin, and will heal their land." For years now, we have quoted, preached, taught and written from this scripture. Yet it is apparent that we have not *done* what the LORD requires of us in order for Him to respond. What are those requirements?

"IF MY PEOPLE"
This is specifically directed toward Christians

". . . will humble themselves . . ."
Have **you** *gone before the LORD and humbled yourself?*

". . . and pray. . ."
Have **you** *prayed for repentance for yourself and this nation?*

". . . and seek My face. . ."
Have **you** *sought the face of the LORD; that is, have you obtained the favor of the LORD?*

". . . and turn from their wicked ways. . ."
Have **you** *turned from the wicked ways that the Holy Spirit has spotlighted in your personal life?*

Only after we have individually fulfilled the above requirements, can we collectively and corporately become victorious. America's pastors and Christian leaders must initiate this in our local churches. If the French historian, Alexis de Tocqueville, who traveled extensively in America once declared that the key to our greatness as a nation was found in our pulpits, then we can and must redeem our nation through pulpits that "flame with righteousness." Do not confuse the eloquence of words in the pulpit with the power of the Holy Spirit. May the LORD forbid that we should resort to such foolishness as trying to preach like Charles Spurgeon without walking in the power of the apostle Paul. It will be through the holiness of our personal lives that the Holy Spirit ignites the flame in the pulpits that preach true righteousness. Pastors must redeem the pulpits in America through personal repentance! Then we, our people and our nation can fulfill America's destiny of leading the world into revival.

Are you alone right now as you read this? Then go before

the LORD and humble yourself before Him right now—do not wait, my friend. Pray that He give you repentance. Give the Holy Spirit full permission to turn His spotlight upon your sins and upon any areas that are displeasing to Him. We often deceive ourselves in thinking we know what is the sin in our lives. Nevertheless, we must depend upon the illumination of the Holy Spirit to bring our sins before us. Seek the face of the LORD as commanded in 2 Chronicles. Ask that the LORD reveal Himself to you on a level you have never known Him before. Keep on knocking! Keep on asking! Keep on seeking! Take this challenge. Sit quietly before the LORD for several moments. Ask the Holy Spirit to spotlight some area in your life that is displeasing to Him. Stop reading. Do this right now.

Then take the advice of Chuck Colson in a recent article that he wrote for Focus on the Family's *Citizen* magazine: "LORD, change me first! I am accustomed to reaching people through the spoken and written word. But God showed me that mere words were not enough. He revealed to me that when so much around us seems hopeless, our prayer, like Isaiah's must be, *LORD, change me first*."[8] Ask the LORD to change you first and then your family, your friends, your flocks and your nation. Reversing the order is ineffective.

In Chapter Eight, The Captives, we discuss captive congregations; however, it must first be asked of our spiritual leaders: "Have you turned your life over to the LORD. Have you asked Him to cleanse and purify you and your works? Is He working true repentance in your life?" Before the LORD commissions you to lead your congregation or various ministry into repentance, He will first expect you to stand clean and holy before attempting to lead others. Do not get the cart before the horse. Let repentance first work in your own life *and then* lead those for whom you are spiritually responsible. Take a silent inventory of your congregation. One spiritual consequence of Hollywood and television is that the enemy has captured the minds of our church members. This will be discussed more fully in Chapter Eight.

Leaders in churches must first move into their own personal repentance and freedom from mind control and *then* seek to lead the flock. "I beseech you therefore, brethren, by the mercies of God, that ye present your bodies a living sacrifice, holy, acceptable unto God, which is your reasonable service. And be not conformed to this world: but be ye transformed by the renewing of your mind, that ye may prove what is that good and acceptable, and perfect, will of God."9 It is hypocrisy for us to attempt to lead others without having first experienced our own repentance and transformation of the mind.

If we question whether our flock is experiencing mind control, look at their ability to listen to sermons. Their addiction to television has conditioned most of them. The consequence is that they have shortened their attention span to that of kindergarten children. They need their commercial breaks. They get irritated and jittery if we stretch them beyond their 30-minute sitcom limitation.

America's Crisis Moment

America's crisis moment has arrived. She faces the Red Sea with the sound of thundering hooves, rumbling chariots and war cries all around her. Satan intends to use Pharaoh's Hollywood to destroy America on the shoreline. With images of approaching violence, dying children and bloody slaughter, some of us might faint at what we see. Yet American Christians have the same choice as the Israelites. We can *look back* and see only the approaching army of the enemy and his works—or, we can look toward Moses, and under his direction, pass through the Red Sea.

Those who stand in the pulpits generally hold the LORD's rod of authority. Are we going to regain our holiness, our righteousness, our power of influence in this nation? Godly men who walk in personal holiness are the only ones qualified to lead the masses to say *No!* to Hollywood. Godly women who walk in personal holiness are the only ones qualified to lead the masses to say *No!* to Hollywood. In Chapter Nine, The Challenge and Chapter Ten, The Conquerors, I specifically outline some things that Christian leaders can do to fulfill their leadership roles in saying *No!* to Hollywood.

Remember...

▶ Hollywood opposes religion through its films. They joyfully attack it.

▶ Michael Medved is an invaluable forerunner in his exposure on Hollywood and the formulas it employs in attacking religion and religious values.

▶ Medved believes that the "tightly-knit creative community" of Hollywood has a deep-seated contempt for religion."

▶ Hollywood produces its own idolatrous religion with films that desecrate Christianity, yet they exalt the devil, demons and powers of darkness.

▶ One spiritual consequence of America's having sat at the banquet table of Hollywood and its twisted view of Christianity is that our nation is guilty of national spiritual adultery.

▶ God has lifted the skirts of American Christianity to expose her sin. Its aim is to cause America to fall on her face before her God and cry out for repentance.

▶ Gypsy Smith's formula for revival is to look to yourself and ask God to start the repentance process for this nation through you personally.

▶ God's plan and formula for America's repentance, renewal and revival is found in 2 Chronicles 7:14. *Memorize* this scripture! Pray it with the first person pronoun, i.e.: "If I, _____, will *humble myself*, and *pray*, and *seek God's face*, and *turn from my wicked ways. . . .*"

▶ Cooperate with other churches in your community to help erase pornography.

January 1997

Friday evening. *January's snow turned into February's slush. Just moments after Brett and Callie concluded their nightly telephone conversation, Granny called. Grandmother*

*and granddaughter chatted warmly about family members
and new recipes for a while. Inevitably, the conversation
turned to Brett.*

"You know I've been troubled about him, honey."

"You worry about everybody, Granny."

*"No, honey, this is different. I keep feeling like the LORD
is having me pray 'specially hard for him. But I don't know
what I'm supposed to be praying for. There's something
wrong—I just don't know what it is. Something's wrong . . . ."*
said Granny, her voice trailing off into her own thoughts.

*Silence crept into the conversation between Callie and
Granny. Callie's heart froze with fear that the LORD may have
revealed to Granny what she and Brett had done. Too often in
the past Callie had witnessed the LORD's revealing things to
Granny about people—not to gossip, Granny had always told
her, but to pray for them, reach out and help them. Tonight,
however, Granny was pondering the problem of exactly what
the LORD was trying to tell her. Callie did not trust herself to
speak so she remained silent.*

*"I woke up this morning and had this heaviness in my
heart. It's got something to do with Brett. I just know it's him.
Is he in trouble at school?"*

"Brett? No, Granny. You know he's a straight A student."
answered Callie immediately.

*She swallowed the lump that kept surfacing in her throat
from fear.*

*"How about his friends? Has he had a disagreement with
some of his friends?"*

*"David and Corey?! Goodness, no! Those three are like the
Three Musketeers—one for all and all for one!"*

*"I know it's not David and Corey. What about his friends
in basketball or football. . . ."*

*"Everyone loves Brett. He's always defending the under-
dog. He's their champion. And the popular kids have always
liked him."*

*"'Course everybody loves him, honey. It's not that. LORD
only knows how smart the child is. I know it doesn't have anything to do with his school work. There's just something
wrong—bad wrong. I was thinking maybe something might be
wrong with some of his teachers or something. It's got something to do with some authority over him though. I've been*

talking to the LORD for too many years. . . I know I'm right.
He's trying to tell me something. I must be gettin' deaf in my
old age. I can't put my finger on it, but it's urgent. You know
what I mean, Callie?"

"Yes, Granny," answered Callie meekly.

"Maybe I need to see him. You children come on by the
house tomorrow. You can eat lunch with me—it's Saturday. I'll
fix us a nice lunch. I froze some of that turkey from
Thanksgiving and I'll get it out of the freezer. I'll make that
peach pie that Brett likes so well. We can visit for a while
together. No, now I won't hear of it, Callie. You and Brett come
on by the house tomorrow afternoon sometime. I know you've
got things you have to do, but I need to sit and talk with that
child for a while. It doesn't matter to me when you get here. I'll
have it fixed early and we can just eat when you get here.
There's something wrong, Callie. I'm telling you, there's something wrong. Maybe the LORD will show me if I can see Brett
in person. Then whatever it is, we can stop it or help it or correct it. We can do something! We've got to do something. I'm
telling you, Callie, there is something wrong!"

Callie's mind raced back and forth to find an excuse. Her
guilt screamed out inside her brain that the LORD must have
told Granny—or was trying to tell her. What was she going to
do? She would die of humiliation if anyone ever discovered
what she and Brett had done. For several hours, she tossed
and turned in her bed that night trying to come up with a reasonable excuse that Granny would believe. She didn't sleep
well that night.

Saturday morning. Callie awakened with a weak, nauseated feeling in her stomach. Her nerves had crashed in the
pit of her stomach. This fear of someone finding out about her
and Brett was literally making her become sick. She rested
quietly in bed with her eyes closed until she heard the stirrings
of her mother frying bacon in the kitchen. Suddenly, the smell
of the frying bacon overpowered her with the urge to vomit. She
barely made it to her bathroom before she became sick. This
fear of being discovered was more than she could handle. She
needed to call Brett. Together, they would think of something.
He would tell her what to do. He always knew how to handle
these things. Brett would take care of this the way he had
always taken care of her. She knew he would be able to take

care of this thing with Granny.

Brett did handle the situation for Callie. The entire problem was solved because he would not be able to go to Granny's with her. He had basketball practice. However, Brett said that he would call Granny and explain everything to her. When he sensed how upset Callie was, he both calmed and surprised her with the sudden announcement that he would go to church with her tomorrow.

"Really?! Oh Brett, that makes me so happy."

It was a decision Brett had made after last night's violent encounter with his father. His quiet desperation finally told Brett that he needed some help. He could no longer ignore the uncontrollable rage residing within his father. An innocent question or any simple comment now sent his father into a berserk rampage of anger. At any given time, his father would transform from the serene, controlled professional into a frenzied, savage stranger. Brett finally realized he had unknowingly become the enemy—in his father's mind.

A warm glow flowed in Callie's heart as she laid in bed later that Saturday night. In his diplomatic manner, Brett had called Granny about their not being about to go to her house for lunch. Even when he had suggested that the three of them have lunch together after church, Callie felt no concern. If Brett made the arrangements, she felt certain everything would be fine. She even looked forward to having lunch with two of her favorite people—Brett and Granny.

She rolled over and hugged up to her pillow. Brett was actually coming to church with her! What had prompted this sudden change? She, of all people, understood how strongly he felt about her church. In the beginning of their high school years, she had pleaded with Brett to come with her. Yet her pleas had always got ignored.

"I want you to come to church with me."

"You mean your preacher. . . ."

"No, I want you to come," Callie answered defensively, while wondering how he always instinctively saw behind her motives.

But things were going to be different now. Brett was the one who had freely volunteered to meet her at church tomorrow. She was too overjoyed to analyze this sudden change of heart.

Sunday morning. *Callie waited just inside the vestibule of the church, looking out the double glass doors to watch for Brett's arrival. Tiffany and Jamie joined her.*

"Can't believe Brett's coming back to church again," said Jamie.

"Yeah, and it was his idea," answered Callie.

"We better go on inside. Mother fusses if we come in after the auditorium doors have already been shut. It's the pits when your Mother sings in the choir and can watch every move you make. C'mon Jamie. We'll save you guys a place. . .on the back pew," chirped Tiffany as she ran toward the auditorium and rushed inside just before the ushers closed the doors.

Callie wished now that she had called Brett earlier that morning. But she had vomited again this morning as she applied her mascara, causing her to be late in getting dressed. Brett assured her in their phone conversation last night that he would meet her at church. Where was he? The choir had already begun singing the special music. The pastor would begin preaching any moment now. David and Corey came up behind her.

"He's not here yet?" asked David.

"No—I'm about to go into the auditorium and let him walk in by himself," said Callie defensively.

"Sure," replied Corey. "I can just see you doing that. Well, go on. David and I will wait here for him. Guess Papa is on his own this morning when he nods off to sleep. I missed getting to choir on time."

"No, I'll wait."

"Yeah, that's what we thought," chimed Corey and David together.

"Hey, there's Granny," said David waving his hand as Granny closed her car door. She walked toward the front of the church. The three of them stood silently watching the bent figure occasionally swipe her eyes and nose with a handkerchief as she moved closer. "What's wrong with her? Is she sick? No . . . Looks like she is crying, Callie."

Callie opened the door and called out, "Granny?"

Granny looked at her young granddaughter and new tears formed in puddles over the blue of her eyes. The swollenness of her lids testified that she had done some serious crying. When Granny embraced Callie at the door, a small sob escaped out of her twisted mouth. Almost simultaneously David and Callie spoke together.

"What's wrong, Granny?"

"Oh children, something terrible has happened. It's awful . . . just awful."

"Granny, what is it?" asked Callie.

"Come on, let's go into the secretary's office. No, you boys come, too. This involves all of us. But we need to get somewhere private. LORD Jesus, please help us!"

Stricken and pale, Granny turned toward Callie. David and Corey stood just inside the door to the church office. Both their faces took on an expression of white fear. They knew Granny as well as all the other kids in church. Something had to be seriously wrong for her to come to church weeping.

"Callie, I had the television on this morning and. . . ." A unguarded moan softly escaped from Granny. In quick response, her wrinkled hand covered her mouth.

Callie wanted to reach out and comfort her Grandmother, but she could not. She suddenly felt as if someone had transported her to a long, empty tunnel where time had ceased to exist. Inside the tunnel, she felt safe. She saw the tears streaking down Granny's smooth skin. Callie heard words echoing back and forth through the long tunnel, but she could not understand them. She did not want to understand them. She refused to hear them. Why was Granny saying these things to her?

". . . that child is dead! Early morning news showed Sheriff Collins standing outside their house. His father took a gun and killed himself after he realized he'd killed Brett with that bat. Oh, LORD Jesus! I knew You were trying to warn me. How could his father beat Brett to death with a baseball bat?"

From behind her, Callie felt David and Corey's hands gently touching her. Why were her two good friends crying? Why was Granny crying? Where is Brett? She needed to go back out to the vestibule. She might miss Brett. Sheriff Collins? . . . reporters from the television station . . . ambulances . . . David, why are you crying?. . . two covered bodies . . . blood all over the bedroom? . . . Granny, hush now—we'll talk later. . . . Granny's words and her friends' tears swelled and bounced around Callie. But her mind retreated from the scene in the church office. It escaped inside the sanctuary of the long tunnel.

Her mind processed only the thought that she must immediately return to the vestibule or she would miss Brett when he arrived.

Then deep inside the cavern of her mind, Callie heard the loud ringing of a telephone. Was she dreaming? She looked around her for a telephone. Where was the telephone that was ringing? With all the life of a mummy, Callie stared at the silent telephone on the secretary's desk, then looked back toward Granny. Callie saw Granny's lips moving. The words started thundering into her consciousness.

". . . Sheriff Collins said he didn't know how Brett managed to crawl to the telephone. LORD Jesus! That poor child was trying to make a phone call to somebody just before he died. That's how they found him. . .holding the telephone in his hand."

Bolts of lightning and crashing thunder bounced off the walls of Callie's mental refuge. Brett? Is that you? She heard Brett whispering in her ear near the Coca-Cola machine. "I promise to call you every night." From somewhere outside of herself, she heard a tormented whimper that progressed to a choked sob and then escaped her trembling lips as a sorrowful scream. The excruciating emotion of grief mercifully swallowed her up into a world of black unconsciousness.

Days merged and swirled into a kaleidoscope of anguish and emptiness. She, along with the entire town, learned the shameful details of one of its respected citizens. She was never allowed to see Brett again. He had been battered so savagely that the casket had remained closed. His closed, pale blue casket was almost hidden from view as flowers from total strangers filled the church auditorium. Callie wept alone in her room at night. She mourned alone. And Callie wept in the company of her friends as they stood beneath the giant oak tree where they buried Brett and his father—side by side—in Oak Lawn Cemetery. Callie mourned in the company of Granny and Aunt Heather standing on either side of her. Callie just wept and mourned, whether alone or in the company of those who loved her. How could she live without Brett? The prospect of such a thought choked her to death. Who would be there to hold her hand after school? How could she ever pick up the telephone again knowing she would never hear his voice at the other end of the line? Who would coach her through calculus? Who would protect her through life? Callie's soul stood as desolate and barren as the giant oak tree that protected Brett's grave.

Almost overnight, Spring began spreading a lush blanket of green grass over Brett's grave. A robin flew into its newly-formed nest on the branches of the rambling oak tree. Callie leaned up against Brett's tombstone, sobbing hysterically.

"Oh, Brett! What am I to do? I'm pregnant!

Part V
The Captives

"The winds of change blew through the dream factories of make-believe, tore at its crinoline tatters...The hedonists, the homosexuals, the hemophilic bleeding hearts, the God-haters, the quick-buck artists who substituted shock for talent cried: Shake 'em! Rattle 'em! God is dead. Long live pleasure! Nudity? Yea! Wife-swapping? Yea! Liberate the world from puberty. Emancipate our films from morality...!

...there was dancing in the streets among disciples of lewdness and violence. Sentiment was dead, they cried. And so was Capra, its aging missionary. Viva hard-core brutality: Arriba barnyard mass rape, mass murder, kill for thrill—shock! shock! To hell with the good in man. Dredge up his evil—shock! shock!"

— Screen Director Frank Capra
The Name Above the Title

Chapter 8

Captured Through Our Senses

Two Weeks Later

Terrified, nervous, Callie sat in the waiting room of the abortion clinic. Her nails were stubs from having chewed them off for the last two weeks. Each time the door opened, she raised the magazine up so high that it covered her face. What if someone came in who knew her? If her mother ever found out. . .Why did Aunt Heather choose to go to England at this time? Callie needed someone to help her. Granny? Guilt suffocated her when she thought of her Granny. It would tear Granny's heart out if she knew. When her thoughts turned to Brett, she choked down a sob and raised the magazine higher so now one could see the tears that insisted on filling her eyes.

This was her second day at the abortion clinic. She had skipped school yesterday and today in order to be here. On her visit yesterday, they had inserted the laminaria into her cervix for dilation. The nurse would insert the second laminaria today and then assist the doctor in the D&E abortion since Callie was now four months pregnant. There was no physical evidence of her pregnancy that could be seen by others. Her waist had begun to thicken slightly, but no one seemed to notice.

The sound of her name being called out by the nurse startled her as if a cannon had just been fired at her. A churning nauseated feeling clung to her stomach. The nurse's smile only *caused the tears to well up again.*

"This won't take long, honey. Come on in here. Get undressed and put the gown on. Turn this switch on when you're finished. It will cause a light to come on outside the room and then I'll be right back with you. Are you okay? They explained the procedure to you, didn't they? It won't take long. This will all be over with soon."

Stricken with fear, Callie stood trembling in the white gown the nurse had provided. When the nurse came back into the room, she instructed Callie to get up on the table.

"The Valium will take effect real soon," the nurse said kindly.

Minutes. Hours. How long had it been since the nurse had inserted the last laminaria? Callie was beginning to lose track of time and the reality of her environment. A stone-faced doctor entered the room just as Callie placed her left leg into the stirrups. She moaned with embarrassment as the doctor sat down on the stool to examine her. The doctor never uttered a word to her. What did it matter? She felt herself slipping away into a world where her feelings were numb, paralyzed, dead. Everything around her seemed to slip into slow motion. Dreamlike. Unreal. At one time, she remembered seeing the nurse bring in an ultrasound machine and attach it to her stomach. It felt icy cold on her naked and exposed stomach.

"There it is, doctor. Right there. I see its movements. Hear the heartbeat?"

Anesthetized, Callie turned her head over to see an illusory nurse handing a pair of forceps to the doctor. She felt a suction and a forceful pulling from inside her uterus. Then she heard something like soft meat hitting the side of a pan that she had earlier seen placed on a table with surgical instruments. Murmurings from the nurse. Cursings from the doctor. Their words and the room began to mercifully swirl around her until she sank into a deep, dark sleep.

Two weeks later. *Callie knelt in front of Brett's tombstone weeping. Her hand slowly and lovingly caressed his chiseled name. The more she spoke, the louder her cries split the still morning air. A knife of guilt cut at her heart, piercing, slashing, stabbing from deep inside her.*

I killed him, Brett—I killed our baby boy. Oh God, forgive me! I didn't know what else to do. I was so scared. . . you weren't here to tell me what to do. Aunt Heather was gone. I tried to wait for her to return from Europe, but she kept extending her time over there. I couldn't tell Granny—it would have broken her heart. It was horrible, Brett, it was horrible. I killed him. I killed our baby boy. I can't stop dreaming about him. Every night. . .Oh God, I can't have anymore dreams. He holds his hands out to me in the dreams and cries, "Mommy, mommy, mommy. . .and then he gets sucked away from me. I scream and scream for him to come back but he doesn't. Something like a powerful vacuum cleaner sucks him away from me. No matter how much I cry and cry in the dream, I can't get him back. Oh, God! Oh, my God, Brett, what have I done? What have I done? Forgive me. Please forgive me. Brett, please forgive me. I killed our baby boy.

Sobbing hysterically, Callie climbed upon Brett's massive marble tombstone. Careful. Steady. Stand up straight. . .reach for the rope she had earlier tied onto one of the branches of the massive old oak tree. For one split instant the image of a chalky white body with empty black eyes flashed before her conscious thoughts. Strange déjà vu. She had seen that picture of the chalky white body somewhere far away in another time. Where? Using the back of her hand, Callie swiped at her eyes to wipe away the tears. Her small shoulders jerked with convulsive sobbing. Her tears blinded her ability to see the rope she now held in her hand. The rough feel of the rope scraped her cheek as she slipped it over her head.

"Oh God! LORD God, please forgive me. I never meant to murder my baby."

Callie stepped off Brett's tombstone.

God Knew The Ending

In the Introduction, I told you that I would return to the thoughts about God knowing the ending from the beginning. Now that you have almost completed the book, I can assure you that throughout the creation of Hollywood, God never slumbered. He did not take an afternoon nap on the day the Supreme Court told America that she could no longer pray in her classrooms. Nothing has ever occurred in our nation's history that caught God by surprise. From the beginning of

America, even as Benjamin Franklin exhorted national dependence upon God through prayer, God knew on that day in 1787 about the cultural corruption into which our nation would fall.

Remember what I told you if the material of this book became "heavy?" I urged you to remember that from the beginning, God knew all about these last days in which we now find ourselves. God did not have to call an emergency meeting of the Triune Godhead to ordain a new strategy just because man invented the telephone, radio, movies, television and computer at the beginning of the twentieth century.

For countless ages, God has observed man and his inventions. He has also observed the devil's crafty attempts to steal those same inventions with the intent to kill and to destroy humans. A telephone helps in lifting up our stumbling brothers or it aids in destroying them through malicious gossip. A piano helps us in praising the LORD or it aids a topless dancer to incite sexual lust. A computer reaches across the Atlantic Ocean and assists in saving a man's life in Europe or it peddles a pool of obscene pornography to a twelve-year-old boy.

From the beginning, the LORD knew the outcome of man's inventions. He knew from the beginning that radio, movies, and television could encourage evil plus good in these latter days. On the same day in human history when God told Moses to write the Ten Commandments, His omniscience understood there would be telephones, radios, movies, televisions and computers. None of this information was lost to God's memory at the different times when He breathed upon holy men of old and inspired them to write the scriptures. God already knew that these instruments of mass communication and entertainment, now so widely used to pollute more than just America's culture, would be contributory causes of our latter-day perilous times:

> "This know also, that in the last days perilous times shall come. For men shall be lovers of their own selves covetous, boasters, proud, blasphemers, disobedient to parents, unthankful, unholy, without natural affection, trucebreakers, false accusers, incontinent, fierce, despisers of those that are good, traitors, heady, highminded, lovers of pleasures more than

lovers of God; having a form of godliness, but denying the power thereof: from such turn away." [2]

While it is true that *God* knew from the beginning about these inventions, *man* did not know about their power to do either long–term good or evil. And it is true that God, from the beginning, knew about the theft of these inventions by the enemy, yet *man* did not know. Satan has never caught the LORD off guard, but he has often done so with the church. The church carelessly slumbered and allowed the thief to steal these inventions and use them for evil rather than good. The moral standards of our society suffer greatly because of the devil's theft. It has always been a Christian's responsibility to "occupy." The word *occupy* denotes a military-type of occupation, commanded by the LORD. Christians must redeem that which the enemy has illegally taken from us. Jesus came and, in a military sense, He occupied. He redeemed that which Satan had stolen. Likewise, our task also is to come to the forefront of this great cultural battle and to courageously occupy that which has been stolen from us. We must right the wrong and redeem that which the enemy has stolen.

The Enemy

Director Martin Scorsese received credit for *The Last Temptation of Christ*; however, he was only a front for the true director behind the scenes—Satan. The devil's abhorrence for Jesus Christ, the One Who defeated him at Calvary, finally had an visual medium for the expression of his great hatred. *The Last Temptation of Christ* became celluloid blasphemy. Scorsese may have been the devil's human instrument; however, there can be no mistake as to who masterminded that profane piece of sacrilege. Without a doubt, Satan is the controlling force behind the dark, desperate films now being forced upon the American public. The devil's first and primary motive is his great hatred for the LORD Jesus and those who follow Him. It is because the LORD authored Satan's judgment when He died on the cross. The Body of Christ will execute the LORD's judgment on the devil in these last days. The devil's strategy and tactics in the entertainment and communication arena need to be exposed. It is imperative that no more victories be allowed for the kingdom of darkness.

The following may be a startling statement, nevertheless, it is a true statement. *"The devil is God's devil."* Before He created man, God created Lucifer. As an archangel, Lucifer belonged to God in the sense that all of God's creation belongs to Him and is under Him. Just as God knew about Adam's fall before it occurred, His omniscience knew from the beginning that Lucifer would lead a rebellion among the angels. Consequently, the *"anointed cherub that covereth"* lost his job of walking *"up and down in the midst of the stones of fire"* and got ousted. In the midst of this heavenly eviction, Lucifer also lost his God–given name and consequently became known as Satan. The first chapter of Job illustrates how God still maintained His power and authority over Satan even after his removal. Satan can only do what God allows. The devil is limited in his power. For this reason, I stated that "the devil is God's devil." This truth is to our advantage in this battle because the devil remains limited under God's power.

Nevertheless, Satan is both a formidable and powerful foe. He has commanded this war against the saints for centuries in comparison to our mere human allotment of *"seventy years."* His experience in this spiritual war is much greater than ours as individuals. That is one reason why we must enter into this arena in the multipled strength of our unity in the Body of Christ. It is not enough to feebly quote our verses about putting on the whole armor of God and teach that *"we wrestle not against flesh and blood, but against principalities, against powers, against the rulers of the darkness of this world, against spiritual wickedness in high places."*[3] It is worthy of note that our enemy has afflicted some sizeable victories over mankind throughout history. This is especially evident in our culture's entertainment and communication in these last days.

During the writing of this book, the devil assaulted me on a level that I had never experienced before in my Christian life. His forces stormed against my mental faculties on one occasion until I almost collapsed. I experienced the reality of Paul's counsel in 2 Corinthians: *"For thou we walk in the flesh, we do not war after the flesh: (For the weapons of our warfare are not carnal, but mighty through God to the pulling down of strong holds;) casting down imaginations, and every high thing that exalteth itself against the knowledge of*

*God, and **bringing into captivity every thought to the obedience of Christ**."*[4] Out of this ordeal, I experienced how crucial our minds and our senses are in this critical battle we wage against the enemy. I came to personally realize that Satan is an adversary that can be neither *ignored* nor *underestimated*. If we, as most of us do, ignore him then he slips in as a thief in the night and sows tares in the wheat fields of our minds. Our thoughts are brought into captivity. We begin to think as the world thinks and do not even realize it. His victory stems from his ability to deceive us into *ignoring* the cultural civil war which rages all around us. We are dyed into the fabric of our culture and blend in with the unrighteous because we look, think and act as they do.

If we, on the other hand, see ourselves as warriors for the faith then there is the possibility of our *underestimating* how proficient the enemy is in his deception toward us. As we proudly quote our verses while feebly holding up our shields of faith, we fail to recognize that we may be standing on the quicksand of presumption. If we think we are standing in faith, the devil immediately pulls us in the opposite direction of faith—that is, presumption. We continue on in our presumption and yet believe we are walking in faith. *The opposite of faith is presumption.* There is such a fine line between faith and presumption that it is often easy for the devil to lure us into crossing over that line. Centuries of warfare has taught him to always move in the opposite direction from the LORD. If our great Captain wants us to stand in faith then Satan deceives us into walking in presumption.

When we are in presumption, we *assume* something is the truth. The Israelites presumed upon God's grace at one time. When the twelve spies returned from walking the promised land, ten of them gave a bad report and only two of them gave the good report that they could take the land as God had told them. They angered the LORD by not believing what He had told them about conquering the promised land. Later, they realized what they had done. They decided to take the promised land anyway and so they prepared for battle. The Bible says they *"rebelled against the commandment of the LORD, and went **presumptuously** up into the hill."*[5] However, the LORD allowed them to be defeated, because they **presumed** He would give them the victory. They had not believed what He had told them previously. The Israelites had moved from a posture of faith into a posture of presumption. Because it is the opposite of faith, presumption can very easily deceive us into thinking we are standing in faith. The scripture in this particular case demonstrates for us that the LORD will allow us to be defeated rather than to honor our presumption. It is only our faith that He honors.

We *assume* or *presume* that we can go to R-rated movies and it will not affect our minds or our personalities. We *assume* that our children are beyond the grasp of the kingdom of darkness when they listen to today's music. In doing these things, we presume upon the grace of the LORD. Yet many of us think we are walking in faith so none of these things can influence us.

The definition of presumption is: an attitude or belief dictated by probability; the ground, reason, or evidence lending probability to a belief. For example, there is reason or evidence in the lives of our families and friends that *our children* simply will not go off into gross rebellion; therefore, we *presume* that we can break certain natural laws and not be affected. The reason is there. Our children just do not do those kind of things. The evidence is there also. Have any of our families' children or our friends' children gone off into some of the horrible things which we read or hear about other children? No! We therefore presume that our children will not step out of bounds either. In that presumption, we deceive ourselves into thinking that certain natural laws will not affect our children. We presume that watching movies that bash America's founding values will not affect our children's patriotism. We also presume that listening to popular songs with themes of sexual depravity and murderous anger will not affect our children's emotional life.

We should never underestimate the tactical strength of the devil. He gets us into presumption, deceives us into thinking we are in faith, and then uses God's natural laws against us—laws that God will not change because of our presumption. When the LORD directed the conception of this book, I did not foresee the violent assault that would be waged against me mentally. I was trapped between both ignorance and presumption in thinking that I could attack the devil's strategic stronghold on Hollywood, music and television without suffering some sort of backlash.

During and after this personal onslaught directed toward me, it reinforced even more to me that one of the major battlefields for regaining America rests in the individual minds of her citizens. If the devil is to control our nation, then he must control our individual minds. He controls our minds by controlling what our senses present to our brains. An unprecedented venue for assaulting our senses with his dark and perverse message is available to the devil through movies, television, music and the media in general.

It appears that Satan is winning in this cultural battle. However, we must return again to the arena of God's Word to maintain the correct perspective. We will win and overcome the devil *"by the blood of the Lamb, and by the word of [our] testimony."*[6] The apostle John says that Satan became the *"prince of this world."*[7] However, the cross judged the *"prince of this world"* almost 2,000 years ago. The apostle Paul continues the story of this judgment where Christ *"having spoiled principalities and powers, He made a shew of them openly, triumphing over them in it."*[8] Christ won. Although we, as a nation, have retreated from certain positions in our culture, we can and must regain that lost territory. As soldiers in the LORD's army, we must occupy as He commanded. In that occupation, we must learn to recognize how the enemy can do nothing but imitate God. There is nothing original about the devil. Furthermore, he can only use that which God has originated. It is for this reason that the devil ***absolutely and beyond a doubt*** uses God's natural laws against us.

The Natural Law of Senses

In the beginning, God said, *"Let us make man in our image, after our likeness: and let them have dominion . . . so God created man in His own image, in the image of God created He him; male and female created He them."*[9] With a few words in the first chapter of Genesis, the LORD gives an account of how He created man. God is very succinct and precise. He uses only a few words to summarize the staggering miracle of His creation of man who was honored to carry the image of his Creator. However, man is not so abbreviated in his words about himself. Man has written volumes on himself—whether concerning his spiritual, emotional or physical aspect.

The written record in the Bible contains only commands for Adam to have dominion, to multiply and to refrain from eating of the fruit of a particular tree. We have no recorded instance of the LORD having ever taught Adam about the importance of his senses. The LORD never said to His new creation: *"Now, Adam, this is your brain. It will do a million things for you throughout the day. Nevertheless, before it can do anything, it must collect information for you. I have created you with specialized ways to collect this information for your brain. They are called senses. These will be the messengers for your brain. They will tell you about the world in which I have placed you."*

In the beginning, the LORD gave no explicit instructions regarding our senses that were recorded in the Bible. However, man has spent centuries researching, analyzing, investigating, searching and studying his favorite subject—himself. This intricate examination of himself has uncovered some important truths regarding his senses. The English word *sense* comes from a Latin word meaning "to perceive," or "to feel." We know immediately then that our senses are given to help us comprehend, to understand, to recognize, to grasp mentally, or to become aware of our world through seeing, hearing, touching, tasting or smelling.

Most of us think that we see with our eyes, hear with our ears and taste with our tongues—but we do not. We see, hear and taste with our brains. Our eyes, ears, noses and tongues are just sensors. These sensors send a jumble of electrical and chemical messages to the brain.[10] In His unsurpassed wisdom, God created the brain to sort and organize these electrical and chemical messages into a picture of the world around us.

The LORD created the brain, then locked it up in silent darkness behind the bony walls of our skulls. Because of this, the brain is forced to depend upon our senses to bring us information about the world in which we live. Elementary teachers use the illustration of a king or a queen who live shut up behind high stone walls of their castle to teach their young students about the brain and senses. The king and queen never leave their castle behind the stone walls. They have to depend on messengers to bring them news about the great, wide world that lies beyond their castle walls. Our senses are those messengers who bring news about the world to our brains that are enclosed behind the bony walls of our skulls.

Like our brains, the queen remains locked up behind stone walls and must depend upon messages from the outside. Locked up behind the bony walls of our skulls, our brains also depend upon messages from our senses to tell us about our outside world.

From the Garden of Eden, the devil has used our senses to cause us to fall. He appealed to Eve through the lust of her eyes when she *"saw that the tree was good for food."*[11] Satan piqued her appetite for the forbidden fruit. In the same way, the devil employs our senses to feast upon forbidden fruit. By using the lust of our eyes, he subtly draws us away from the Word of God and entices us into the arena of the lust of our flesh with its powerful urgings, making it more difficult for us to resist. The lust of our eyes sees what the world has to offer and we desire that more than our obedience to God or our relationship with Him.

The word "senses" is used only once in the New Testament. It refers to senses being important in knowing how to discern both good and evil. *"But strong meat belongeth to them that are of full age, even those who by reason of **use** have their senses exercised to discern both good and evil."*[12] We translate the word **use** from a Greek word that refers to a habit of the body or mind. The Hebrew writer speaks of mature Christians as having the habitual use of their perceptive faculties—that is, they are exercising their senses that result in their ability to discriminate between good and evil. Did you understand the truth of that? *It is with our senses that we discern good and evil.* But if our senses are nothing but sewers carrying the garbage of the world, they are backed up cesspools. How can they operate in their God-given function of discerning good and evil for us?

Most of us do not monitor our own senses. We are therefore poorly qualified to protect our children. For too long, we have allowed our children's senses to be assaulted. Television, movies and popular music bombard them with daily doses of violence, filthy language, and sexual eroticism. Messengers continually crawl over that stony wall of the skull and slide unguarded into the brains of our children. In truth, our children's senses are being dulled to the point that their minds cannot discern between good and evil. If the only message that the brain receives from the outside world is that of violence, blasphemy, filthy language, perversion, and immoral sexuality then it assumes that is the standard. With a never-ending stream of such messages flowing into the brain, it eventually becomes less shocked by the content of what the senses feed it. That is when *process adaptation* begins..

The Brain and Body Always React

All of our senses cause the brain and the body to respond to their messages.[13] Sometimes we are consciously aware of a message sent to our brains and we act upon it. For instance, if we are stepping off of a curb on a street corner and suddenly hear a car horn blare out at us, we will instantly jump back onto the curb. Our sense of hearing has consciously heard the horn honking at us. Our body reacts immediately by jumping back onto the curb. We have the same automatic reaction when we burn our hand on the stove. Our sense of touch feels a searing pain. Our body reacts instantly by jerking our hand away from the hot burner. Many messages sent to our brain by our senses cause us to be consciously aware of their information.

Yet there are other times *when we consciously do not notice all of the messages.*[14] This one particular natural law where we do not consciously notice all the messages transmitted by our senses is constantly used by the devil. He seeks to get us into this system of familiarization. We have become so desensitized to the messages of sex, violence and foul language that we have entered into what scientists call *process adaptation.*[15]

If a strong stimulus lasts a long time it soon appears to grow weaker and weaker. Our brain then responds to it less and less. In other words, we become *desensitized.* For example: Our clothes stimulate touch receptors on our bodies all day long, but most of the time we do not notice the feel of what we are wearing. For understandable reasons, we become desensitized to the feel of our clothing. A strong smell can also fade quickly from our consciousness. How often have we stepped onto an elevator with someone bathed in perfume or aftershave? Yet that person, having spent hours inside the cloud of the odor, is quite unaware of its powerful impact on a new nose. That heavily-perfumed individual's senses has already moved into *process adaptation,* or they have become *desensitized.* The initial strong stimulus of smelling the perfume has adapted itself and has almost faded into non-existence for the individual. The person is no longer sensitive to his own smell.[16]

It is important that we realize that the brain and the body always respond to these messages whether or not we are conscious of them.[17] So whether we are consciously aware of the message or whether *process adaptation* has taken over, *the brain and the body always respond.* The LORD created us so that our brains and bodies will always respond to the messages sent by our senses. Sometimes we consciously realize that we are responding; at other times, we are unconscious of a response, yet nevertheless, there is a response. What that means is that if we continually hear God's name used in vain in movies or hear crude four-letter words, then *process adaptation* takes over in our minds. Our brains adapt so as not to pay any attention to what we are hearing. If we continually watch explicit sex scenes in movies or on television, *process adaptation* takes over again. Our brains adapt so as not to pay any attention to what we are seeing. We become desensitized.

The Lord created us so that our brains and bodies always respond to the messages sent by our senses. With each succeeding year, our society becomes more and more desensitized to the messages we receive from Hollywood. The evidence of how much these messages have changed our society is all around us. *Our sixth sense is proprioception and governs the movement of the body or its parts.

The enemy has used the truth of this natural law against us and our children. The first time our senses assault our brain with messages of explicit nudity, filthy language, or violence, we normally react with an automatic, instantaneous *jerking our hand away from the hot burner,* so to speak. That is, we quickly changed the channel on television or some of us actually got up and walked out of theaters. However, the danger comes for us when our brains become accustomed to the same sensory messages. *Process adaptation* is a natural law and it will be activated. Our society has become desensitized to nudity, foul language and visual violence. Nudity in movies has stimulated our sight receptors so often that we have become less responsive to the immorality of it. A continual barrage of filthy language carried by our sense of hearing to the brain has eventually caused our brains to respond less and less vigorously. The natural law of process adaptation has desensitized us to the culture in which we live.

Americans have ignorantly fallen into the trap of the enemy through his use of this natural law of God—*process adaptation* or *desensitization.* The real danger in becoming desensitized, however, is that our conscience can become seared. The context of a seared conscience is especially in conjunction with "latter days" in the Bible. ". . . having their **conscience seared** with a hot iron."[18] *If our brain is in process adaptation, then we become desensitized, then we are open to the perils of Paul's latter day prophecy of seducing spirits and doctrines of devils—the final step is a seared conscience.* The Holy Spirit deals with us through our conscience. If it is seared, we cannot feel the promptings of the Holy Spirit. If you are scorning the truth of this as you read it, there is the great possibility that your conscience has already been seared. That is a perilous situation for any Christian. I would suggest you prayerfully read I Timothy 2:1,2. To have fallen into the deception of the enemy is not good; however, there are few of us who are not guilty of having been deceived by the enemy to some degree at some time in our lives. If we stay in that deception, we are opening wide a door for our conscience to become seared.

Captive Congregations and the Law of the Mind

Most of us, in some form and to some degree, have been

taken captive through the use of our senses. One major spiritual consequence of Hollywood is that the enemy has captured our minds. *Do not fear to learn about mind control.* If the devil can get you into fear, you are assuredly taken captive. "For God hath not given us the spirit of fear; but of power, and of love, and of a sound mind."[19] We are not talking demon possession here; we are talking about church members who struggle silently as their minds are daily bombarded with hostile, angry thoughts, with ungodly, sexual temptations. People are paralyzed with fear about sharing how cluttered their minds are with such thoughts. They succumb to the traffic of their thoughts and walk around in guilt. Much of it is because they have allowed the natural law of their minds to be fed a steady diet of Hollywood's perversion through the route of their senses. These are Christians we are talking about here— not the unsaved. They have no idea that there is a constant battle going on to win their minds. Most walk around in daily defeat.

The "prince of the air" who fills our nation's airways with such trash has one strategic plan: to control the minds of those who see and listen to his messages. He and his army work relentlessly to establish negative, ungodly, immoral patterns of thoughts in our minds. *How does he do this?* He rides in daily on our sense of sight and hearing. If he is successful in doing this until process adaptation takes over, he succeeds in establishing negative, ungodly and immoral patterns of behavior in our lives. This battle for the minds of Christians is clearly taught in the Bible as we mentioned earlier: "For the weapons of our warfare are not carnal, but mighty through God to the pulling down of strongholds; Casting down imaginations, and every high thing that exalteth itself against the knowledge of God, and bringing into captivity every thought to the obedience of Christ."[20] These "strongholds" or "fortresses" are negative patterns of thought. These strongholds may have also stemmed from a one-time traumatic experience for some of us, such as abuse as a child. Far too many of these negative thought patterns, however, are the consequence of our sense of sight feeding our brain with messages of graphic sex and violence. Or these negative thought patterns stem from our sense of hearing that fed messages of foul language to our brains. Also, negative patterns of thought are fed to us through the subliminal messages as discussed in Chapter Seven about "killer-Christians" or "dangerous Christians from the South" or "ignorant Christians."

The apostle Paul wrote that he saw "another law in my members, warring against the *law of my mind*, and bringing me into captivity to the law of sin which is in my members."[21] The apostle Paul realized that God had established a *law of the mind*. What are some points to this *law of the mind*?

▶ Our senses are the only messengers that can penetrate the mind

▶ Our mind and body always react to these messages

▶ If process adaptation takes over, we become desensitized to sin

The center of all spiritual bondage is in the mind. That is why Satan seeks to influence and control our minds. That is why Paul summarizes his profound epistle to the Romans with: "I beseech you therefore, brethren, by the mercies of God, that ye present your bodies a living sacrifice, holy, acceptable unto God, which is your reasonable service. And be not conformed to this world: but be ye transformed by the renewing of your mind, that ye may prove what is that good, and acceptable, and perfect, will of God."[22] The battle must be fought in the mind and it must be won there if you are to experience the freedom of your inheritance in Christ Jesus. It is crucial that you understand the devil, first of all, wants you to fear this, and secondly, if you do not fear it, he wants you to believe the lie that you are not susceptible to any form of mind control. The Bible clearly teaches that we are at war against principalities and powers, but they are part of a kingdom of darkness that has already been defeated! It is only when we believe their lies that they gain any measure of victory over us. Some walk around in such defeat that they posture themselves alongside the enemy in beating up on themselves. Others close their eyes to the truth and walk deeper into the clutches of deception. Paul wrote to Timothy and told him that "Now the Spirit speaketh expressly, that in the latter times some shall depart from the faith, giving heed to seducing spirits, and doctrines of devils. . . ."[23] Especially in the latter days, demons will seduce believers. How do you suppose a demon can seduce a believer? *By using the senses and the law of the mind!* These doctrines of devils are nothing other than lies. One of the biggest lies is when these *thoughts*, that are the result of mental strongholds, are considered by us to be ours. Scripture clearly teaches that Satan can put thoughts in our minds even as he did King David in the Old Testament and Ananias in the New Testament.

If Hollywood has continually slithered in like a snake in the grass via your senses, Satan has successfully established "strongholds" in your mind—whether you realize it or not. That is part of the law of your mind. Your mind consequently adapted itself to what your senses allowed to enter.

However, there is freedom in Christ Jesus. By the time Paul penned the book of Romans, he was an established apostle. Yet it was he who cried out, "For the good that I would I do not: but the evil which I would not, that I do."[24] This portion of scripture is in the context of the "law of the mind" operating after the flesh. If the apostle Paul still struggled at this point in his life to control his mind, are we going to be so foolish as to deny the reality of that struggle in our own lives? The limitations of this book prevent any further discussion on mind control, but there are several excellent books that address this issue listed in Appendix D. Some of these lead you through personal prayers and detailed guidance on receiving help in the areas of spiritual bondage and how the enemy seeks to capture you through controlling your mind.

None of us are exempt as targets of the devil's deception. The ultimate goal of the devil in using Hollywood is to *gain control of your mind!* The LORD told the apostle Peter, "Simon, Simon, behold, Satan hath desired to have you, that he may sift you as wheat."[25] Satan has gotten enough control of Peter's mind that the devil demanded to sift him. What made Satan so assured that he could *demand* to sift Peter? He had successfully established a stronghold of pride in Peter's mind. What sensory message did the devil use to get a stronghold of pride into Peter's mind? Was it the *touch* of water beneath his feet as he held onto the LORD's hand and walked on the water to get back into the boat? We often forget to mention that truth. Peter may have started down into the water and cried out for help—but he did not swim back to that boat. He held the LORD's hand and they both walked on the water back to the boat. None of the other disciples felt the waves splashing around their ankles. Only Peter's sense of touch could relay that message to his mind. Or was it when he *saw* the glory of the LORD on the mount? Peter's sense messages may be different from those which you receive today through the media of Hollywood and television, but the law of the mind operates the same regardless of the time frame.

I stress again the need for you to honestly examine your own life. Write down on your "To Do" list the names of the books in Appendix D. Call your bookstore and order them or get in the car and go purchase them. Sit down and prayerfully read them when you are not rushed. Allow the Holy Spirit to set you free. The LORD came to set the captives free—in some degree, that includes all of us.

Remember...

▶ God knew from the beginning what we would face in these latter days.

▶ We win! However, we must do our part by occupying that captured by the enemy.

▶ The real enemy is the devil, although he uses people as his instruments.

▶ We must not be guilty of the presumption that we and our children will not be affected by the message of Hollywood, television, popular music and the media in general.

▶ The devil uses the natural laws of God to defeat us. He has successfully flooded our culture and society with so much immorality that our senses are constantly bombarded.

▶ Our brains and bodies *always react* to the messages sent them via our senses.

▶ We do not wish to destroy Hollywood, but we must demand reasonable responsibility for the effect of the entertainment they produce.

Oak Lawn Cemetery - Late Spring 1997

"Heather, take your sister home. I need to stay here by myself for a while. No, run along now—I'm fine. She needs you more than I do. . .I'm glad you decided to move back home. She'll need you more than ever now. The two of you should never have been separated anyway. . .twins need to be together more than regular sisters. We're all going to need each other—"

Granny's voice broke on her last few words when she remembered the forlorn, poignant, childlike way her daughter, Callie's mother, had said: "Mama—Callie's dead."

The blood supply to Granny's brain had ceased in that split second. Her heart hemorrhaged at the sound of those words. Sudden unawareness of her surroundings smothered her like a suffocating blanket. In the immediate hours which followed, Granny's thoughts moved in tortured circles always bringing her back to that moment of emotional strangulation:

"Mama—Callie's dead." Unmitigated wrath. Anger. Excruciating pain. Anguish. Unparalleled grief. Fury. Paralysis.

"Mama—Callie's dead." Unmitigated wrath. Anger. Excruciating pain. Anguish. Unparalleled grief. Fury. Paralysis.

"Mama—Callie's. . . .

Granny moved like a traumatic shock victim. The entire family entered into the intensive care unit in a state of numb paralysis. Remorse. Sadness. Sorrow. Unbearable heartache. Why? Why? Oh, LORD why did she do it? Why? Truth trickled in gradually. Pregnant? Granny's laughing, lovable Callie was pregnant? Granny's heart entered the torture chamber of agony. Abortion?! How? When? Where? Callie, oh, Callie! Who destroyed your innocence? Who failed to protect you?

The black clad figures moved slowly away from the gravesite of Callie. The family had made the decision to bury Callie next to Brett beneath the old oak tree. Now Granny walked slowly over to the gnarled old oak. She stood, head bowed, hands touching the bark of the tree, with her back toward the departing mourners. Her heart bolted over the same track of emotions it had run on for days now. No matter how hard she tried, Granny could not deafen the torment of those initial words.

"Mama—Callie's dead." Unmitigated wrath. Anger.

Excruciating pain. Anguish. Unparalleled grief. Fury. Paralysis.

Oh, Father God! don't let my heart get as hard as the bark on this tree. Man of sorrows, come through for me now. I can't go on. I can't keep going on because no one listens. . . .

*Oh, LORD—I am so angry! Why? Why did she do that? How did we fail her? Where did we go wrong? God, please. . . please, Father God show me how this happened. Show me. . .I can't do anything about it if I don't understand how or why. That innocent child didn't stand a chance being raised in the catacombs of dead religion. O God, forgive me! I should have stood up in that dead church and screamed **FIRE!** at the top of my lungs. We're killing our kids with dead religion. We're so smug and self-righteous. . .we're so spiritually proud of preparing a Sunday School lesson every week that we don't realize we're the blind leading the blind. We're nothing more than dead sepulchers. We have a "form of godliness but deny the power thereof." Well, our "form of godliness" has murdered my granddaughter. It's not just this dead mausoleum I attend . . . the whole country is playing church. O Father God, my Callie—they've bowed down to their idols and murdered my Callie. My granddaughter. . . my granddaughter, O merciful God, my granddaughter. They've destroyed my granddaughter with their despicable complacency.*

Sobbing beyond control, Granny feebly pounded on the oak tree. *Callie, oh, Callie. They've destroyed you and don't even have the spiritual sense to accept the blame and try to reverse it.* Granny bowed her head on top of her hands and wept softly for a moment, but the anger and sorrow gathered within her heart and burst forth like a great fountain of lamentation. Helplessly, she sank down to her knees in a crumpled heap of black linen. Pitiful, wailing cries choked the air and drifted up through the new spring leaves on the oak tree. She felt like a trapped animal that would have to gnaw its own leg off to escape. *Satan had gotten to her granddaughter and she could do nothing about it now. Too late. The devil had slipped into Callie's life; he had stolen from her, he had destroyed her and he had killed her. Callie, oh Callie, my innocent Callie. . .*

From behind her, Granny heard a soft, tremulous voice. *Granny? Someone* called out to her. Instantly, her heart responded with resurrected hope. *Callie? Is that you, Callie?*

This was just a bad dream after all?

"Granny? Granny, are you okay?. . . ."

Granny raised her tear-streaked, swollen face and turned around to see a semi-circle of six young people—Tiffany, Jamie, Corey, David, Darla, Laura—and aging Brother Bosher all standing there together. Drawn pinched faces. Concern creased the teenagers' young brows. A sympathetic well of deep compassion swam in old Brother Bosher's eyes.

"I'll be a granddaughter to you now, Granny," whispered Tiffany, lower lip trembling. "Me and Jamie—I mean Jamie and I—we both want to be a granddaughter to you now. We can't take Callie's place, but we'll come over and help you bake bread every Thursday just like Callie used to do. After school. . .we'll ride our bikes."

"Yeah, Granny. I told Mother I'd help you finish sewing our new choir robes like Callie was doing," promised Jamie.

Jerking, loud sobs tore at Granny's heart as she looked at the pathetic little group that surrounded her. Jamie and Tiffany inched closer. David and Corey followed.

"We love you, Granny. You've always been a Granny to all of us," said Tiffany.

"We're nothing more than waste water treatments walkin' around, Granny—so we need you to help us," said David, with a lopsided grin in his customary humor. "Think of all the plaque and cholesterol that will leave that old heart of yours once we start doing what's right for the LORD."

Several murmurs of stifled laughter rippled through the small group. David's humor was the key to unlock Granny's heart. How could she not be there when the kids needed her? At David's words, Granny bowed her head onto her chest and wept aloud once more.

"Callie, oh Callie. . . my grandchild. . .oh, Callie!"

The young people began to cry unashamedly with Granny. Slowly, with timid awkwardness, they all inched in closer. Somewhere in the emptiness of her soul, she felt enough strength to stretch her hand out to Brother Bosher who gently assisted her up onto her feet. When she rose up, she reached out, still weeping, and wrapped her arms around Tiffany and Jamie. She motioned for Darla and Laura to come on inside the circle of her arms. Brother Bosher, David and Corey lingered on the outskirts, the three of them wrapping their arms around the huddling, crying group of females. For several minutes, a chorus of male and female, old and young, sorrow and grief moved up through the branches of the old oak tree.

Satan and his demonic legions of darkness had broken through the defensive line of her family. The victory of their treacherous, demonic theft had branded Granny's heart with a scorching iron from the pits of hell. Something more precious than gold had been stolen from her—her granddaughter. But the old prayer warrior knew her weapons. Generational curses. Spiritual warfare. Prayer. Fasting. Humbling herself before her God. Diligence in guarding those whom she loved. Never again, devil. Never again. I've lost Callie, but you will not steal these children from me. Oh, LORD Jesus. . .You are the Captain of the hosts of heaven. . . the Warrior of the ages. . . teach me afresh and anew how to guard my family from the enemy. Never again, satan! Never. Never! Never again!

A movement to her left brought Granny's thoughts back to the moment. Brother Bosher coughed and sputtered from behind Darla and Laura.

"We've been talking amongst ourselves, Granny. The kids and I think maybe we need to get a little closer to the LORD," he said, giving Granny a stolen wink. "So we were wondering if maybe we could all meet at your house a couple times a week. . .you know, maybe pray a little bit. . .read our Bibles. Who knows—I might teach some. Like I used to do when George and I took care of the young people. Think I can still pull out some of my old lessons. These young'ns don't seem to mind if I'm as old as I am. What do you say, Granny? Think maybe you could manage to put up with all of us scalawags being over there several times a week?"

A glow of hope surged into Granny's heart. She looked from Brother Bosher's smiling face around the sea of young eyes. Questioning eyes. Eager eyes. Granny's shoulders squared instinctively at the sound of Brother Bosher's words. With her own blue eyes, she queried Brother Bosher. "Really?" Grinning, he nodded affirmatively "Yes, it's true."

Granny took her handkerchief and cupped it over her mouth for a minute as she looked at each of them. Tears glistened in her eyes. Yes! Somewhere from deep within her, she would find an empty reservoir that the LORD could fill with His strength for this task. Her ragged, torn heart had enough fragments that could be mended in order to help these young people. She would teach them the fear of the LORD. Yes. Then in due time, she could leave the work of the LORD to these ones who would become mighty men and women of valor. Mighty warriors for the LORD! YES! They were ready to learn now. The death of Callie had opened their eyes. They would become leaders of a new generation. They would become the generation chosen to usher in the Kingdom of God. . . to witness the return of the LORD!

"I think so, Brother Bosher. Yes, I think that's a fine idea," said Granny softly. She pulled Tiffany and Jamie even closer to her.

Together, with Brother Bosher on one end, Granny on the other, the four girls and two boys linked arms and walked out of the graveyard. Together, they walked away—away from Callie's grave. Away from Brett's grave. Away from the oak tree's shadow that guarded the graves. But never away from the memory of the innocent child Callie who had been stolen from them.

The End

The story of Callie that has been interspersed throughout the previous chapters is fictitious. Yet it is disturbingly prophetic in the sense that you may personally know a *"Callie."* Our nation is filled with *Callie* stories. They watch television in our homes. They sit on our church pews. They walk down the halls of our nation's schools. *Callie* has been given to you with the hope that she may somehow deflect the damage that Hollywood causes in the lives of our young people—your children. Hopefully, the story of *Callie* will sound an alarm and signal a wake-up call if you are a parent. As an accountable parent, you carry the God-given responsibility to protect your children from the works of the enemy. If *you* do not protect your children—who will?

Part VI
The Challenge

"The studios now have clean toilets and dirty pictures."

—Owner of Warner Bros. Studios
Jack Warner on the demise
of the Production Code
in the late 1960s.

Chapter 9

Consignment to Save America

Try to read these last chapters when you will be alone and uninterrupted to receive the greatest benefit from them.

Don't Blame Us!

When any form of criticism is laid at the doorstep of Hollywood, their instant answer is, "Don't blame us!" Repeatedly, they tell us that it is not their fault. "Don't blame us! If you don't like what you see, turn the channel." Or like programmed robots, they repeat, "Don't blame us! If you don't like the movie, don't go see them. It's the public's fault. You're the ones who go to the movies and make them box office hits!" One of Hollywood's all-time favorites is: "Hey! Don't blame us! Our art is just a reflection of the world in which we live."

Well, guess what? As decent citizens of America, we assuredly have the right to expect some *reasonable and responsible actions* from Tinsel Town.

If the purpose of this book has been successful, then by now you should be experiencing some kind of emotional response. Are you shocked? Let me say this. Out of an ocean of literature documenting Hollywood's indecency, I have shared only a thimble of the wickedness that exists. Are you angry? Good! You have been given eyes to see the cultural carnage of the devil's work on America. You have been given ears to hear the sound of the trumpet calling concerned Americans to rebuild your nation's foundations. Are you overwhelmed with frustration? Don't be! Remember . . . in the beginning, God knew the ending. We can win this battle! Nevertheless, we cannot win it without YOU.

You will notice immediately that the *voice* and the *style* of this chapter will differ slightly from the other chapters. The reason for this is that I want to speak to you personally. I am purposely writing this chapter to YOU—not to your spouse, your child, your parent, your pastor, your family, your friend, your boss . . . I am writing this to you as a personal letter. No. Actually, I want to get closer than that. I want to sit right there next to you as a concerned friend. I want to share something with you as you read these words. I want to tell you that only YOU can make a difference in what needs to be done regarding the cultural crisis now facing your country. I do not want to challenge you with anything *more* than what God has equipped you to do. Yet, I do not want to challenge you with anything *less* than what God has equipped you to do either. Above all, I plead with you to avoid Hollywood's attitude of: "Hey! Don't blame me! It's not my fault America has lost all her traditional values." This chapter is your personal challenge to do something. Help get America back on track. Do not think that you are alone in this battle. The enemy who seeks to destroy America will be delighted if you believe that *you personally* cannot make a difference.

I Want YOU!

Remember the famous World War II poster? The one of Uncle Sam, with puckered brow and pointed forefinger, and the words beneath stating: I WANT **YOU**! Those words ring as true today as they did during "the war to end all wars." A grandfather, whom I never knew, died of wounds from one of Hitler's soldiers. My grandfather died for one purpose—for freedom. As a child, my mother never knew what it was like to have a father because he answered the call of that poster. Uncle Sam wanted *him*. He, and thousands more, responded. Like my grandfather, America not only *wants* YOU—America desperately *needs* YOU. Yes, YOU. The one who sits there holding this book in your hand at this very moment.

Are you thinking, "What can *I* do?" Hey! That is a good place to start. Hopefully, this chapter is going to outline some things that will help you answer that question.

Before America ever used my grandfather to defend the cause of freedom, she prepared him. His preparation was not an option. It was nonnegotiable. Absolutely essential. America would not send my grandfather until she had equipped him, furnished, provided, strengthened, briefed, exercised, trained, fortified—made him ready! Neither will the Holy Spirit send you onto the battlefield until you are prepared. "Aha!" you are thinking, "that means *I* don't have to do anything. I'm not equipped, furnished, provided, strengthened. . . ." Are you thinking that you have an automatic excuse because you believe yourself to be neither equipped, nor trained nor fortified—nor any of the other things listed above? You may be surprised.

As a Christian, the Holy Spirit has equipped you. He resides within your spirit. *You have been furnished* a heavenly strategy for overcoming: "They overcame him (the devil) by the blood of the Lamb, and the word of their testimony; and they loved not their lives unto the death."[1] *The Holy Spirit has provided you* spiritual gifts, talents and abilities. The LORD provides spiritual gifts "to every man".[2] *He has strengthened you* for any earthly task. "I can *do all things* through Christ which strengtheneth me."[3] You have been *briefed* that a war is going on. ". . . we wrestle not against flesh and blood."[4] *You have been exercised* in detecting the enemy's tactics. ". . . those who by reason of use have their senses *exercised to discern both good and evil*."[5] *Prayer has trained you* to receive your marching orders from your Commander-in-Chief, the LORD of hosts from the moment you uttered your first petition to Him as a child of God. Your training for this battle is *habitual, humbling* prayer. *You have been fortified* through the whole armor of God found in Ephesians. *The LORD has made you ready!* This book has made you ready!

Make a mental note on those two adjectives that I placed before the word prayer. *Habitual. Humbling.* Do not forget these two words. Tattoo them onto the memory of your heart. Those two words are as crucial as two railroad tracks are for a train. If one of those tracks is discarded—America will have another train wreck. The *H&H* Railroad is the only way for America to arrive at her destination. She must travel on the tracks of the *H*abitual *& H*umbling Railroad. Splendid and

desired by all nations, America took a wrong turn in 1962.
Now she must return to that crossroad and turn right.

I Saw America the Other Day[6]

God married America as surely as He married ancient
Israel. In centuries past, He greatly desired a new country to
love. He sought a nation that would love Him and honor His
Word. So—"in 1492, Columbus sailed the ocean blue." A careful study of Columbus' journal leaves no doubt that he
believed that God commissioned him to sail where none others had dared. The trinity of the Nina, the Pinta and the
Santa Maria carried Columbus into the waters of an ancient
continent, undiscovered, unbirthed, except in the heart of
God. From her Plymouth Rock conception and her Pilgrims'
formation in the womb of God's plan, He loved this land. He
concealed her in His journal of greatness until that moment
in time when she would be born into her destiny. On the day
of her birth, He swaddled her in the red, white and blue of the
Fourth of July. Crowning her with the Spirit of 1776, He
named her the United States of America. God Himself conducted the choir to sing its first song over this new nation. He
shortened her name and spoke fondly of her as "America."
Shortly thereafter, He lingered around Philadelphia at her
Constitutional Convention and constructed His marriage contract between Himself and her forefathers. Then He carried
her into His bridal chambers as a virtuous young country and
spoke tender words of a covenant with her. He provided for
her. He protected her. He assuredly prospered her. In return,
she pleased Him. As a modest young bride, she reverenced
Him in every way. In the early years of their union, she openly wrote about her dependence upon Him. "We hold these
truths to be self-evident, that all men are created equal, that
they are endowed by their *Creator* with certain unalienable
Rights, that among these are Life, Liberty and the pursuit of
Happiness." "In *God* We Trust." "One nation under *God*."
Out of love for Him, America openly honored Him. Endlessly,
she bragged about Him. Throughout the land, she promoted
His words everywhere—in her court chambers, upon her
buildings, down her school hallways, above her national mon-
uments, on her Liberty Bell. The fruit of their union expand-
ed and enlarged until it reached from the Atlantic to the

AFFIX TRANTYM STICKER
DCJS-552.1 (4/89)

☐ CORRECTIVE ACTION   ☐ RECHECKE

NAME SEARCH POSSIBILITIES

☐ 1 AUTOMA
☐ 2 RECHECK
☐ 3 AUTOMA
☐ 4 FIELD HIT
☐ 5 NON-IDE
☐ 6 MANUAL

OMMENTS:

TRANSACTION CONTF

America and her God conquered all
 land." Vigilance taught her to keep
taints of what was lewd.
ith diverse fashion for her wardrobe.
efore Him in a cool cotton, embroi-
and genteel hospitality of the South.
er sensible gabardine produced by a
 industry from the North. Or decked
rted a breezy and informal indepen-
he West. Yet, she just as likely draped
d linen, tailored to perfection by the
holarship of the East. Adorned in the
 red, English white, African black,
hinese yellow, America dazzled the
geous, she nevertheless stressed
 and purposed to keep her home free
from debasement or vulgarization. It was the chastity of her
beauty that caused nations to gaze upon her with envy. She
blossomed into maturity before her God.

The strength of His protection kept her house from being
torn asunder during a Civil War. Holding her tightly within
His arms, He whispered divine wisdom in her ear that a
"house divided against itself shall not stand." With aching
heart she witnessed her children fighting among themselves,
yet she stood firm and obeyed His commandment, all the
while firmly holding onto the North with one hand and the
South with the other.

After that great civil trial, the LORD clothed her in rai-
ments of compassion as He instructed her to receive the
stranger and the immigrant. One of her favorite pastimes
was to slip unawares down to the harbor in New York City
during the midnight hours. She splashed her skirts in the
Atlantic Ocean and savored the favor of His presence there
with her. These were special moments between her and her
God. Then wading further out, she postured herself with a
torch of liberty and held it high enough for all to view
through the night. Ships sailed safely into her ports. America
welcomed them to her home of independence and democracy
and freedom for all. Often she spent days mingling among the
Jewish and the Polish and the Italian and the Irish and the
Russian and the German and the—just among all the various

national immigrants who arrived on Ellis Island. These were great moments as America nurtured her growing family. Her breasts swelled with the nourishing milk of her morality. Even the trials of her Great Depression offered no temptation for her to forsake the purity of her marriage to God. Ripened into maturity through two World Wars, America rose up in fearful, and yet majestic, splendor. She had matured into her full stature in those initial postwar years. And God granted her the awesome authority of world leadership in the atomic age. Because of the LORD's favor upon her after World War II, she prepared a banquet of lavish prosperity before the nations. Her technology surpassed all others. Freely, she shared her industrial secrets with a hungry world. All nations sensed the perfume of her democracy. Then God granted her superior knowledge and she rocketed up into outer space.

Stop and consider. America had fought two World Wars—and won both of them! What a ticker tape celebration she held for her returning heroes after the Second World War! Whew! She could relax a little now. It was such a good time for America in those post-World War II years. Her children were home. Always so prudent in her past, this mother began now to ease her vigilance regarding her own domestic household. In her mind, she had nothing to fear. Hitler could not cast his dark shadow of senseless murder over *her* home. No holocaust would ever touch *her* shores! It was inconceivable to her that the enemy would ever hurt her children again. The enemy—who was *out there, over the sea, far away*—had been defeated. America had fought a fierce battle. She had sacrificed her sons and daughters. Yet there would be no more Pearl Harbors. No more Hitler. Not for this Lady of Freedom.

Nevertheless, lovely, desirable America became halfhearted in those years of God's prosperity toward her. Indifferent toward Him now, she ceased talking about Him so often. Why should she speak about Him so much? She had bragged on Him for so long that everyone knew all about Him. Even Hollywood honored her God in its movies. Children prayed to Him in her schools. Senators and Representatives honored Him in her legislative chambers. His Ten Commandments gazed down from a wall in her Supreme Court. This was—after all!—a *Christian* nation. Her forefathers assured that before they gave America to Him in marriage. In her younger years, she had diligently taught her children about the documentations that recorded her courtship with God. Yet, how often can a child listen to the same old stories about George Washington, James Madison, John Quincy Adams and their deep convictions about God? She still loved God. Naturally. She was America! How could anyone ever question *her* love for God? She and her God were inextricably bound up with one another. She never doubted that she would always and forever love Him. But—and still yet—she *was* older now. It's just that she—well. . . .

Besides, America was ready for a change. She had been so traditional for so long. And so proper! Decent, clean, moral— she was all these. So her eyes started to wander—just a little bit. Not much. Just a little. Then she became more relaxed. Less restrained. She deserved a little relaxation . . . maybe, even a little fun. Before long, she began listening to authorities other than God. She dutifully held the Supreme Court's hand and listened as they doubted the historical significance of her relationship with her God. Maybe she did need to be more broad-minded. She sensed no danger. Why should she? These were *her* judges. Supreme. Sovereign. Absolute. In the past, she had always trusted them, but blindness covered her eyes now. Her memory failed. The lessons she had learned from her forefathers escaped her. She forgot that only her God was to be Supreme, Sovereign and Absolute. Her dependence on God was bound up in her prayers to Him. Since she depended upon Him in prayer, He granted her unparalleled independence. Unsuspecting of the consequences, America gave no thought to the purity of her *supreme* judges and their decision. There was nothing evil in this, they told her. By upholding this decision, she would be assuring "freedom for all." Freedom? Well, goodness, yes! Freedom was America's middle name. So she offered no struggle in 1962 when they told her she could no longer pray in her public school. Sadly, she embraced that *supreme* decision and went quietly into the night.

By that one act of acceptance, she turned away from prayer. This action was foreign to the very nature of her character. Never before had she so obviously contaminated her national and public relationship with God. In her past, she had always purely and publicly acknowledged her love for Him and her dependence upon Him. Now she polluted their relationship by agreeing with her judges that she would not support her children praying to her God in public places anymore. She consented to removing her young children's dependence upon her God. It was America's first act of spiritual adultery. She committed her first act of national, illicit unfaithfulness to God. With lukewarm apathy, she breached her contract with God. She barely felt any guilt.

As with most first hidden acts of adultery, it also escaped the attention of others. At first, America remained in the eyes of the world as chaste as always. Yet her ideal character, almost overnight, became transformed into hedonistic carnality. The purity of her relationship with God, her covenant to walk as a Christian nation had been adulterated. Soon, America could not hide this change in her character. After 1962, her modesty became an artifact. Decency became outdated. Almost at once, she began boldly and openly to display her newly-awakened promiscuity. She threw off the restraint of her old coverings. She squirmed and complained through her news media when forced to wear her former garments of moral responsibility. After all, the Supreme Court and media declared to her that she was FREE! Freedom of expression! Why hadn't her forefathers told her what liberty they had truly given her? What a glorious thing now finally to realize just how FREE freedom was! How could she have been so morally righteous? Where was the fun in all of that?

America became so involved in just "letting it all hang out," that she carelessly entered into another skirmish—a small one in a remote region of the world. *Vietnam.* In the beginning, this presented no problem to her. Her boys would clean this little mess up and return home within a year. One more victory, one more medal of valour to display in her Pentagon Hall of Fame. The war did not end in a year. It dragged endlessly on. That war began to irritate her. After all, she was trying to have a party and news of the war began to aggravate her. Peace, brother! Sing songs about love and flowers. Smoke Mary Jane and love everybody under the age of thirty. Yea! Get high, baby. Nudity? Oh yeah! These were her glorious years of "far out, man, Woodstock" years of rolling naked in the mud. Overnight, she started resenting this Vietnam interruption to her agenda of changing the country. Another casket! And another and another and another. All these caskets she had to cover! These deaths began to annoy her. America wanted to party with her young boys, not go overseas to fight in some stupid war. She grew moody and discontent with this governmental interference. Ultimately, she turned her back on the boys who dared to leave this Woodstock festivity of free love. With unholy and vindictive punishment, she openly shamed them once they returned home. Not once did it occur to her, that for the first time she lost a war because of her breach of contract with God. This war did more than signal failure on the domestic front. It announced to the world that her God had turned His back on America. Even had she been able to recognize it, however, she did not seem to care.

With reckless abandonment, she took on a new lover in those years—his name was Hollywood. America had flirted with Hollywood often, but now she openly lusted after him. She frolicked and tumbled between Hollywood's satin sheets on his bed of sexuality. Sin *was* fun! America suddenly gloated in being Hollywood's most notorious mistress. This new love of hers taught her how foolish she had been in her past. He showed her through his movies how she had been so religiously self-righteous in her past. Yet He justified her Baby Boomer actions as she tried to destroy the legacy of her old traditions, institutions and establishments. Hollywood convinced America that it was politically proper to sneer at her institutional relics of family, country and God. She needed to be a little more cynical and condescending. America was so infatuated with her new lover that she believed him.

Yet she was blind to the fact that Hollywood was twisting and distorting the truth. He taught her contempt for morality and decency. The First Amendment restricts nothing to you, he bragged to her, through the creative technology of his movies. Hollywood told America that the First Amendment of her forefathers approved her nakedness for all to see. Isn't this great fun that you can show all your private body parts? You're free to openly produce anything you want regarding sex. Be as crude as you want. Talk vulgar? Yeah, it's okay, America. This is cultural and sophisticated. Then he declared to her through his promotions, "This is art. You are free to express anything you want." While Hollywood spoke to her, she was unaware that he had a sharp, surgical instrument in his hand performing a cruel, radical mastectomy on her American breasts. Eaten up with cancer, they were no longer capable of providing wholesome nutrition. Hollywood laughed to himself as he administered a large dose of graphic anesthesia to America. His brutal surgery on her was making him wealthy and powerful beyond comprehension. Even had America known about the surgical operation, the Supreme Court had canceled the insurance of her God in 1962.

Soon, America became overtly selfish. She thought only of her freedom of expression and her need to satisfy her sexual perversion. The more she gratified her desires, the more she craved. She could sleep with anyone and do anything she pleased. No one could tell her what to do—she was free to express herself in whatever manner she chose! Almost overnight, America became brazen, insolent, presumptuous in her sexuality. The skilled, creative and wealthy gigolo, Hollywood, succeeded in his mind control over America. She thought as he thought. She dressed as he dressed. She spoke as he spoke.

In addition to giving her a lifetime membership into the country club of sex, Hollywood also initiated her into his technical wizardry. Before her hungry eyes, he constantly showed bizarre mutilations and murders that glorified violence and human suffering. "This is humor," he told her, echoing his words when he had earlier told her that graphic sex was art. At the same time, her compassion for human suffering became callous and uncaring. She joined in with Hollywood and together they laughed at his distorted ideas. He displayed his sadistic humor so often that she adopted it as her own. She supported his addiction to savage brutality. After all, he repeatedly told her, there is no more Mayberry RFD—who would want it anyway? Yet the relationship between America and Hollywood was one-sided and Hollywood was the controller. Her need to replace the God she had once known, placed Hollywood, lofty and exalted, upon a new pedestal. Hollywood was her god now. He taught her to speak a new language—crude and vulgar and nasty. Yet she mastered it quite easily. Within only a few decades, America changed dramatically. Much of the change occurred from her having an illicit love affair with Hollywood. Some of her own children no longer recognize her as the mother they once knew. Some are so young that, from birth, they have only known her only as being violent and wanton and promiscuous. Yes. America is different now.

I saw America the other day. Walking down a street, I stopped at the corner and observed America emerging from an alley. She had been digging in a dumpster, pillaging for a bite to eat. At first, I must admit that I did not recognize her myself. There was a permanent hunch to her shoulders as she tried to hide the conspicuous truth of her radical mastectomy. By all indications she was accustomed to digging through the garbage in order to find food, and doing it openly in the sad twilight of her years. In a vain effort to stay warm, she had torn up her flag and wrapped herself in the rags—shredded, tattered red, white and blue rags. She had the appearance of an ancient corpse staggering about in graveclothes. Her tangled hair was a frizzed-out mop. She had reddened it with henna trying to look young. Her brows were knotted and her mouth was set in hard painted lines. Then she caught a glimpse of herself reflected in a store window. I watched her as she smiled at her own disheveled reflection, a twisted sardonic grin that she intended to light up her face. In a flash of revelation, I realized that she had deceived herself into seeing only the image of herself when she had been the vibrant young country that had hungered after her God. She was blinded to the truth of herself as a repulsive rag doll. In her hands, she carried a piece of molded bread and rotten fruit. Flies swarmed around the fruit, but she—well, she didn't even seem to notice. When she raised the fruit to her mouth, there were decayed and missing teeth. I dropped my gaze in shame. Oh, America! How can you eat from the garbage? Yet as a magnet, drawing my attention back to her, I looked up again. She was staring in my direction with a vacant, empty expression in her eyes, munching idly on her rancid fruit. Over one eye, a lid drooped down like a lizard, puffy and purple. Purple? The color worn by royalty? America's only indication of royalty now was upon her swollen eye.

I looked closer. It startled me to see just how very bruised and battered and beaten she was standing there before me. Wrinkled skin covered her wanton face. She did not realize how pitiful she appeared and yet there was a licentious and vulgarness that hovered around her. Not one trace of her former beauty existed, well, perhaps faintly. At first, I thought she was walking toward me but then I noticed that she was approaching a man. He was dressed in the same rags as America. As she walked toward him, she dragged one of her feet, crippled and damaged, in her red, white and blue rags. A vile smell of filth assaulted my nostrils as she came closer. I was aghast to see how she approached the man. With brash impudence, she offered to please him with her obscene favors. The scene happening before me was so pathetic. I realized with sudden horror that *America could not see her true self.* Then I also understood that the man in rag clothing did not realize, or was not willing to admit, that he wore the same clothing as she.

At that moment, a car with the windows rolled down stopped at the red light where America stood on the corner. A rap song blared from the car radio. She started singing the filthy lyrics aloud and moved her hips in a vain display of suggestive sensuality. America was repulsive and repugnant in her attempts to be youthful and sexually desirable. Yet in her mind's eye, she saw herself as still being the reigning queen of nations whom God had crowned in 1776. Cringing inside with shame for her destitute and decadent condition, I watched the man ignore her and walk casually past her. She called out to him. She would be there if he wanted her later.

Yet even the apparent rejection of the man was not enough to stifle her shamelessness. America then turned boldly in my direction and called out a suggestive invitation to me. When I failed to respond, she shrugged her shoulders and slouched toward a very large, outdoor commercial toilet. Horrified, I realized that huge porta-potty had become America's home. Her living room had become nothing more than a dumping station for waste material. Yet in a moment of twisted compassion, I realized that living in the porta-potty was the only place where she could stay warm. Fallen from the height of her glory, America was not even wise enough at that given moment to realize that she was now suffering the consequences of her spiritual adultery. She had left the company of God's presence and she had no other place to inhabit. Apparently, she saw no need to change her situation.

Desperate and heartbroken, I wanted to get her attention. So I cried out to her.

I pledge allegiance to the flag
of the United States of America.
And to the Republic, for which
it stands; One nation under **God!**
Indivisible, with liberty, and
justice for. . . .

America hesitated outside the toilet. She turned to look at me when I shouted out **God!** For a split moment, I saw a melancholy love flicker unmistakably out of her eyes as she stared in my direction. For a long while, she scrutinized me with eyes that peered out from beneath swollen lids and scraggly hair, questioning, remembering. Then America's chin dropped sadly to her chest in silence. Slowly, she moved her head from side to side several times. Was it helplessness or unbelief? Her hand reached for the knob on the toilet. Rotted, star-spangled stench belched forth from the porta-potty. Quickly, she closed the door behind her and disappeared into the putrid bowels of the porta-potty.

I wait. No one joins me as I linger on the corner. Moments later, I glance over to the street sign. Filth and Hollywood Boulevard. A street block away is Prayer Avenue. Will America merge from that porta-potty on the corner of Filth and Hollywood? I cannot follow her inside that door marked R-rated because the slime and sludge inside will overcome me. Tears choke my heart. What can I do? A couple of men pass by me. They crane their necks over their shoulders to throw a backwards smirk at me. They think I'm a fool standing here on this street corner yelling at America to come out of that porta-potty. A fool? Yes. I look foolish, but someone needs to do something! Hope swells urgently within my chest. America! America! you've got to hear me. Someway, somehow, someday I'll get your attention. I love you, do you hear me? I love you!—still. . . I don't care where you've been sleeping. I don't care how far you've fallen. But please come out of that toilet! It is not a fit place for you to live.

Hours pass. The twilight colors of magenta and blue swirl like a kaleidoscope over my head. The evening Wind gusts through the street corner like a crisp Colonel, then pauses before me in a gentle breeze. Nostalgia grips him as he hears my pleas to America. He remembers blowing across a different

America. The Wind picks up my words and tucks them inside his air pockets. He promises me that he'll carry my cries to the four corners of the United States. With a drafty farewell, he leaves me alone once more on the corner of Filth and Hollywood. I notice he gusts, puffs, blows and blasts for the longest time on Prayer Avenue after leaving me.

Listen to me! I start to shout out again. I love you, America. God will forgive, I know He will. But you must humble yourself before Him. He'll restore you back to your former glory. No! No, America! He'll restore you to even greater glory! He's longing to give you another chance. Are you hearing me from inside that door rated R and NC-17? Have the raunchy lyrics deadened your sense of hearing? Has pornography blinded your sense of seeing? Come out of that toilet, America. Cry out to your God! He's your only hope for survival. America! Are you listening? Can you hear me?

After night covers the street corner with a black cloak, a desperate melody rises up within me in the spirit of 1776. Hoping my voice rushes forth like the rocket's red glare—like bombs bursting in air—giving proof through the night that her flag *is* still there, I start to sing as loudly as I can. My right hand reaches over and embraces the patriotism within my heart. Yankee Doodle Dandy goose bumps march up and down my arms. O America, America, your song is a sad song. I choke occasionally on streams of salty tears as I sputter out her song:[7]

O beautiful, for spacious skies
For amber waves of grain,
For purple mountains majesty,
Above the fruited plains,
America! America!
God shed His grace on thee,
And crown thy good
With brotherhood,
From sea to shining sea.

Yet America never comes out. She stays inside. Can she even hear the sound of my voice? If I sing louder—or perhaps a different song. Maybe if I get others to help. Help! Help me, somebody! Jeering laughter comes from a woman as she crosses the street to avoid me. Pointing fingers. Mockery. Scorn. Insults. People pass me on their way to Hollywood. I cry yet louder. Help me somebody! Please. . . help me get America out of that stinking porta-potty. Together! We can do it together! She is worth any effort we can put forth. Help! She doesn't hear my solo. It might take all of us singing together in unison. Hey! Can anyone hear me in this dark hour of the night? Will you please come and join me? Sing this song with me, won't you? You there! Yes, you, the one reading these words. Sing with me? Together, our voices will be strong enough so America cannot fail to hear us. Come on—sing it with me![8]

God bless America, land that I love
stand beside her and guide her,
through the night, with the light
from above.

From the mountains, to the prairies,
To the oceans, white with foam,
God bless America! my home sweet home,
God bless America! my home sweet home.

America Still Needs You!

Wow! If you're reading these words and not crying for America at this point, you can probably close the book right now. Reading any further may not be necessary for you. Oh. . . you love her, too? Then did you sing the song aloud as I asked you? If you did not, go back right now and sing America's song out loud to her.

I guess you thought I had forgotten how I began this chapter. Just the two of us talking rather privately. Well, I did not forget. Nevertheless, before I could continue our private conversation, I needed to share that story with you about America—about our country—yours and mine. She belongs to us. We are her children. It is our responsibility to be there for her now that she needs us so desperately. The tragedy of her story is monumental. She looks rather disgusting right now. You and I both realize the truth of how America still has a need—a great need for both of us.

Don't you agree? Good. Then stop and consider the truth of these words I am about to speak to you, my friend: "**YOU** are America!" Now, don't get defensive. Just pause with me for a moment. Let these words sink in upon your heart. Say these words aloud, "*I am* America!" Think about the responsibility of those words.

The wretched state of America is YOUR condition because YOU are America! You are in that porta-potty with her.

Okay. Okay, I can hear some of you, saying, "Not me, buster! I'm not like that." Then answer this for me. Is America the Smoky Mountains? Or the Mississippi River? The wheat fields of Kansas? The Grand Canyon? Or perhaps Pike's Peak? "It certainly is," you might answer in smugness. Okay, I agree with you. There's some truth to that. Still, you must agree with me that God did not make a covenant in 1776 with the Yellowstone National Park or Niagara Falls. He makes covenants with people. If you are an American—YOU *are* America! The Giant Redwood trees in California cannot vote. The Great Lakes do not make legislation. The Shenandoah Valley does not support Hollywood.

The tragedy of the man America accosted on the street corner is that he did not realize the condition of his garments. How sad if you were to walk past America in her decadent, dying condition and not understand the truth. For by reason of your American citizenship, you are clothed as poorly as she. You are partakers of her either through birth or by naturalization. Your citizenship is certified proof that *you are* America.

Some of you young people might be saying, "Yeah! That's okay for you to say, but don't blame me for America's condition. It's not my fault this country is like it is today. I was not even *born* when all of this mess started happening back in the late Fifties." That is a good point, young person. Let me ask you a question. But before I do, travel back with me for a moment. With your mind's eye, visualize America again in her current condition as you stand with me outside the porta-potty. Do you see her? Remember how she looked? Now, if that were YOUR mother, the one who gave you birth, standing there in that condition, would you turn away in disgust or would you stand on that street corner and try to get her attention? I hope that you would love your mother enough to withstand the shame of her current condition and sing your heart out for her. Can you at least agree with me that, although you are not to blame, that America is at least YOUR mother? You were born in her household and raised in her neighborhoods. She needs YOU right now as much as she needed my grandfather to go to fight for freedom during World War II. You may never have known America during the days when she was unsurpassed in her national beauty, but she needs you to help cleanse her right now. She was not always the foul-smelling, vulgar old hag described above.

Your challenge—my challenge—without a doubt, is probably greater than any experienced by preceding generations. Others fought for liberty. You fight for life—America's life. The battle to restore America to her former state is greater than any war fought by her soldiers on foreign soil. What a challenge for today's generation! Consider the honor. You are part of a chosen generation that will open the doors for God to pour forth His repentance to America. Do you know how to do this? First, by honestly admitting that YOU truly are America. By taking an honest evaluation of your personal habits regarding Hollywood, television, movies and music. If repentance comes to America, it must first come through YOU. Only then will true change occur in America. So we are agreeing now, right? Right? You will first open your heart to the Holy Spirit so He can cleanse and purify your personal connection to Hollywood. That's good. You and the Holy Spirit sit down and reason together on this subject. Go ahead. Ask Him to spotlight the areas where He has been grieved in your own life regarding Hollywood. Sit quietly for a moment. Stop reading. Listen to Him.

Did you ask Him? Okay, we're getting somewhere now. Are you ready to get on board the **H&H** train. Destination? America Restored. Don't worry about the ticket. America's God has already paid the cost of your ticket. It's waiting for you in the Throne Room of Heaven. You will get it the first time you get on your knees before the LORD.

AMERICA needs you!
America *NEEDS* you!
America needs *YOU!*

Part VII
The Confession

"Man has forgotten God — that is why this has happened."

—Russian author Alexander Solzhenitsyn who explained America's moral collapse when he observed her national impoverishment in 1983.

Chapter 10

Confessing Our Sins and Failures

Fasting and Prayer

Remember the **H&H** train stands for **H**abitual and **H**umbling. The purpose for the **H**abitual part of the **H&H** is to let you know that America is not going to repent without your *habitual* prayers. One or two haphazard prayers are not going to get the job done. *America has committed adultery against God Almighty!* Do you realize the truth of those words? America cannot go sashaying up to the Throne Room of God and flippantly think that His holiness will ignore the filth of her current ways. She has blood dripping off her hands from having murdered more innocent children than Hitler himself. Yet mercy triumphs over justice! Absolutely. But think about the circumstances that would surround physical adultery.

If a wife has defiled the purity of her marriage bed by taking on, not one, but dozens of illicit love relationships, can she go up once to her former husband, murmur a quick "I'm sorry" and expect him to welcome her back with open arms? I think not. Oh! But I'm forgetting Hosea, you tell me. Not at all. The glory of Hosea's forgiving love will anchor America as she perseveres in her prayers to her God. She has that hope. God will cleanse her and purify her and take her back. I wish space would permit us time to study national spiritual adultery. You do that for yourself. Prayerfully, ask the LORD to show you this truth. Then you will understand why it is that missionaries come home with strange stories of miracles in other countries. Yes. It is true. Some people on the mission field have actually had their blind eyes healed. Yeah?! asks the skeptic. Why doesn't it happen here in America? Because America is guilty of spiritual adultery. From her beginning, she experienced God, she partook of the purity of having "known God" in the most intimate sense. Africa was never founded upon the Word of God. Argentina? Nope! These nations may have been guilty of *spiritual fornication*, but not *spiritual adultery*. Big difference. Serious difference this business of a covenant. You study this for yourself. It will make you see how great is the need for you to practice *habitual* prayer.

That second track is **H**umbling. America can only travel that track if YOU humble yourself as an individual. Again, because of limited space, I am not going to detail physical fasting for spiritual purposes in this book. In Appendix D, I have recommended a book entitled *The Coming Revival* by Bill Bright, President of Campus Crusade. In that book, Dr. Bright states, "Fasting is the only discipline that meets all the conditions of 2 Chronicles 7:14. When one fasts, he humbles himself; he has more time to pray, more time to seek God's face, and certainly he would turn from all known sin. One could read the Bible, pray, or witness for Christ without repenting of his sins. But one cannot enter into a genuine fast with a pure heart and pure motive and not meet the conditions of this passage."[1] Get this book and read it! The LORD is using Dr. Bright to raise up an army of Christian who will habitually and humbly pray for America's restoration.

The Power of Fasting

In 1994, Dr. Bright called together some notable Christian leaders, from all denominations, to meet for the specific purpose of fasting and praying for America. In *The Coming Revival*, he trumpets the call for two million Christians to fast for forty days. When I first read his book (January 1996), I began the forty-day fast as prescribed in the book. Then because some gouty arthritis developed in my foot after sixteen days into the fast, the doctor required me to stop. The medication for the arthritis required food in my stomach.

However, those sixteen days absolutely changed my walk with the LORD. It opened the door for the LORD to reveal another kind of forty-day fast.

Whereas, Bill Bright is calling America to fast from food for forty days, I am calling America to fast from Hollywood, movies, television, and all music other than classical music or praise and worship music for forty days. Whoa! That might be as difficult for some as it is to not eat solid food for forty days. Just think of it! If you can get America to stop rummaging in the garbage for her food for forty days, maybe she will return to the banquet halls of her God and eat the *spiritually solid food of the Word of God*! Yes! That is the greater purpose for fasting from Hollywood. To return America to a diet of righteousness, renewal and revival.

Dr. Bright has been commanded to lead America into fasting for forty days as evidence of their desire to restore America. What is the reason for two million Americans going without solid food for forty days? God Himself desires America to return to Him, but until she fulfills 2 Chronicles 7:14. "If My people, which are called by My name, shall humble themselves, and pray, and seek my face, and turn from their wicked ways; then will I hear from heaven, and will forgive their sin, and will heal their land."

It is my belief that a mandate similar to that of Dr. Bill Bright has been issued to me. The difference? Through this book, I am inviting pastors, church leaders and individuals to stand with me on that street corner of Filth and Hollywood. Join me in a forty-day fast from movies, television, and all music other than classical, or praise and worship. During those forty days, America can eat all the spiritual food from His Word that she wants! God invites her to do so. I pray that America gorges herself until she cannot rise from the table during those forty days. Then I pray she never leaves God's banqueting table again.

If you can fast from Hollywood for forty days, its power over you will be broken. However, you might also discover during the first week or so—maybe the first few days—how addicted you have become to Hollywood. Part Eight, The Conquerors offers guidelines on how to fast from Hollywood for forty days.

Prayer Warriors Who Conquer

Fasting and prayers go together. It does no good to go without food on a fast without praying. You will only be punishing your physical body to fast without praying. One is the right arm and the other is the left arm. They are both needed to wield the sword and hold up the shield. For right now, however, I want to talk to you specifically about your prayer life. It will do you no good to fast from Hollywood unless you get on board the **H&H** train of *habitual* and *humbling* prayer.

You have been uniquely and definitely gifted by God from all others. Do not attempt to wear someone else's armor. Young David could not slay Goliath in Saul's armor, but he could slay him with what he had mastered—the unlikely weapon of a slingshot and five stones. You must be wise enough to walk in your own God-given abilities and gifts. However, you might not recognize your own *unlikely weapons*. The LORD had already used David to kill a bear and a lion before he stood in front of the Israeli army. You must search your heart and honestly answer these questions. How has the LORD gifted you? What are your greatest abilities? Up to this point in your life, have you slain the lions that have come against you when you are all alone and not with the rest of the Army of God? Now be honest with yourself! No one is listening to you answer these questions except the LORD. Is your life clothed in prayer and dependency upon the LORD? Have you ever humbled yourself and gone to others to ask for their forgiveness because you offended them or sinned against them?

Those trained in spiritual warfare and those who are dedicated intercessors have already come face to face with these questions in their personal lives. They have already wrestled with the powers of darkness. They have learned that *their fight* was with the devil and not the people he was using. However, if you feel that you do not qualify to go to the front line, do not think for a moment that your words of prayer against Hollywood's works of darkness are not necessary. There is no truth at all in that.

In the natural army, it takes soldiers to cook, soldiers to build roads, soldiers to plan strategy, soldiers to carry out the tactics of that strategy, soldiers to nurse the wounded and soldiers to fire the nuclear weapons. How well could a soldier, trained in using artillery, fire his weapons without food to strengthen him? The artillery expert might never meet the soldier who cooked his meals, but he could not survive long without him. *Absolutely* they need every child of God in His army! We need each other—even more so in these perilous times. Those who man the submarines or those who fly the fighter jets are no more important than those who sweep the barracks or peel potatoes.

It is God pointing His finger at you from that poster and saying HE needs you for America. God is the General who has equipped you and He is the Shepherd who has led you in the experiences of your life. You must keep our eyes turned upon Him—not upon others. Do not fall into the snare of the enemy before you even fire the first shot by measuring yourself by another Christian. If He had wanted you with different abilities, talents and gifts, He would have endowed you with them. You give Him pleasure by *being* whom He created you to be. My mother keeps a poster in her office that sums this up quite well:

**What you are is God's gift to you,
what you make of yourself,
is your gift to God**

Whatever gifts, talents or abilities the LORD has given you, He works through your prayers. It is His ordained medium for our dependency upon Him. It proves our need for Him. He did not need America's prayers in 1962—*we* needed prayer. He gave us prayer for *our* benefit, not His. God waits to see how serious America is about prayer. One serious and dedicated intercessor shared her testimony regarding a particular prayer incident she had in 1988:

"I had decided to 'pray through' and so one night I covenanted with the LORD to lock myself away in a room. For eight hours, nonstop, I prayed. In the past, I had prayed nonstop for several hours. From those experiences, I had learned to keep bottles of water with me because my mouth would become so dry from speaking. So with my bottles of Evian, I began my prayer vigil. I stopped pleading and praying to the

LORD only long enough to take a drink of water. The night hours began to take their toll on me. My emotions somersaulted from hope to despair to weariness to feeling like a conceited fool thinking my prayer could make a difference. Once, after five hours, I stopped for about three minutes from the sheer weight of what I had undertaken. I was so tired. I considered giving up in those brief moments. But then a rush of energy flooded from somewhere within me. It was as if prayer itself took hold of me. I was no longer struggling just to finish. At that point, I knew I *could not stop.* Something had happened! I got up off the bed and began to pace the floor with new zeal. About the seventh hour, which was around three o'clock in the morning, there was such a strong sense of the LORD's presence that I paused in my prayer and just sat quietly. Momentarily, there came a definite, strong sense of hearing the LORD speak to my heart: "I cannot hear the prayers of America because of the sound of her babies crying in My ears." Instantly upon hearing those words, I *knew* He was talking about the abortion holocaust in America. Suddenly, I felt as if every abortion done in America was somehow *my* fault. I remembered where I was and what I had been doing on the day the radio announced the Supreme Court ruling on *Roe vs. Wade.* My reaction on that day was, "That is terrible!" Yet, I had never gone before the LORD and prayed for Him to intervene in America. I spent the last hour that night repenting of my own sin. It was so real to me that, as a Christian citizen in America, my hands were stained with the blood of innocent children I had never tried to save. From that experience forward, the LORD has continued to show me the importance of persevering prayer. Abortion and America were two subjects that never entered my conscious mind when I decided to "pray through." However, I learned a valuable lesson that night. What I think is important and what I'm always praying for is not as important to God. He never answered the petitions that I thought were important that night. Yet He mercifully answered me and honored my futile attempt at praying for eight hours straight by showing me what was truly important to Him: America and the degradation of how low she had fallen. The weight of her sin is unbearable for one individual; it will take all of us fasting and praying together."

Daniel's Prayer for America

The scriptures speak favorably about Daniel. You remember his story. As a Jewish young person, he purposed not to defile himself with the king's meat. Daniel understood how the food served to him by the world would defile him. Yet there is no spiritual arrogance found in him. Rather, he humbled himself and actually included himself as the problem for Israel's troubles. Daniel, like the LORD Jesus, was a true intercessor. Daniel grieved as if everything had been his fault. He personally identified with the sins of his nation. Jesus grieved over our sins. He then took those sins upon Himself and paid for them. In heaven, He no longer does miracles or preaches or heals people as He did while on earth. He sits at the Father's right hand and "ever liveth to *intercede* for us."

I have taken the liberty to paraphrase Daniel's prayer for Israel as a prayer for America. It is best if you read this prayer as a personal petition to the LORD when you are by yourself. If now, you are reading this in the company of others, do not continue by reading the prayer below. Turn the page until you go beyond the prayer and return to it later. Do not cheat! The prayer will be there when you return to it. Leave the blank for your name empty until you can return. For the prayer to be fully effective, *you must speak the words aloud*; therefore, it is necessary that you be alone when reading the prayer. Read the words aloud. Take your time. This is serious business you execute between you and the God of America. Let the words sink deep into your heart. Allow the Holy Spirit to work with you. He will begin to graft them deep within your spirit. Write your name in the blank where Daniel's name was originally placed in the scriptures.

And I, _____, set my face toward you, LORD God. I want to seek You through the words of my prayers. I want to plead with You for America; with fasting from Hollywood and sackcloth and repentance for our sins against You;

I pray unto You, God of America, and make my confession, and say, O LORD, the great and dreadful God, keeping the covenant and mercy to them that love Him, and to them that keep His commandments; We have sinned and have committed iniquity, and have done wickedly, and have rebelled, even by departing from thy precepts and from thy judgments:

Neither have we hearkened unto thy servants the prophets, which spake in thy name to our presidents, our senators, and our spiritual fathers, and to all segments of our nation's culture. O LORD, righteousness belongs to You—but our faces are confused and ashamed at this time in America's history; to those who praise Your name, to those who sit in the church pews, and unto all Americans, to those who are in church and to those who are out of church, through all the different areas of our lives where we have been divided because of our sin and because we committed spiritual adultery against You in 1962 and did not immediately repent.

O LORD, as a nation we wear confusion and shame on our faces before the world; even our political leaders, our entertainers, and our spiritual fathers, because we have sinned against You.

To You, LORD our God, belong mercies and forgiveness, although we have rebelled against You, forgotten You, openly shamed You. Neither have we obeyed Your voice, LORD God, to walk in Your laws, which You set before Your servants, our founding fathers, after they had fasted and prayed for Your guidance to establish our nation's government.

Yes, all America has transgressed Your law, even by departing, that we might not obey Your voice; therefore the curse is poured upon us, and the oath that is written in the law of Moses the servant of God because we sinned against You. And You confirmed Your words which You spoke against us, and against the Supreme Court that makes our laws, by bringing upon us a great evil: for under the whole heaven there has not been a nation more guilty than America of defiling her own culture plus other nations with her entertainment harlotry.

As it is written in the law of Moses, all this evil is come upon us: yet we have not prayed before the LORD our God, that we might plead with Him to show us the personal sin in our lives, give us true repentance, and understand Your truth of why all of this happened to us. Therefore, You LORD, watched the evil that happened in America in 1962 and You brought it upon us: for You, LORD our God, are righteous in all Your works which You do: because we failed to obey Your voice.

And now, O LORD our God, You established this nation with a mighty hand. Your name was prominent, as we stood "one nation under God" before the world, and yet we have sinned, our hands are stained with the blood of innocent, unborn children. O LORD, according to all Your righteousness, I beseech You, please turn Your anger and Your fury away from America, the nation founded upon Your principles: because of our sins and the iniquities of our fathers, America and Christianity are reproaches to everyone around us.

Now therefore, O our God, hear my prayer and my requests, and cause Your face to shine upon the churches in America that are desolate, for the LORD's sake. O my God, incline Your ear, and hear; open Your eyes, and behold our desolations, and the nation which was founded upon Your Son, Jesus Christ, for we do not present our supplications before You because we are righteous, but because we know how merciful You are.

O LORD, hear; O LORD, forgive; O LORD, listen to our prayers and act on our behalf; do not postpone answering us for Your own sake, O my God: for Your nation and Your people who are called by the name of Your Son, Jesus the Christ.

Remember...

▶ Fasting and Prayer are two essential elements for turning America back to God.

▶ That means we get on board the **H&H** train of habitual and humbling.

▶ America has committed spiritual adultery against her God.

▶ Following the concept of Dr. Bill Bright's forty-day fast agenda to turn America back to God, we propose the forty-day fast from Hollywood. It is the only way to break the mind control of the devil that is over our country and is destroying our family and children.

▶ Whatever gifts, talents and/or abilities the LORD has given you, He works through your prayers.

▶ What you are is God's gift to you; what you make of yourself is your gift to God.

▶ Repeatedly pray Daniel's Prayer for America.

America's beginning was God's gift to her, America's ending is your gift to God.

Part VIII
The Conquerors

"Nay, in all things we are more than conquerors through Him who loves [America]...." (Authors paraphrase)

—Jewish Apostle Paul (formerly Saul of Tarsus), writing under the inspiration of the Holy Spirit and can be found in Romans 8:37.

Chapter 11

Corporately Confronting the Problem

Fasting From Hollywood

The singular term of "Hollywood" will be used in this chapter to include the broad categories of theater movies, video movies, television, magazines about movies or television (*TV Guide, Entertainment Weekly*, etc.), any music that is not classical music or praise and worship. When we speak of fasting from Hollywood then, we mean that we are fasting from watching movies either at home or in theaters, watching television in our homes or the homes of family or friends, reading magazines that describe or discuss movies or television programs, or listen to any music that is not classical music or praise and worship.

Computers. If you have read Chapters Three and Four, The Crisis, then you are aware of the possibilities of how the devil can use this invention of man. Yet there are great benefits with the computer. At this very moment, I am typing these words to you on a computer. Many use the computer as an instrument of work, so naturally, I am not referring to computers used in that capacity. However, it will serve no real benefit to fast from movies and television and then spend hours playing games on the computer. A fine line must be drawn in your fast from Hollywood regarding computers. I strongly urge you to include games on the computer as part of the forty-day fast. This is especially needful for breaking habits with young children, yet this does not apply to necessary time spent at the computer doing homework.

Before going further, let me encourage you to go the full distance in the forty-day fast. You no doubt realize the significance of the number forty in the Bible. Most Biblical scholars generally teach that the number forty symbolizes testing. Forty days also equals six weeks. Psychologists will tell you that to break a habit, it takes a consistent and concentrated effort of six weeks before you can truly establish a new habit or an old habit can be broken. You will experience a transformation of your mental faculties after you finish this forty-day fast from Hollywood. Fasting and prayer can destroy strongholds. Now—having said that, let me say this.

If you have been submerged and saturated for years in Hollywood, you will be surprised how difficult the forty-day fast will be for you. Your mind and your flesh are going to scream with loud protests. Your family and friends are going to be just as vocal. You must prepare yourself beforehand to resist comments such as the following:

"This is stupid! You are Mother Teresa now? The Pope maybe?!"

"There is nothing wrong with cartoons! You are really going overboard on this. That's not fair for your children. What are they supposed to do just because you're trying to prove something?"

"How are you going to know what is going on in the world if you don't watch the evening news? You're really going off the deep end now. You are taking this thing a little too far."

"Tell you what, buddy! Nobody is going to convince me that God minds if you watch the Dallas Cowboys. You crazy or something?"

"Look—you are totally exhausted. You've had a long day at the office. You're beat to a frazzle. One little program is not going to hurt you? Touched by an Angel?! Come on, sit and relax for a minute. Even the preacher says that's a good show!"

"Who is going to know if you watch one little soap opera? You're here by yourself. The kids are at school. Lock the door if it will make you feel better. No one can walk in on you then. Just hold the remote in your hand. Keep the volume turned down real low. You can always click it off if someone knocks on the door."

Be prepared to handle different situations. These are only a few of the comments you will hear from your family and friends and from inside your own head. Ideally, the entire family will undertake this fast together. However, you must be prepared with how you will handle any situation that could arise when you are a guest in someone's home. Be forewarned. The forty-day fast must not begin unless there is preparation and decisions made beforehand how to handle different situations that can arise.

Be prepared to try again if you fail. You might not be able to complete the forty-day fast the first time you attempt one. This chapter is to help you do everything you can to prepare for a successful and full forty-day fast from Hollywood; however, I do not want you to beat yourself to death if you fail. You might have to work up to it. You might need some counsel from another Christian who has succeeded. Nevertheless, whatever you must do to help get yourself through the forty-day fast from Hollywood—do it!

Be prepared for the enemy's deception afterwards. If you prepare for your forty-day fast and then successfully complete it, the rewards are going to be great. You will have succeeded in breaking some habits and strongholds that you might not have even realized were there. Your mind might feel as if someone had gone in and swept out many dusty old cobwebs. Yet a great temptation awaits you at the end of your fast. If you fall for it, you will have lost all the sweetness of your victory. Do not strut around in superior pride and foolish arrogance, thinking you are a really spiritual Christian. At the beginning of your fast, ask the LORD to give you His cloak of humility. Once you have completed the forty-day fast, go find someone and share with them how the LORD gave you the grace to break some bad habits. Then encourage them to do the same. Keep yourself covered with His cloak of humility. Remember! You started this to free America and not to exalt your stature as a Christian over everyone else. You do not want the success of your fast to become an avenue for legalism or pride. You do not want to condemn others who have not yet experienced freedom from the bondage of Hollywood. You do want to do everything you can to help and encourage others. The LORD told us we would be known by the love we have one for another, not by having such sharp discernment faculties that we condemn one another with as much zeal as Hollywood condemns religion. Keep these few admonitions in mind before you as you begin the preparation of your forty-day fast from Hollywood.

Practical Preparations

The success of your forty-day fast may depend on following some of these practical guidelines.

Family vs. Individual: To do this as a family is going to strengthen your ties as a family to the LORD and to America. The husband and wife need thoroughly to discuss these preparations and agree to carry them out together. When the youngsters begin to fuss about having their pacifier taken from them, it may take both parents to get through the storm. Be prepared, parents. I can assure you this will happen. Let me also encourage husband and wife to decide the parameters for this fast before announcing it to your troopers. Trust me. Even a four-year-old will protest vigorously when you take his daily diet of cartoons and Disney movies away from him. You don't want an unnecessary mutiny on your hands before you get the strategy in place. Spend at least several days going over this chapter together before calling in the children and making the announcement. Together, you will need to decide things like: How are you going to monitor Johnny and his car radio? What about when he drives home from school and, out of sheer habit, turns the radio up to 150 decibels? It will take foresight and preparation to succeed and make it a family adventure that can be fun, not torment, for you and your children.

There may be a different set of problems for the single parent. Remaining firm in a situation where you are totally exhausted might be harder as you enter a house when the winds of teenage boredom are blowing at gale force. The temptation will be to plop down on the couch with your children and let them plug in the TV for your own peace of mind. If you wisely plan before the fast begins, you can eliminate many situations that might arise. However, you might also secure a support system of other single parents beforehand. It is especially helpful if you are doing this with your church. You will not feel so isolated in your efforts. Single parents should follow the same advice for a husband and wife and make certain that you have most of your preparation on paper before you tell your children.

Fun vs. Torment: The built-in "fun" that you and your children have depended upon for years is about to be eliminated. You can compare it with a wife having her built-in stove taken out of the house and then the family still expects to eat the same type of meal they ate in the past. Your entertainment diet is about to undergo a drastic change. Movies will be gone. TV will be gone. Most music will be gone. How boring life will be without these. This is why you must use common sense and make some preliminary and practical preparations before attempting to fast from Hollywood for forty days. One book to help you is *Married to Television?* Do not announce to your children that you are about to *starve them to death* until you have made some tentative plans for other nourishment. These activities will strengthen you as a *family.* With a little forethought, you can extend some suggested activities to include grandparents, aunts, uncles. It can be a beautiful and uniting experience.

Corporate Strength: Achieving corporate unity and prayer is one primary purpose for this book. "And if one prevail against him, two shall withstand him; and a threefold cord is not quickly broken."[1] If one family unit prevails against Hollywood, then that is a great achievement. Yet if two family units prevail, how much greater. However, if those two family units *and* the corporate church prevail together, you will see how much more excellent is their strength! When families and the corporate church begin to prevail against Hollywood together, you will witness a spiritual phenomenon in America. Shifting in the cords will occur. The individual family unit will be the *one*; the corporate church with her families then becomes the *two*; and the LORD Himself will move onto the scene as the *THIRD* cord. A *THREEFOLD* cord is not quickly broken. I encourage every individual and every family to fast for forty days from Hollywood. It is essential for you and for America. However, I beseech, I plead, I beg the local churches in America to undertake this on a corporate level. Corporate preparation for the "Fast From Hollywood" is discussed later in the chapter.

Organization vs. Flying by the Seat of Your Pants:

If one of your spiritual gifts is administration, you probably have already organized your forty-day fast in your head. For some of you without that gift, however, I offer some brief guidelines.

1. Count the cost as an individual and as a family. Let it season for several days. Ask the LORD to begin supplying His grace and give you guidance on how to do this for yourself, your family and/or your church.
2. Let your pastor read this book and discuss the possibility of doing this on a corporate level.
3. Order and purchase some books in the Recommended Reading List.
4. Take a notebook and make a "Fast From Hollywood To Do List." Include possible snares that your flesh or the devil could use. I encourage you to keep your notes, preparation, insights, etc. in a permanent notebook for future reference. You may be called upon two years from now to help someone else begin their fast from Hollywood. Include some items listed below in your "To Do" List.
    1) How to handle family/friends visiting my home.
    2) How to handle visiting family/friends in their homes.
    3) Construct honor system or accountability system for times when not with family.
    3) Purchase a calendar (American/patriotic themes would be nice) with large blocks for posting special events so that you can see a "week" and/or a "month" at a glance. It helps the children to see that they are not going to be "bored to death." Make certain that you block out certain times for eating spiritually solid food. Let the children help with this project.
    4) *Purchase an American flag* and drape it over your television set in the living room. Find a flag large enough to cover the entire set. You will save that much money in video rentals and movie tickets. It

makes for a great conversation piece when you have company. It serves a dual purpose. Most people will not ask you to move the American flag so they can watch television. Secondly, they will not be as scornful if you can honestly answer: "I am doing this for America." If you have additional sets in the house, and you can afford it, purchase smaller flags to cover them up—it is best to cover them entirely. If you cannot drape the sets with flags, then unplug the TVs and store them in the closet where you cannot see them. At least completely cover its "black eye" with a large piece of fabric—preferably something red, white and blue.

5) Keep your "Fast From Hollywood" notebook in a convenient place.

5. Go through your video movies, audio cassettes and CDs. The Holy Spirit would delight to oversee your choices. Those that are not decent and beneficial for you and/or your family will need to be put into a box. If you are fasting as an individual or a single family, then throw them away or burn them immediately. If you are participating in a corporate fast with your church, box them up and put them in the garage or somewhere outside your house until the "Burn, Hollywood, Burn" Celebration at your church.

Spiritual Preparations

Again, I suggest that you purchase Bill Bright's *The Coming Revival* and read it *before* going on your forty-day fast from Hollywood. Actually, if you are a strong individual, you can assuredly combine these two fasts. They complement each other. While you are fasting from food, why not slide the Hollywood fast in on the same forty days? Dr. Bright makes excellent suggestions in his book regarding spiritual preparations. There is no need to repeat them here.

Repentance. However, I do want to undergird the truth of repentance concerning your spiritual preparation. If you fasted from Hollywood for forty days and yet you did not truly repent, then you are headed straight back to the porta-potty. May I suggest that one of your most sincere and constant petitions as an individual and as a church should be: "LORD

God, please show me my sins; have mercy on me; and give me
the gift of repentance." Learn to sit before the LORD and He
will reveal your sins. There is nothing more glorious than to
come into His presence. Spend time alone with Him. He is
such an Awesome God. While there, He will cleanse you and,
if necessary, apply the healing balm of Gilead to any old
wounds. This is all part of the process of repentance.

Forgiveness. The final admonition concerns forgiveness.
If there is unforgiveness in your heart toward someone else,
then you must put it under the blood. Again, you must allow
the Holy Spirit to spotlight any areas of unforgiveness. Trust
Him—He will never fail in this. Let me encourage you so
much in this. You may have been raped or molested or abused
as a child. There is no greater sin that they could have
assaulted you with as an innocent child. Certainly, you were
someone's victim. Gossip that was nothing more than vicious
lies may have destroyed you and your family's good reputation. They could have kicked you out of a church because of
jealousy. You may have had someone steal money from you or
even destroy your business. These are serious things!!! From
a *human* perspective, they seem unforgivable. And trying to
conjure up forgiveness for someone who has so grievously
sinned against you cannot be done—*from a human perspective*. When you have been the victimized so grievously, you
might not be able to conjure up forgiveness! You must experience a divine forgiveness that can flood your soul with peace
and joy. I can promise you this. The LORD Jesus Christ has
enough grace literally to drench your soul with forgiveness.
Only the LORD can *give to* you that forgiveness. However, you
must trust Him enough to believe that you will be better off
after you forgive than you are keeping unforgiveness hidden in
your heart. The LORD commands us to forgive. He sternly
warns us about the consequences of not forgiving. Yet, it is He
Who provides the grace for forgiveness. However, He will not
force any forgiveness upon you. This is your choice.

Let me help you with this. Come on. Who is that individual that came to your mind as you read these words? You
might not realize it, but your entire body, mind and emotions
changed when that individual entered your thoughts. This
unforgiveness is actually hurting your life more than
his/her/their lives. I am going to help you pray as if it were a

man who had hurt you so deeply. You can change the pronoun accordingly. Pray this with me.

"LORD, just now, I don't feel like forgiving _____. He hurt me and I just hate him at times. He sinned against me, LORD. I cannot forgive him. I don't even want to forgive him. *But if will pleases You to give me forgiveness in my heart* for him, then *I want to please You.* I want to keep Your commandment to forgive because I love you. I choose for *You* to help me with this and to forgive _____."

Do not leave the presence of the LORD until you wrestle this thing through with Him. Forgiveness is an essential, nonnegotiable, prerequisite for repentance. After Jesus taught the people how to pray in the LORD's Prayer, He said: "For if ye forgive men their trespasses, our heavenly Father will also forgive you; But if ye forgive not men their trespasses, neither will your Father forgive your trespasses."[2] Do not allow bitterness to rob you of your victory. A primary reason that America is in the porta-potty is because a root of bitterness has sprung up among her citizens. This is evident in our society that has gone "litigation crazy." There is no forgiveness anymore. Everyone wants to sue someone else for any small reason.

Again, this does not detract from the tragic truth that you may have truly been a victim of someone's sin. I tell you this for your benefit and because I want you to be set free.

Corporate Preparations

Obviously, leaders in local churches can implement most of the prior suggestions. The *"threefold cord,"* forty-day fast from Hollywood is by far the most powerful. If organized and prepared for properly, it can be a wonderful experience for the entire congregation.

1. Pastors, you need to spend time before calling the forty-day fast in preparation for teaching your people. Check Appendix B Christian Sources and Appendix D Recommended Reading List immediately. Begin to assemble and collect your resources so they will equip you to

teach your people and answer questions. Another option is to contact the author at his ministry address given below and inquire regarding his church meetings on Hollywood. Whether you choose to contact the author or seek to undertake this on your own, the video by Michael Medved, *Hollywood vs. Religion*, is an essential starting point.

> Gene Wolfenbarger, Jr.
> Gene Wolfenbarger Evangelistic Association
> Post Office Box 450938
> Garland, TX 75045
> (972) 840-3600
> (800) 876-4932
> (972) 864-1492 Fax

2. Organize the forty-day fast by delegating certain tasks.
   1) *Organize a prayer team.* If you do not already have an active prayer team or time designated for intercession, then do so at this time. Do not let this be a regular Wednesday night "prayer meeting." Come organized with specifics to pray regarding America. Keep this prayer time in front of the people. Mention it weekly in your bulletin. Stress that this is not a regular prayer meeting. This one is different! This one is for America! You are fasting from Hollywood to get America out of her wretched, foul-smelling porta-potty!
   2) *Be creative.* This is going to continue for forty days. Begin something that your people will want to participate in—after all, they're not watching television now. This helps fill the gap that will automatically be created during this time. Whatever you do and however you do it, *focus on prayer.* Break into groups, go off as individuals, walk around the auditorium or the gym as you pray, but do not let it be the same old prayer meeting.
      Call in your creative people and have them make flags for different segments of America, such as Education, Government, Hollywood, etc. Designate different people to study the different statistics (crime, education, etc.) of your community, report

them and then pray about them.

Have a "Pray Around America." There are many ways to do this. Create a mammoth plastic map of America and place it in your gym or church parking lot. The states can be either separated or pieced together as one large map. Then allow different groups of people to stand in different states as they pray for America. Make certain that someone stands in every state. Allow different people to go to the microphone and read aloud "Daniel's Prayer for America" as written in Chapter Ten. You might consider allowing individuals who were born in different states to offer prayer for their particular home state. Another suggestion to "Pray Around America" is to obtain pictures or the actual flags of each state. Place them around the auditorium or gym so that people may gather in groups at each flag. Have an individual in each group pray as they "travel" through the states.

Incidentally, the younger children will love doing a "Hopscotch America." Let them take turns tossing a small homemade bean-bag (red, white and blue, please) onto the plasticized map of America. Then that particular child receives the honor of standing in that state as prayer is spoken for it. Make a game of the fact that they must include every state before you offer refreshments. The kids love it and it makes a lasting impression on them.

Youth departments are great at sponsoring, "I Saw America the Other Day" contests. (Please—if you have a contest, let all of the participants be winners in some way.) Allow some of them to dress up as America the way she was in her beginning and then characterize her the way she looks today. Show the two sharp contrasts. If done properly, this is a graphic picture that will greatly affect your church. If you have a drama department, turn this over to them. When the genius of youth gets involved—look out! They can be superior in these interpretations. You can show America as she was in her beginnings and then progress down to the porta-potty stage. You might see that adults love doing this as much as the young people.

Have a *Burn Hollywood—Birth Hollywood* celebration at the close of the forty days. Take the indecent videos, cassettes, CDs, literature, books, etc. and have a bonfire.

These are only a few directions to point you in the general direction. The various gifts and abilities of the local church will manifest once the leadership gets excited.

3) *Serve a banquet of spiritually solid food.* The success of any corporate fast will be in guiding the people into eating different food. Seek the LORD on what He wants to feed your particular flock at that season in their lives. The food (preaching) you serve from the pulpit will be a private issue between you and the Holy Spirit. However, *teaching is crucial during this time also.* Saturate your people with such topics as establishing a relationship with the LORD, transformation of the mind, prayer, fasting, repentance, forgiveness, humiliation, etc.

Writing this almost seems unnecessary because pastors understand better than anyone the need to feed people the word of God; however, let me encourage you again in the importance of *feeding the flock* during this fast. Most will be going through various *withdrawal symptoms* that can be likened to withdrawal from a drug addiction. If they are craving (and they will be) the food of their habitual television and movie watching, then you must feed them the nourishment of the Word of God. Likewise, you must encourage, support and teach them to do this for themselves at home. As you well know, this is no small task. America must go back to eating the Word of God and not the regurgitation of hell that comes through Hollywood. Fasting from Hollywood will be most beneficial, but *it will be the Word of God that cleans the cobwebs out of their minds.* Keep this thought foremost in *your* mind as you lead your flock. Set as number one, the goal of tearing down the spiritual strongholds that the enemy has fortified in their minds.

Do you want to have fun? Absolutely! Be creative? Yes. Stir up patriotism and love for America? Hallelujah! But what is your goal, pastor? *To set the captives free.* And by doing so, you get America out of the porta-potty. "The Spirit of the LORD is upon me, because He hath anointed me to preach the gospel to the poor; he hath sent me to heal the brokenhearted, *to preach deliverance to the captives*, and recovering of sight to the blind, to set at liberty them that are bruised."[3]

Are you capable of such an undertaking? Oh, I definitely believe you are, pastor. That is the reason the LORD placed you in your current position. The extent of your influence can have great effect. God has given you the leadership ability to lead an entire congregation back to that PRAYER crossroads of 1962 when America went the wrong direction. *If you do not stand against the tide now, in another decade you may not have the right to pray within the walls of your own church!* But right now, there is no Supreme Court that can stop you from leading your people in a massive, organized prayer effort to save America. Do it now! Do not wait until it is too late!

Corporate Prayer: Getting America Out of The Porta-Potty

I was standing at the edge of an enormous dirt field. It stretched in all directions almost as far as the eye could see, acre upon acre. Somehow I knew I was supposed to go and work that field. I also knew that the Owner of the field, for whom I worked, wanted the whole thing cultivated and planted and prepared for harvest. I looked across that expanse of earth again just to see if it was as vast as I thought. It was. But upon closer inspection, I saw a few others far off in the field. Separated by wide distances, these individual workers were tending their respective patches of land with diligence. I felt such a responsibility to my Boss. Although I did not think that there was much chance in succeeding at this task, I thought I would do what the others were doing and work my little spot of land as well as I could. Maybe my Boss would send in more workers. "He'd better send in a lot," I thought to myself.

I looked down and saw that I was holding a small handheld shovel. Something was written on the shovel in tiny letters. I had to hold it up close to my face to read it. Squinting, I made out the word *PRAYER*. That inscription told me three things:
1)   Prayer was definitely the tool to use in this field.

2) Something was lacking in the quality and quantity of my prayer life.

3) Everyone else in the field had a tool more or less like mine.

Then thinking that someday I might get a bigger shovel to work the field better, I bent down and went to work.

Just like in a movie, time elapsed and there, instantly in front of me, were two tomato plants. One of them actually had a little green tomato on it. The second plant seemed to have some potential and I was beginning to work on a third plant.

"Aha!" I thought, "Two and a half feet! Progress! Sure—sure, hundreds, maybe thousands of square acres to go, but this is nothing to sneeze at!"

Actually, I was proud of my little tomato plants. They were not of the hardiest stock, but they were something! I returned to my labors with my tiny prayer shovel in hand.

Suddenly, I heard the deafening growl of a gigantic engine. "Vroom! Vroom!" I popped my head up like a startled gopher. And there it was on the edge of the field—reverberating with power. Smoked billowed out of its exhaust pipe. The most enormous tractor/combine piece of farm equipment I had ever seen. It was not just impressive, it was scary it was so powerful! I was totally dwarfed by its enormity. I looked at that machine, then I looked at the field. By my calculations, what I and others could not finish in a lifetime, this thing was able to do in only a few days.

Just then, a kind and jolly gentleman poked his head out of the driver's compartment and called out to me.

"Working the field?" he asked.

"Yes, sir I am."

"Need any help?"

"Well, yes sir. I really do. Can this rig of yours do the field?"

"Yep!," he replied.

"Plough?" I asked.

"Yep!"

"Fertilize?" I asked, thinking this was too good to be true.

"Yep!"

"Water as well?" I asked incredulously.

"Yep! It's real good at that."

I thought of one thing it would not be able to do. "Can this thing weed?"

"Yep! It does it all. C'mon—you better get on board now."

So even though I hated to leave my little tomato plants, as puny as they were, I climbed up and joined the nice man in the huge machine. To my surprise, there were hundreds of other people in there with him.

"Hey," I asked suddenly. "Who are you?"

His eyes twinkled. And then with a grin, he said, "The Boss sent me."

"Well," I asked, "What is this thing?"

"Oh! This?" He patted his giant machine with true affection. "This baby is *Corporate Prayer!*"[4]

This is my last reminder to you, so don't forget...

▶ To come and join me! Remember? I'm still standing on that corner where "I Saw America The Other Day," praying for her to come out of her porta-potty.

▶ Oh yeah! The BOSS sent me! He wants to know if you'll sing along with me?

> God Bless America! land that I love;
> stand beside her and guide her,
> through the night, with the light
> from above.
>
> From the mountains, to the prairies,
> To the oceans white with foam;
> God Bless America! My home sweet home.
> God Bless America! My home sweet home.

Appendix A

The Production Code[1]
Crimes Against the Law
1. *Murder*
   a. The technique of murder must be presented in a way that will not inspire imitation;
   b. Brutal killings are not to be presented in detail;
   c. Revenge in modern times shall not be justified.
2. *Methods of Crime*
   a. Theft, robbery, safe-cracking and dynamiting of trains, mines, buildings, etc. should not be detailed in method;
   b. Arson must be subject to the same safeguards;
   c. The use of firearms should be restricted to essentials;
   d. Methods of smuggling should not be presented.
3. *Illegal drug traffic* must never be presented.
4. *The use of liquor* in American life, when not required by the plot or for proper characterization, will not be shown.

Sex
The sanctity of the institution of marriage and the home shall be upheld. Pictures shall not infer that low forms of sex relationship are the accepted or common thing.
1. *Adultery*, sometimes necessary plot material, must not be explicitly treated or justified, or presented attractively.
2. *Scenes of passion* should not be introduced when not essential to the plot. In general, passion should so be treated that these scenes do no stimulate the lower and baser element.
3. *Seduction or rape*
   a. They should never be more than suggested, and only when essential for the plot, and even then never shown by explicit method;

    b.   They are never the proper subject for comedy.

4. *Sex perversion* or any inference of it is forbidden.

5. *White slavery* shall not be treated.

6. *Miscegenation* is forbidden.

7. *Sex hygiene* and venereal disease are not subjects for motion pictures.

8. *Actual child birth*, in fact or in silhouette, are never to be presented.

9. *Children's sex organs* are never to be exposed.

Vulgarity

The treatment of low, disgusting, though not necessarily evil subjects, should be subject to the dictates of good taste and regard for the sensibilities of the audience.

Obscenity

Obscenity in words, gestures, reference, song, joke, or by suggestion is forbidden.

Dances

Dances which emphasize indecent movements are to be regarded as obscene.

Profanity

Pointed vulgarity or vulgar expressions, however used, are forbidden.

Costume

1. *Complete nudity* is never permitted. This includes nudity in fact or in silhouette, or any lecherous or licentious notice thereof by other characters in the picture.

2. *Dancing costumes* intended to permit undue exposure or indecent movements in the dance are forbidden.

Religion

1. No film or episode may throw ridicule on any religious faith.

2. Ministers of religion, in their character as such, should not be used as comic characters or as villains.

3. Ceremonies of any definite religion should be carefully and respectfully handled.

National Feelings
1. The use of the flag shall be consistently respectful.
2. The history, institutions, prominent people and citizenry of other nations shall be represented fairly.

Repellent Subjects
The following subjects must be treated within the careful limits of good taste.

1. *Actual hangings* or electrocutions as legal punishments for crime.
2. *Third Degree* methods.
3. *Brutality* and possible gruesomeness.
4. *Branding* of people or animals.
5. *Apparent cruelty* to children or animals.
6. *Surgical operations.*

Appendix B

Christian Sources

To say no to Hollywood is no small matter. The most essential way to pull down the assistance of heaven in this battle will be for Americans to pray and fast from "Hollywood" as described in the book. However, there are other ways in which we can be effective in this war. Yet we must be prepared. We must be thoroughly equipped. Listed below are some sources that can assist you through their experience and their materials. Many have been actively involved in resisting the immorality that has molested America. These organizations are established to help you! Contact them.

Christian Organizations

Some of the following are organizations that are actively involved in the cultural war to win America back from the immoral influence of Hollywood, entertainment, music, television, etc.

> Al Menconi Ministries
> P. O. Box 5008
> San Marcos, CA 92069
> (619) 591-4696

This ministry evaluates today's popular music for young people and keeps the parents informed on it.

> American Family Association
> Donald E. Wildmon
> P. O. Drawer 2440
> Tupelo, MS 38803
> (601) 844-5036

AFA will supply you with detailed information on how to take action against the cultural pollution pouring out of Hollywood, television, etc. This organization promotes the Biblical ethic of decency in American society with primary emphasis on television and other media. They fight against indecency through boycotting the products of companies who sponsor offensive programming. They actively battle pornography. This organization is extremely generous with their time and information. Their publication, *Journal*, is both informing and motivating for the concerned Christian community.

> Christian Coalition
> Pat Robertson
> Box 1990
> Chesapeake, VA 23327
> (757) 424-2630

This organization promotes Christian values through a network that reaches into numerous states and counties throughout the nation. They monitor legislative enterprises and actively promote traditional Godly principles. One of their major goals is to train and equip individuals to become involved in the political arena and to run for local offices.

> Concerned Women for America (CWA)
> Beverly LaHaye
> 370 L'Enfant Promenade, SW
> Suite 800
> Washington, D. C. 20024
> (202) 488-7000

Their double focus is prayer and action. They organize united, effective prayer chapters to pray for our nation. CWA is a valuable resource for information regarding the status of various movements, bills and/or laws that would weaken or threaten the American family.

> Family Research Council
> Dr. Gary Bauer
> 801 G Street, NW
> Washington, D. C. 20001
> (800) 225-4008

This organization sends free of charge a monthly newsletter, *Washington Watch*, which contains the latest updates on different issues, policies and bills. The newsletter keeps church and community leaders informed on a national level. The organization is actively involved in stopping the deterioration and pollution of our national culture. Contact them regarding their cultural studies project.

Focus on the Family
Dr. James Dobson
Colorado Springs, CO 80995
(719) 531-3400

One of the most well-respected Christian organizations in the world today. They stand on the front line in regards to protecting the family unit and fight vigorously against any threat to its stability. All of their products are unsurpassed in quality and content; however, I list only those that are especially pertinent to our topic. It would be inconceivable to wage a battle against the pollution of Hollywood without some of the resources from Focus on the Family in your library. Contact this ministry and ask them about the following materials and inquire if they have any additional materials that might assist you in this area.

Michael Medved's video *Hollywood vs. Religion*
Public affairs journal *Citizen*
Popular culture journal *Plugged In*

Anti-Pornography Groups

Contact the following groups for more information on how to fight pornography in your local community.

American Family Association
Donald E. Wildmon
P. O. Drawer 2440
Tupelo, MS 38803
(800) 326-4543 or (601) 844-5036
(See information above)

Citizens For Community Values
11175 Reading Road, Lower Level
Cincinnati, OH 45241
(513) 733-5775

This organization has been particularly effective in helping major cities to eliminate pornography and obscenity through the proper legal channels.

Morality in Media (MIM)
475 Riverside Drive, Suite 239
New York, NY 10115
(212) 870-3222
FAX (212)-870-2765
E-Mail: mimnyc@ix.netcom.com
Web Site: www.netcom.com/~mimnyc/index.html

National Christian Association
P. O. Box 40945
Washington, DC 20016
(202) 822-7933

National Coalition Against Pornography (NCAP)
800 Compton Road, Suite 9224
Cincinnati, OH 45231
(513) 521-6227

This organization's particular focus is directed toward the elimination of pornography and obscenity in relation to child pornography. They educate the public and community leaders through research and case studies.

Historical Groups

Our prayers for America will spiral up and escalate with a fervent urgency if we can grasp again the truth of just how far our nation has been moved away from its foundation. When the battle rages hot and we have been stung by the enemy's arrows, we will need the courage of our forefathers to persevere for our children as our ancestors persevered for our sakes. A honest study of our national, spiritual roots will hold us steady in this battle to regain our nation. The following organizations are dedicated to the task of educating us to this essential truth: America was established as a *Christian* nation!

The Foundation for American Christian Education
2946 25th Avenue
San Francisco, CA 94132
(804) 978-4535

This organization dedicates itself to the recovery and restoration of true American historical information. They produce "Redbooks" which are filled with photocopies of original American documents that prove how Christian principles guided our past leaders in education and government.

Plymouth Rock Foundation
Jack Coffield
P. O. Box 577
Marlborough, NH 03455
(603) 876-4685

This ministry focuses our American Christian heritage in their research and publishing. They also address current affairs from a Biblical viewpoint.

Wallbuilders
David Barton
P. O. Box 397
Aledo, TX 76008
(817) 441-6044

A Christian ministry that has published several books that proved to be pivotal turning points in my understanding of American history. They search for portions of American history which has been removed from contemporary texts and then republish that information in its original form. I highly recommend two books from this ministry: *America: To Pray Or Not To Pray* and *The Myth of Separation*.

Another book that is essential study for America's spiritual foundation is *America's God and Country* by William J. Federer and is also listed in the Bibliography. This book should be available in any Christian bookstore.

Legal Groups

American Center for Law & Justice (ACLJ)
Jay Sekulow
P. O. Box 64429
Regent University Drive
Virginia Beach, VA 23467
(757) 579-2489

Started by Pat Robertson, this is a network of attorneys throughout the nation who willingly and courageously stand up for God and decency in our courtrooms and legal system.

Although they do battle in many different legal arenas, the ACLJ actively confronts the ACLU in its systematic attempt to destroy America's religious and moral foundation.

Christian Law Association
P. O. Box 30
Conneaut, OH 44030-0030
(330) 493-3933

The National Legal Foundation
P. O. Box D
Chesapeake, VA 23328
(804) 424-4242

A law firm committed to freedom of religion, speech, assembly and the press with particular preservation of First Amendment rights in these areas.

The Rutherford Institute
P. O. Box 7482
Charlottesville, VA 22906-7482
(804) 978-3888

A non-profit organization founded to defend the civil rights and liberties of religious persons.

Appendix C

Television and Movie Studios

Often we do not take action because we do not know how to contact certain individuals and/or companies. Writing letters is one way to make a difference in the cultural direction of our nation.

Major Motion Picture Companies

The first address listed below is that of the Motion Picture Association of America (MPAA), headed by Jack Valenti. This is the non-profit group that provides the ratings for all major releases. This is the organization that replaced the Production Code.

The second address is that of the National Association of Theater Owners which represents theater owners nationwide. The remainder of the addresses represent the major motion picture companies.

Most parents do not realize that a local theater does not have to legally enforce the MPAA rating system (PG, PG-13, R, and NC-17). If a movie is rated "R," it does not mean that the management of a local theater must enforce this provision. In other words, our 14-year-olds can walk into an R-rated movie without a parent. It may be beneficial to contact the local theaters in your community and ask if the management enforces this voluntary guideline and if they do not, request that they do so. This applies to the new NC-17 rating also. This new rating was implemented so that filmmakers could produce soft pornography without having the X-rating attached to it. Local newspapers and multiplex cinemas normally make the decision whether to promote and screen the NC-17 films. It is mandatory that we apply pressure on the management to keep the NC-17 films out of our community's theaters. The National Association of Theater Owners is listed for this purpose.

Motion Picture Association of America (MPAA)
15503 Ventura Blvd.
Encinco, CA 91436-3140
(818) 556-6567

National Association of Theater Owners
4605 Lankershim Blvd.
North Hollywood, CA 91602
(818) 506-1778

Columbia Studio
10202 W. Washington Blvd.
Culver City, CA 90232
(310) 280-8000
MCA/Universal
100 Universal City Plaza
Universal City, CA 91608
(818) 777-1000

MGM, Inc. (Metro-Goldwyn-Mayer United
   Artists)
2500 Broadway Street
Santa Monica, CA 90404-3061
(310) 449-3000

Orion Pictures Corp
1888 Century Park East
Los Angeles, CA 90067
(310) 282-0550

Paramount Pictures
5555 Melrose Avenue
Los Angeles, CA 90038-3197
(213) 956-5000

20th Century Fox
P. O. Box 900
Beverly Hills, CA 90213
(310) 277-2211
Warner Bros. Studios
4000 Warner Blvd.

Burbank, CA 91522
(818) 954-6000

Major Television Networks

The average amount of time spent watching television per household per day in 1950 was **4 hours, 35 minutes**. In 1995, the time spent watching television per household per day was **7 hours, 20 minutes**. America has become a nation of *watchers* and not *doers*. The television industry, of course, wants to keep us that way. However, some are beginning to rise up and exhibit concern about the indecent programming of television's sexuality, violence, foul language and anti-Christian messages. If Christians would *consistently persevere* in an organized effort to write the networks, we would begin to change the tide of immorality now washing upon the shores of our nation and being exported to other nations around the world.

The "big four" networks are listed first.

American Broadcasting Company (ABC)
Vice President, Television Broadcasting
77 West 66th Street
New York, NY 10023
(212) 456-7777

Columbia Broadcasting System (CBS)
Vice President, Television Broadcasting
7800 Beverly Blvd.
Los Angeles, CA 90036
(213) 852-2855

FOX Television Network (20th Century)
1999 South Bundy Drive
West Los Angeles, CA 90025
(310) 584-2000

National Broadcasting Company (NBC)
Director of Public Affairs
30 Rockefeller Plaza
New York, NY 10112
(212) 664-4444

Cable Television

The average number of households that tuned to different cable television networks continues to spiral upward. The Federal Trade Commission (FCC) does not restrict cable television in the same sense as it does the major networks; therefore, its channels sometimes tend to offer more R-rated and X-rated movies. Some are nothing other than explicit pornography.

The average number of households tuned to **NBC** during prime time in the second quarter of 1996: **10 million**. The numbers are not as large, but there is a considerable audience that tunes into cable television.

ESPN: **1 million**
Discovery Channel: **747,000**
MTV: **404,000**
ESPN2: **150,000**
E! Entertainment Television: **125,000**

When major cable networks listed below show offensive programming, one thing we can do is turn the station. The best thing to do is to write a letter. Likewise, when they present beneficial programs, we should acknowledge that in a letter also.

Arts and Entertainment Network (A&E)
235 East 45th Street, 9th Floor
New York, NY 10017
(212) 661-4500

Black Entertainment Network (BET)
2801 West Olive Avenue
Burbank, CA 91505
(818) 566-9948

Christian Broadcasting Network (CBN)
977 Centerville Turnpike
Virginia Beach, VA 23463
(804) 424-7777

CNBC
2200 Fletcher Avenue
Ft Lee, NJ 07024
(201) 585-2622

CNN
Turner Broadcasting System Headquarters
P. O. Box 105366
Atlanta, GA 30348-5366
(404) 827-1700

Data Broadcasting Corporation
120 Wall Street, 9th Floor
New York, NY 10005
(212) 208-7705

The Disney Channel
3800 W Alameda Avenue
Burbank, CA 91505
(818) 569-7500

The Sports Network (ESPN)
935 Middle Street
Bristol, CT 06010
(203) 585-2000

HBO/Cinemax
1100 6th Avenue
New York, NY 10036
(212) 512-1000

Lifetime Television
2049 Century Park East, Suite 840
Los Angeles, CA 90067
(310) 556-7500

Music Television Network (MTV)
Vice President of Public Affairs
1515 Broadway
New York, NY 10036
(212) 258-8000

The Nashville Network
2806 Opryland Drive
Nashville, TN 37214
(615) 889-6840

Nickelodeon
Vice President of Public Affairs
1515 Broadway
New York, NY 10036
(212) 258-8000

Public Broadcasting Service (PBS)
4401 Sunset Blvd.
Los Angeles, CA 90027
(212) 666-6500

Showtime
1775 Broadway, 8th Floor
New York, NY 10019
(212) 713-7300

TBS/TNT
1050 Techwood Drive, NW
Atlanta, GA 30318-5264
(404) 827-1717

Telemundo Network
2470 West 8th Avenue
Hialeah, FL 33010
(305) 882-8700

The USA Network
1230 Sixth Avenue
New York, NY 10020
(212) 408-9100

Univision Network
9405 NW 41st Street
Miami, FL 33178
(305) 470-2323

Miscellaneous Organizations

A single letter will doubtless serve a purpose. Hundreds and thousands of letters declare a determined, corporate effort to make a difference. Listed below are the addresses of miscellaneous organizations that can assist in the fight against indecent radio and/or television.

The first one is the governmental agency (FCC) that enforces the standards for radio and television broadcasting. The United States Criminal Code, Section 1464, allows criminal penalties for uttering "any obscene, indecent or profane language by means of radio (includes television) communication." The FCC states that any: "language or material that depicts or describes, in terms patently offensive as measured by contemporary community standards for the broadcast medium, sexual or excretory activities or organs." The FCC asks that if a complaint be forthcoming that it be specific and detailed as to what was actually viewed or heard. Details should include the date, the time of day, and the call letters of the radio or the name of the television station. The FCC must have specific details and it is therefore helpful if there is an actual video or audio recording of the offensive material. If that is not possible, then a detailed transcript should accompany the complaint. In order for the FCC to take action against a potential violation, there must be documented evidence.

Federal Communications Commission
Mass Media Bureau
Enforcement Division
Complaints and Investigations Branch
1919 M Street, NW
Washington, D.C. 20554
(202) 418-2600

The National Coalition on TV Violence
Robert Gould, M. D., Chairman
33290 West 14 Mile Road, Suite 498
West Bloomfield, MI 48322
(810) 489-3177

Appendix D

Recommended Reading List

The following are only a few of the books, and one video, that will validate the premise of this book and serve to educate the reader. Needless to say, this is not an exhaustive list. Most of these books should be available through your local Christian bookstore. They are listed alphabetically and not in order of importance.

America's God and Country by William J. Federer. An encyclopedia of quotations which highlight America's noble heritage. Profound quotes from the Founding Fathers, presidents, statesmen, scientists, constitutions, court decisions, etc. Available in most Christian bookstores.

America: To Pray Or Not To Pray by David Barton. A statistical look at what happened when religious principles were separated from public affairs. The focus is specifically from the year 1962 when the Supreme Court ruled that prayers could not be offered at school. If this is not available through a local Christian bookstore, then check David Barton's ministry, Wallbuilders, under Appendix B.

Hollywood vs. America by Michael Medved. The author powerfully argues that the entertainment business follows its own dark obsessions, rather than giving the public what it wants.

Hollywood vs. Religion by Michael Medved (Video available through Focus on the Family)

Married to Television? by Dale and Karen Mason. A challenging book directed toward those who are concerned about their families. It is a practical guide and mandatory reading for you if you are serious in saying "no" to Hollywood.

The Bondage Breaker by Neil T. Anderson. Overcoming negative thoughts, irrational feelings and habitual sins.

The Coming Revival by Bill Bright. A practical handbook and guide in understanding that America's only answer is to "seek God's face" through fasting and prayer.

The Myth of Separation by David Barton. An examination of the quotes of the Founding Fathers and of Supreme Court rulings from 1793 to 1952 which establish that Christian principles were to be the basis for the governing of this nation and its schools. If this is not available through a local Christian bookstore, then check David Barton's ministry, Wallbuilders, under Appendix B.

Victory Over the Darkness by Neil T. Anderson. Realizing the power of your identity in Christ.

Notes on Sources

Chapter 1
Casting Its Shadow

1. David Parkinson, *History of Film* (New York: Thames and Hudson, Inc, 1995), p. 23.
2. Kenneth Anger, *Hollywood Babylon* (San Francisco: Straight Arrow Books, 1975), p. 3.
3. Ibid.
4. Ibid, p. 9.
5. Ibid.
6. Ibid, pp. 15-18.
7. Ibid, p. 21.
8. Ibid, p. 25.
9. Ibid, p. 22.
10. Ibid, p. 22.
11. Ibid, p. 25.
12. Ibid, p. 33.
13. Ibid, p. 46.
14. Ibid, p. 185.
15. David Barton, *The Myth of Separation* (Aledo, Texas: Wallbuilder Press, 1992), p. 245.
16. Gerald Gardner, *The Censorship Papers* (New York: Dodd, Mead & Company, 1987), p. xiii.
17. Ibid.
18. Information derived from a quote an hour-long documentary regarding Hollywood. The documentary had already started before the video began taping. The video is owned by Elizabeth Collins.
19. Ibid.
20. Ibid.
21. Ibid.
22. Ibid.
23. Ibid.
24. Ibid.

Chapter 2
Contempt for Morality
1. Gene Brown, *Movie Time*, (New York: The MacMillan Company, 1995), p. 50.

2. Ibid,
3. Information derived from hour-long documentary regarding Hollywood.
4. Ibid, *Time* magazine 1956.
5. Michael Medved, *Hollywood Vs. America* (New York: Harper Collins Publisher, 1992),
    p. 279.
6. *Movie Time*, p. 30.
7. Ibid, p.
8. Ibid, p.
9. *Hollywood Vs. America,* p. 283.

Chapter 3
Catastrophe of the Sexual Revolution

1. Raymond Chandler quoted from *Details*, November 1996, p. 28.
2. *Hollywood Vs. America*, p. 112.
3. Charles Rose Show aired on PBS.
4. Ibid.
5. *Entertainment Weekly*, September 20, 1996, p. 11.
6. This film for has already been viewed on national television.
7. *Entertainment Weekly*, November 22, 1996, p. 22.
8. Ibid, p. 19.
9. Ibid.

Chapter 4
Corrosion of Our Culture

1. Job 38:3.
2. Dr. James Dobson and Gary Bauer, *Children At Risk: The Battle for the Hearts and Minds of Our Kids* (Waco: Word Publishing, 1990), p. 50.
3. *Rolling Stone*, October 3, 1996.
4. Ibid.
5. *Hollywood Vs. America*, p. 101.
6. Ibid.
7. *Children At Risk*, p. 72, 73.
8. *Plugged In*, March 1996.

9.   Daniel 12:4.
10. Rolling Stone, October 3, 1996.
11. Ibid.
12. Ibid.
13. Ibid.
14. Ibid.
15. Ibid.
16. Ibid.
17. Ibid.
18. Ibid.
19. Ibid.

Chapter 5
Consequences of Our Actions

1.   Tabitha M. Powledge, *Your Brain: How It Works,* (New York: Maxwell McMillan International, 1994), pp. 3-5.
2.   Hosea 8:7.
3.   Josh McDowell and Dick Day, *Why Wait? What You Need to Know About the Teen Sexuality Crisis* (San Bernadino: Here's Life Publishers, 1987), p. 40.
4.   S. Robert Lichter, Linda S. Lichter and Stanley Rothman, "Hollywood and America: The Odd Couple," *Public Opinion*, December/January 1983, p. 58.
5.   *Hollywood Vs. America*, p. 294.
6.   Kenneth Woodward, "The Elite and How To Avoid It," *Newsweek*, July 20, 1992, p. 55.
7.   Ibid.
8.   David Hocking, *The Moral Catastrophe*, (Harvest House Publishers, 1990), "A Pornographic Nightmare."
9.   *U. S. News & World Report*, February 10, 1997, pp 42-49.
10. David Barton, America: *To Pray Or Not To Pray* (Aledo, Texas: Wallbuilder Press, 1988), p. 33.
11. Adelle Banks, "Some Kids Agree in Survey: Rape OK If Date Costs Money," *Los Angeles Herald Examiner*, May 8, 1988, Section A-14.
12. *America: To Pray Or Not To Pray*, p. 33.
13. *Why Wait?* pp. 205, 206.
14. Ibid, p. 207.
15. Ibid, p. 208.

16. Ibid, p. 214.
17. Ibid, p. 216.
18. Ibid, pp. 222, 223.
19. Ibid, p. 223.
20. Ibid, p. 259, 260.
21. Galatians 6:7.
22. *Why Wait?* p. 218.

Chapter 6
Call of the Church

1. Alexis de Tocqueville, *The Republic of the United States of America and Its Political Institutions, Reviewed and Examined*, Henry Reeves, trans, (Garden City, NY: A. S. Barnes & Co., 1851), Vol. I, p. 334.
2. *Hollywood Vs. America*, p. 19.
3. American Family Association, July 1996, pp. 12, 13.
4. Psalm 11:3.
5. *The Myth Of Separation*, pp. 108, 109.
6. Psalm 33:12.
7. *America: To Pray Or Not To Pray*, p. 109.
8. *The Myth Of Separation*, p. 11, 12.
9. Ibid, p. 102.
10. Focus On The Family, *Citizen*, July 22, 1996.
11. *America: To Pray Or Not To Pray*
12. *The Myth Of Separation*, p. 245.
13. Ibid, p. 35.

Chapter 7
Commitment of the Clergy

1. Michael Medved, Video entitled *Hollywood Vs. Religion*
2. *Entertainment Weekly*, October 11, 1996, p. 99.
3. Ibid, November 8, 1996, p. 49.
4. Ibid.
5. *Spin*, September 1996.
6. Jeremiah 13:25, 26.
7. I Peter 4:17.
8. Focus On The Family, *Citizen*, July 22, 1996, p. 7.

9. Romans 12: 1,2.
10. II Corinthians 10:4,5.
11. Romans 12: 1, 2.

Chapter 8
Captured Through Our Senses

1. Frank Capra, *The Name Above The Title*, (New York: The MacMillan Company, 1971).
2. II Timothy 3:1-5.
3. Ephesians 6:12.
4. II Corinthians 10:3-5.
5. Deuteronomy 1:43.
6. Revelation 12:11.
7. John 12:31; 14:30; 16:11.
8. Colossians 2:15.
9. Genesis 1:26, 27.
10. *Your Brain*, p. 49.
11. Genesis 3:6.
12. Hebrews 5:14.
13. *Your Brain*, p. 51.
14. Ibid, p. 52
15. Ibid.
16. Ibid.
17. Ibid, p. 51.
18. I Timothy 4:2.
19. II Timothy 1:7
20. II Corinthians 10:4, 5
21. Romans 7:23.
22. Romans 12: 1,2.
23. I Timothy 4:1.
24. Romans 7:19.
25. Luke 22:31.

Chapter 9
Consignment to Save America

1. Revelation 12:11.
2. I Corinthians 12:11

3. Philippians 4:13.
4. Ephesians 6:12.
5. Hebrews 5:14.
6. Elizabeth Collins, Unpublished manuscript, Copyright 1997.

Chapter 11
Corporately Confronting the Problem

1. Excerpt taken from the bulletin of New Covenant Fellowship, Knoxville, TN.

Appendix A
1. David Chagall, *Surviving The Media Jungle* (Nashville, Tennessee: Broadman & Holman Publishers, 1996), p.p. 142-145.

17
116
203 3
49
250

66
52
60 / 2
2